Is Rape a Crime?

Is Rape a Crime?

A Memoir,
an Investigation,
and a Manifesto

Michelle Bowdler

FLATIRON
BOOKS
NEW YORK

IS RAPE A CRIME? Copyright © 2020 by Michelle Bowdler. All rights reserved. Printed in the United States of America. For information, address Flatiron Books, 120 Broadway, New York, NY 10271.

www.flatironbooks.com

Grateful acknowledgment is made for permission to reprint excerpts from the following:

"Tonight No Poetry Will Serve." Copyright © 2016 by the Adrienne Rich Literary Trust. Copyright © 2011 by Adrienne Rich, from *Collected Poems: 1950-2012* by Adrienne Rich. Used by permission of W. W. Norton & Company, Inc.

"A Litany for Survival." Copyright © 1978 by Audre Lorde, from *The Collected Poems of Audre Lorde* by Audre Lorde. Used by permission of W. W. Norton & Company, Inc.

Designed by Devan Norman

The Library of Congress Cataloging-in-Publication Data is available upon request.

ISBN 978-1-250-25563-1 (hardcover)
ISBN 978-1-250-25575-4 (ebook)

Our books may be purchased in bulk for promotional, educational, or business use. Please contact your local bookseller or the Macmillan Corporate and Premium Sales Department at 1-800-221-7945, extension 5442, or by email at MacmillanSpecialMarkets@macmillan.com.

First Edition: 2020

10 9 8 7 6 5 4 3 2 1

For Mary, Ben, and Becca

Contents

The ordinary response to atrocities is to banish them from consciousness. Certain violations of the social compact are too terrible to utter aloud: this is the meaning of the word *unspeakable*.

Atrocities, however, refuse to be buried. Equally as powerful as the desire to deny atrocities is the conviction that denial does not work. Folk wisdom is filled with ghosts who refuse to rest in their graves until their stories are told. Murder will out. Remembering and telling the truth about terrible events are prerequisites both for the restoration of the social order and for the healing of individual victims.

—Judith Lewis Herman, *Trauma and Recovery*

"Hope" is the thing with feathers
That perches in the soul

—Emily Dickinson

Is Rape a Crime?

Introduction

Is rape a crime? It's a startling question. Most people would answer emphatically, "Of course it is." They might even add, "What kind of a question is that?" This question, though, is a fair one to explore given how rape is treated in our country and around the world—underinvestigated, trivialized, and excused. Is anything else enacted as an international weapon of war and referred to for a sure laugh at a comedy club? Rape in the United States is a felony, in theory, but evidence of rape is largely ignored and victims are expected to prove their veracity. This reluctance from law enforcement to use its valuable resources does not seem to extend to other felonies—the kind where evidence is tested and witnesses interviewed, the kind DAs prosecute readily, the kind where arrest and conviction are more than a remote possibility. We are left with a central contradiction here: most people, when asked, will agree that rape is one of the most horrific violations that can happen to a human being, yet somehow society appears to stand aside while crimes of rape are minimized or dismissed, if they are reported at all, if they are investigated at all.

The crime of rape sizzles like a lightning strike. It pounces, flattens, and devastates its victims. A person stands whole, and in a moment of unexpected violence, that life, that body, is gone. If the eviscerated individual somehow rises, incredulous bystanders shout with relief, "They're alive! They are a survivor!" not realizing the victim's organs are incinerated, her brain runny scrambled egg.

And what of those internal scars? Does time allow regeneration? Can medical care fully repair the bodily damage the lightning bolt so violently imprinted? Since the injuries are largely unseen by others, how does the victim carry on? How are the scars attended to and softened rather than made hard and immovable?

To answer those questions, to really answer them and not turn away, we need to consider the role we play in dismissing the experiences of victims of sexual violence. This collusion by omission occurs, in large measure, to protect our own vulnerability. The challenge of confronting a power structure so entrenched that its full impact is unseen lies in the insidiousness of our need to look away. What we accept as a normal response to sexual violence is anything but. We must make space for each individual story, creating a larger mosaic of what has emerged as an all-too-common experience: the delegitimization of rape as a crime. Only then can we begin to change how rape is addressed in our society.

This is a difficult task I ask of you—to look at these violent crimes full-on and listen as I tell my story and what it implies about a collective disregard for victims of sex crimes. But I hope you will listen, and I hope you will consider engaging in a shared and urgent task: to both recognize and raise awareness about the many ways rape is treated differently from all other felonies and to demand change. Our collective efforts are needed in this essential task and the work cannot be done in isolation.

—

The term "rape culture" was introduced by second-wave feminists in the mid-1970s to describe how pervasive and normative violence against women was in the United States.[1] Twenty years later, the problems identified by the term not solved through naming it, the editors of *Transforming a Rape Culture* described it as "a complex set of beliefs that encourages male sexual aggression and supports violence against women. . . . [It] condones physical and emotional terrorism against women and presents . . . as the norm . . . that sexual violence is a fact of life . . . inevitable."[2] Today, the "me too" movement and a charged political environment continue the struggle to define rape culture, address its impact, and effect change. Rape culture is the subject of a number of books, essays, and inspiring speeches.[3] What is it we continue to name over fifty years' time that is so recalcitrant, its damage tolerated? Centuries ago, violent sexual crimes committed against women were considered crimes against their husbands—a harming of *their* property, a stain on *their* honor.[4] In contexts where rape was perceived as affecting men by proxy, it was often addressed with more gravity than it is now.

The "me too" movement, which was founded by activist Tarana Burke and spurred the subsequent viral hashtag, ushered in a wave of news about sexual assault, harassment, and abuse of power. These stories were followed by weak apologies and promises to get help from the perpetrators but few repercussions. It is commonplace that men, famous or not, experience no consequences for these behaviors, whereas those alleging harm pay a much steeper price. Just ask the forty-fifth president of the United States.

In this book I present my story alongside research on the criminal justice system's treatment of rape in the United States to argue for the importance of acknowledging and treating rape like the felony crime it is. I assert that rape does not hold status as a crime largely because the victims are overwhelmingly women, children, and persons from marginalized populations. One in six U.S. women and one in thirty-three men will experience rape or attempted rape in their lifetime.[5] I generally use the feminine pronoun throughout this book to describe victims of sexual assault, but it is imperative I acknowledge that many people experience sexual assault who don't identify as female. Twenty-one percent of transgender, genderqueer, and nonconforming college students have been sexually assaulted, compared to 18 percent of cis females and 4 percent of cis males.[6] It also cannot go unmentioned that sexual violence disproportionately affects women of color.[7]

Race and racism have shaped the U.S. response to crimes of rape over the centuries. In this country, it was legally impossible for a white man to rape an enslaved black woman because the act was "not a crime."[8] In contrast, a black enslaved man accused of raping a white woman would be subject to death, including by lynching or castration, often before a trial took place.[9] According to a study from the National Registry on Exonerations, "a black prisoner serving time for sexual assault is three-and-a-half times more likely to be innocent than a white sexual assault convict."[10] Our ugly history of systemic racism impacts every aspect of our society, and rape culture cannot be defined or analyzed without addressing the influence of racial bias. In the courts, racism affects whether a case ever makes it to trial, the likelihood of a conviction, the severity of the sentence, and whether a plea bargain is offered.[11]

I am not advocating for more incarceration and longer prison sentences in a country that already has the highest incarceration rates in the world.[12] But it is clear to me as a long-term survivor of rape that there is a striking disproportion between the severity of the crime's lifelong consequences for survivors and the seriousness with which it is treated by society and, specifically, by the criminal justice system. It is this disparity I question.

Data from this current decade shows that close to 25 percent of all rapes were reported compared to over 60 percent of robberies and assault and battery crimes.[13] The Rape and Incest National Network (RAINN)—using an amalgamation of federal data[14]— estimates that 230 out of 1,000 rapes are reported. Of those, 46 lead to arrest, 9 to prosecution, and 5 to felony conviction. Only 4 percent of all *reported* rape cases ever see the inside of a courtroom, translating into 1 percent of every 1,000 rapes committed. About 2 percent of rapes reported and one half of one percent of every 1,000 rapes lead to conviction and/or incarceration. Recent data showed a spike in reported rapes—up to 40 percent in 2017 and then down again to 25 percent in 2018.[15] A 2018 *US News and World Report* article speculates that victims may have felt more comfortable coming forward because of the "me too" movement and notes that it is too early to know whether changes in how cases are handled will also result. The article quotes Karen Weiss, a sociology professor, who asserts that the increase is likely attributable not to victims' growing trust in the law enforcement system but to "a confidence in their ability to be heard."[16] Rape victims still are routinely discounted, and our pleas—first for the rapist to stop and then for law enforcement to help us seek justice—are largely ignored.

Studies estimate that between 2 and 8 percent of rape claims are deemed to be either false or baseless.[17] But we must ask what that means, exactly. These determinations are most often made by the detectives to whom a rape has been reported. Many police departments use categories of "exceptionally cleared" and "unfounded" to dismiss rape allegations.[18] "Exceptionally cleared" indicates that a case was investigated but cleared by certain standards—for example, because of an uncooperative witness or the death of the offender. But this category may also be used when district attorneys decide they cannot successfully prosecute or when officers don't believe they have a strong case—before an investigation even moves forward. The term "unfounded" in rape cases is supposed to be used when officers find a case is false or baseless. This label is often applied before an investigation commences at all and makes law enforcement's "solve rates" artificially higher than they actually are.[19] In 2019 the city of Pittsburgh deemed almost a third of its rape cases unfounded.[20] In both Scottsdale, Arizona, and Oxnard, California, almost half of rapes reported between 2009 and 2014 were classified as unfounded.[21] Additionally concerning is that victims risk being charged with a false report if their case is dismissed in such a way—yet another disincentive for victims to go to law enforcement.[22] This classification system should give us all pause, as it stands in stark contrast to the data showing low rates of false reporting. Are there other crimes where the first question asked is whether the victim is being truthful, and where there is no ensuing investigation to determine if that presumption can be backed up with facts?

If you have ever had a rape kit done or tried to report a sexual assault formally, you understand it is no one's idea of a good time. Describing in detail sexual humiliation and unimaginable violence is not something a human being would choose to do if they had any other option. And yet the fact that we even have the phrase "he said, she said" in our vernacular—as if it's as likely as not that a woman would lie about sexual violation—is itself instructive about the status of this crime in our society.

Rape in this country is not treated as a crime of brutal violence but as a parlor game: his word against hers, regret sex, revenge against a scorned lover. Politicians in state and federal offices have been widely quoted saying such abhorrent statements as, "Rape is kinda like the weather. If it's inevitable, relax and enjoy it," "If a woman has [the right to an abortion], why shouldn't a man be free to use his superior strength to force himself on a woman? At least the rapist's pursuit of sexual freedom doesn't [in most cases] result in anyone's death,"[23] and "You can do anything . . . grab 'em by the pussy."[24] These are merely a few examples in a long list of egregious comments delegitimizing rape as an act of violence. It's a game of it didn't happen or it's not serious even if it did. The victim is painted as unstable or unreliable, wanting attention or money, hoping to destroy the rapist's life, perhaps even part of a well-crafted political conspiracy to discredit the perpetrator. It might be laughable if it didn't work so much of the time.

So how do rape victims "survive" in an environment when everywhere around us we can reasonably conclude that what we went through is largely a trivial matter?

—

Twenty years after a violent home invasion and sexual assault so terrifying that I could barely function in the aftermath, the memories of violence and terror returned. While I recognized the assault occurred two decades in the past, my body and brain were not aligned, and I spent most days feeling as if there were still a knife at my throat. I anticipated its strike, my heart beating hard even when at rest. Fortunate to live in Boston, where some of the best trauma experts practice, I got help and came to understand that I was not alone, that my experience was far from unique. Unprocessed memories too overwhelming to feel at a moment of terror have to go somewhere. It is like a cancer that goes into remission—not disappearing but lying in wait for the most inopportune time to resurface.

After years of floundering in temp jobs and trying to hold on to hope that I would someday return to any semblance of a career, I found meaningful work in the public health field. Eventually, I earned my master's degree at Harvard University and worked at a university as the director of health and wellness at a time when colleges' responses to sexual assault survivors had become front-page news. Daily, I witnessed young people suffering both from their experiences with sexual violation as well as from the secondary pain of being disbelieved, shunned by friend groups, and unable to complete their studies. Most schools had inadequate remedies for survivors, and rarely were students accused of sexual misconduct held accountable. During this period, I read that Massachusetts had thousands of untested DNA samples in its state crime lab going back as far as the mid-1980s and wondered about my unsolved case. Then I read further that there were untested, abandoned rape kits in cities everywhere—hundreds of thousands of them.

Old memories flooded my body, and I got busy, very busy. I learned whatever I could about how rape evidence and rape complaints were treated around the country. I did so to feel better, to understand my case, and later to be a voice for victims who wondered and wonder still why they feel so alone and unseen.

As my wife once said to me on a day when my own intractable memories grabbed me hard, "You aren't crazy; what happened to you is crazy." I must believe change is possible, despite all the facts that could lead me to conclude otherwise. I must believe that, this time, a reckoning toward justice will occur. Otherwise, it is simply too crushing.

This is the reason I speak about my experience, the vast amount of untested rape evidence and uninvestigated rapes nationally, the flaws in our criminal justice system that perpetuate this state of affairs, and the mass acceptance of misogynistic laws, policies, and practices. This book tells the story of one rape victim's experience and its impact over years in terms of job loss, displacement, post-traumatic stress, interrupted education pursuits, and more. The pervasive and constant nature of the impact of sexual violence on every aspect of my life is contrasted with the scant response from the law enforcement officials to whom the rape was reported. Many years later, when I had become an advocate at work and nationally for changing the way rape cases were addressed, I returned to the Boston Police Department to find out what happened with my case. What I found confirmed what I feared: that even with the availability of DNA technology and increased funding for rape investigations, the core of the problem related to my case remains largely unaddressed in the present day. Too many cases are dismissed with no investigations and victims left to feel that justice for them is out of reach.

My manifesto is not a rallying cry for *victims* to act but a rebuke of current norms and a plea for change and accountability from law enforcement, whose job is to investigate and prosecute sexual assault, and from legislators, who speak too often about rape as if it is something other than a devastating crime of violence requiring a serious response. We can no longer allow the indifference toward sexual assault that leaves victims unable to rely on seeking justice for the crime they endured. We must try to move the needle, but our flawed world doesn't make it easy. Every voice that challenges these norms is essential and reminds us that there is still much work to be done. Change is not optional, since it affects the safety, rights, and dignity of human beings who are violated by a crime of violence and by society's diminishment of the seriousness of that crime. Freedom is still a concept given only to a select few, and the right to our bodies and their sovereignty is not yet secured. I hope this story can help move us a little closer to that distant claiming of power—power that includes full legitimacy, respect, and equal treatment under the law, power that I believe is within our grasp.

Part I

A Memoir

Tonight I think
no poetry
will serve

—Adrienne Rich

One

1984

I am sitting in the back of a police car, like someone accused of a crime. It is the first night of summer in Boston. I do not have on handcuffs; I have not been read my rights. I am a victim, not a prisoner, but the difference between the two has completely escaped me tonight and will for the rest of my life.

My wrists and ankles are red and bruised from the phone cord that tied them together behind my back, attaching them to my ankles and pulling my knees up behind me—a position I've heard called "hog-tied" when referring to steer in a rodeo. There is a deep bite mark on my neck, and I am torn from my vagina to my anus. In about thirty minutes, a doctor will note that this tear is like one a woman might get while giving birth for the first time. I am headed to an emergency room for a visit that will take several hours and am aware that they may want to admit me. Over my dead body, I think.

I will need stitches, a pregnancy test, and antibiotics to treat any sexually transmitted infections that can still be prevented. In about a year, we will know enough about HIV for me to think I might have contracted it from one of these two men. They were likely IV drug users. I bled. When I finally summon the courage to get an HIV test a couple of years later, the wait for the result seems endless. It is one thing that goes in my favor.

Later, I'll remember this moment and think of it as the easy part.

"I don't need one," I say about the pregnancy test.

"That's what everyone thinks," the examiner says. "It's just a baseline. If someone learns they're pregnant in a few weeks and didn't get a test done, it might be harder to know for sure who the father was."

Father. That couldn't possibly be what she meant to say, I wonder. It turns out that, legally, it is indeed a relevant term. At the time of my attack, most states gave men who "fathered" through rape the same custody and visitation rights as other male parents. As recently as 2012, thirty-one states still allowed these rights, and in the present day a few have yet to change them.[1] The existence of these laws means a woman impregnated through rape may have no choice but to "bargain away her legal rights to a criminal trial in exchange for the rapist dropping the bid to have access to her child."[2] According to those who write our laws, the perpetrator is a father who has rights that must be honored. The victim and her needs and rights, not so much.

—

The ride to the hospital lives in shadow. I look around the police car and stay as quiet as possible. It is daybreak, and as the sun rises, the cold steel surrounding me slowly illuminates, softening from black to gray. There is a metal cage and bulletproof glass between the back and front seat of the car, and I wonder how the police officers would know if I needed them for anything. All I can see is the balding head of the driver, stray wisps of hair peeking out from his cap. If only I had some scissors, I think. His partner has a short ponytail and isn't wearing her hat. Her head keeps whirling around to look at me and she is saying something, but all I can hear is the timbre, not the words. At least her voice is soft; my ears are ringing.

Just moments before, these officers had come into my apartment building with their guns drawn. They found me sitting on the floor in a corner of the apartment across the hall from mine. I tried calling the police from my apartment, but the cord had been sliced with a knife, and the phone was dead. I hadn't met my neighbors across the hall before this and must have been a disturbing sight when I knocked. "I need to make a call," I croaked out, walking through the threshold uninvited, barefoot, and disheveled. They asked me no questions, led me to the phone, and disappeared quickly into their rooms.

I tried to make myself as small as possible in the unfamiliar apartment. Perhaps I would be mistaken for a speck of dust and the police would leave me be. I'm not even sure why I called them.

Are you injured? Are you safe? What is your name?

I hear a voice from somewhere inside my body say *Michelle,* and the word startles me. It sounds vaguely like a curse. The female officer puts her gun away and stands next to where I'm sitting on the floor. I lean on her leg and start to shake. The other person I call is my friend Laura, who lives about five blocks away. She arrives, having run the whole way, and opens her mouth as if to speak, but no words emerge. I reach up for her hand and we trek the distance from the apartment to the police car, a few feet at most; my legs feeling like they're traveling halfway around the world.

I think about kicking the thick glass in the police car and getting a bit rowdy just to make sure I can elicit a reaction. I am a little worried I am a ghost. Laura is silent; her eyes dart about. Her red flannel nightshirt is buttoned wrong and she keeps pulling it away from her neck, not realizing that she is sitting on it and that a slight tug of the tail would give her the comfort she is seeking.

That I am dead seems completely probable. This thought is more connected to reality than any thought I've had since several hours before, when two men came rushing toward my bed in the middle of the night hissing at me.

Don't move. Is anyone else home? Put this over your face. Be quiet!

Maybe they did use the knife I saw before the blindfold went over my face. Maybe they did tie that scarf around my neck and strangle me instead of stuffing it deep into my mouth and tying it tight. It's what I expected and waited for throughout the night. Perhaps these things really did happen, and my consciousness mercifully moved itself to another place while I died.

I'd love to hand my brain over to the officers so they can find out what happened without my having to say another word. My blindfolded eyes saw only the darkness, but perhaps I have a scrap of memory that can be mined. What secrets, what evidence, do I hold that fear has so elegantly pushed away?

I suddenly feel myself rise out of my body, and I notice from my new vantage point that the siren and blue lights of the police car are on, and the officers are driving as if we are on a high-speed chase. What's the rush, I think.

Other cars are pulling over so that we can pass, although everything around me is completely silent. Boston is ugly in the first light of morning. There are overflowing trash barrels and a fine layer of soot covering the sidewalks. I float above the traffic and follow an early morning T train going down Commonwealth Avenue, until I am on my street. There is crime-scene tape blocking the front-door entrance of my apartment building, and the neighbors are staring as they go about the business of their day.

"I wonder what happened there?" they ask one another.

My eyes close and the vibrations of the police car hum through me. Everything is a blur. My glasses are gone. The men didn't need to blindfold me since I'm almost blind without my glasses anyway, but they did. Perhaps knowing I never saw their faces is what saved me in the end, but the absence of my sight already has me feeling like I missed a huge part of this night. How can I fully explain to anyone what happened if I didn't see it for myself? How can I help the police find these men if all I have to rely on is the description offered by my other senses? I even hesitate to share the details I do have for fear I will sound confused or somehow complicit, so I keep quiet.

The clothes I am wearing feel unfamiliar, but they are soft and warm. After the rapists left and I managed to untie myself, I crawled on the floor trying to find my glasses. Drawers had been emptied, books thrown off shelves. I grabbed something to cover my naked body. It feels like terrycloth and smells of the vegetable curry we had for dinner.

My glasses, I hope, are somewhere. They are no longer on the little spot by the nightstand, where they sit perched every night when I am done reading, next to a glass of water and a tiny desk lamp I recently purchased. Now, the nightstand lies tossed on its side. Someone may have trampled on my wire frames by now or the police collected them as evidence. I have no idea where I will get new ones or how I'll pay for them.

Rape is not sex, they say, but this was certainly some kind of horrible imitation. I can't even begin to absorb this part of the evening, so it sits crudely at the front of my mind. What am I supposed to do now? I have only been with women since my freshman year in college, which started out as a complete surprise and then became an identity. I'd never had much experience with men before that: a few kisses, maybe, a little teenage groping. I had intended to get around to men someday. It seemed like an experience in life I shouldn't miss altogether. Now, I am not so sure. It feels final. The door slams shut, hard. This was the first and last time a penis will enter my body or be in my mouth. Later, this particular loss will make me ache, no matter how happy I am in my marriage and with the choices I've made over the years. There remains something unfinished, taken away, forged from brutality and timing rather than my own free will. When people ask me in a moment of curiosity if I've ever been with men, I just say no.

I wonder whether I'll be able to describe what happened to me as torture when my attackers seemed so at ease, so relaxed.

One of them acted like he was on a date and asked if I'd mind if he stayed the night.

"Sure," I practiced saying in my head.

———

I have a thought even before arriving at Beth Israel Hospital that I am going to call my ex-lover and have her come up from Manhattan. Maybe having sex with her might help repair what has just happened, prove to me I'm alive after all. I'm not thinking clearly, and this thought intrudes every time I close my eyes and feel the blindfold being placed.

The police car stops suddenly. We have arrived at the hospital. The emergency room is quiet. I can see empty plastic blue seats in the waiting room beyond the glass. Laura jumps out of the car before I've even registered that the engine is off. She runs through the hospital doors at full speed, and I trudge along behind. My arms and legs feel like they have sandbags on them, but I press on, trying to keep track of Laura as she races through the hallway.

"I'll try to check you in. You go with the police."

I stare back at the police car, frozen. Thinking I may still be naked, I stroke the outlines of my body until convinced that I feel fabric on my skin.

Wait up, I think. *Come back. Don't leave me here with them.*

Laura has given my name to a woman who instructs us to wait until she finishes checking someone in. Soon, she gestures us over. "Can I have your name and your insurance card?" the intake person asks, sitting behind a tiny desk with a Formica top in the corner of the emergency room.

I look at Laura, speaking to her and ignoring the stranger in front of me. "I'm going to sit over there." I wave in the direction of the waiting room. "I don't have anything with me. Get me when I'm supposed to do something." Pulling whatever I am wearing around me, I walk to the nearest empty seat.

Laura must do an adequate job providing the requested information, because now a person in scrubs is standing over me. "We would like to take a look at you," she says, her hands clasped behind her back. She knows touching me would be a most grave error. "As it stands, we seem to only have male physicians in the emergency room right now. That happens sometimes. Do you mind me asking if that would be acceptable to you?" I don't respond, and she adds, "I'm more than happy to page a female. You might just have to wait awhile."

"I'll wait." My voice does not offer the usual apology.

I'm distracted by the ugliness of the chairs, and daylight coming through the windows. People are waking up, I think. Soon, more of them will know.

When my name is called, Laura springs forward, pulling me up with her.

"You can bring your friend," the nurse says.

Something nags at me. The sun is up, and I picture my room-mates walking into the shambles the night left behind. Since the phone in the apartment is dead, I'm not sure how to reach them to soften the blow. "Laura, maybe you should go and meet them at the apartment," I say. "You can look for my glasses."

Laura nods but doesn't move. "I'm staying here with you."

The exam will take hours. A rape kit will be taken as a matter of procedure. Unknown to me at the time is that this evidence-collection tool has been available for the last few years: it was first introduced in 1978 in a Chicago emergency room and then ad-opted by multiple ERs in the surrounding area by 1980.[3] Soon, emergency rooms in other larger cities adopted its use.

Over the years, I've been asked what a rape kit is and what it looks like. Simply put, a rape kit is the package of materials that contains the evidence gathered from victims of violent sexual fel-onies. The victim's body is a crime scene, holding invaluable evi-dence of the assailant's identifying biological characteristics. The exam is lengthy and painstaking, often taking four to six hours to complete. When the evidence is retrieved by a trained pro-fessional and attended to with respect, the perpetrator may be possible to identify, as well as link to other crimes.

Some kits look like a shoebox labeled with the name of the state in which the test is performed and the words RAPE EVIDENCE written on the outside. Some states prefer a large manila envelope, also properly labeled. Inside, there are clean swabs for retrieving DNA from multiple orifices, a chain-of-custody form, envelopes to hold materials collected from the victim, and a piece of paper that looks like the silhouette of a body, which the examiner uses to document where the victim was cut, scratched, or otherwise injured.

To prevent evidence contamination, clinicians are instructed to change gloves frequently and to wear scrubs, surgical hats, and netting for hair and beards. All the evidence is gathered and placed in the box or envelope, which is then sealed by wide tape to show that the contents have been secured. The kit may be kept in the hospital if the person getting the exam is not yet sure she wants to report the assault. Otherwise, following the chain-of-custody standards, it will be given to and transported by law enforcement should the case ever reach trial. This means that the transfer of the rape kit and documentation of who touched it at every stage of the process should be carefully controlled. These standards are critical to ensuring that evidence of a DNA match cannot be challenged at trial because of shoddy documentation, poor labeling of the samples, or transfer done by someone not qualified to handle the evidence.

As the package leaves the hospital for its new destination, the victim might hope, might expect, that the items gathered are quickly analyzed by a crime lab so that the person or persons whose DNA has been left in and around their body can be identified. That's how it's done on the TV crime shows, anyway. Perhaps that rape victim is buoyed imagining a "good guy" like Olivia Benson from *Law and Order: SVU* rushing the evidence to a crime lab to augment the investigation she has already begun, soon leading to the capture and conviction of the rapist and the resolution that brings to the victim. But real life does not mirror TV shows, which contribute to a false narrative that rape victims' complaints are investigated routinely and seriously.

The exam I am about to endure will be performed by a sexual assault nurse examiner (SANE). The SANE program began in the late 1970s, when ER nurses in some cities decided standards for treating rape victims were inadequate.[4] While their numbers have grown over the years, there is still a national shortage. In 2017 a writer in *The New York Times* observed, "The Violence Against Women Act guarantees rape victims the right to a sexual assault examination. But rights mean very little if they are un-available based on your physical location, or are inaccessible be-cause of your socioeconomic class, or are delayed because of the excessive violence that occurs against your gender."[5] A person who cannot receive an exam because they are unable to travel hours to get to a facility that has a SANE or who forgoes an exam because it will take hours for a SANE to arrive will find prosecution of the crime difficult should they decide to pursue charges.

While some medical schools and residencies include training on appropriate care for sexual assault victims, it is not yet part of physician training nationally.[6] In 2017 a group of medical profes-sionals created online modules for medical students and physi-cians on trauma-informed care because, as they state, "Training to provide appropriate, compassionate care for this population is lacking in most medical school curricula."[7] Knowledge of how to treat a trauma survivor matters enormously in the survivor's will-ingness to seek medical care over a lifetime. As one primary care physician who teaches trauma-informed care explains, "A medical office or hospital can be a terrifying experience for someone who has experienced trauma. . . . The perceived power differential, being asked to remove clothing, and having invasive testing can remind someone of prior episodes of abuse. This can lead to anx-iety about medical visits, flashbacks during the visit, or avoidance of medical care."[8] Yet trauma-informed medical care, something that's been written about and discussed within the mental health field for years, is not yet a uniform standard in medical training.

Laura and I follow the person who beckoned me into a small exam room full of people waiting with gloves and masks on, holding metal trays. I suppose the person examining me introduces herself, tells me her name, explains all that will happen. I suppose she smiles hoping to seem kind, instead of showing the pity she feels. There are bright fluorescent lights on every side of the table on which I lie—to illuminate my bruises and ensure no small trace of evidence is missed.

They scrape under my fingernails and comb my pubic hair. Someone is dictating a description of a bite mark on my neck, and I hear a pencil moving furiously. People are talking about me and being instructed on what to do next to this body part and that. My legs are spread. My eyes are shielded with large wraparound sunglasses to protect them from the light. I am above my body on the ceiling once more, looking down on a person I do not recognize. She is a tiny girl with no control, eyes covered, feeling like nothing more than an object for the second time in less than a few hours.

I think about all the people who don't know yet and how they might react when they find out. Their faces appear under my eyelids, distressed and silent. The paper gown draped over me is scratchy, and I feel naked and alone with a dozen people in the room. Laura is somewhere. I wonder if she is looking away. I think about how worried my roommates will be, how frantic.

They hand Laura a cylinder of antibiotics for me. "The instructions are on the bottle," someone says. Someone else asks me again if I could be pregnant, and I'm more specific this time. "No," I say. "I've never had a male partner, only women." This information seems to sting the person examining me; she says she is sorry, as if what has happened is suddenly so much worse.

What exactly is she so sad about, I wonder? My attackers didn't target me because of my sexuality, and I was careful to hide it from them, fearing even more brutality. Still, I learn years later that rates of rape and sexual assault are higher in the LGBTQ population because of marginalization, higher rates of poverty, and hate-motivated violence, and I feel a kinship to people I don't even know.[9] Bias must be acknowledged whenever we find there are higher rates of violence targeted at marginalized or disenfranchised groups. There is a marked difference in how law enforcement responds to crimes largely perpetrated against people of a common demographic, such as race, sexuality, or gender. In *Identifying and Preventing Gender Bias in Law Enforcement Response to Sexual Assault and Domestic Violence,* the Department of Justice acknowledges that "even where law enforcement officers harbor no explicit biases or stereotypes about women or LGBT individuals, an officer's unconscious bias towards these groups can undermine an effective response to sexual assault and domestic violence incidents."[10]

And so I am combed and swabbed and have my bruises documented on the silhouette of a naked woman's body on one page of the forensic record. I am poked and entered and asked hundreds of questions. And I sign papers that allow the collected evidence to be sent to the police.

The pen will sit heavy in my hand as I try to remember how to write my name.

"I think we are just about done," the examiner says, pulling off her gloves. "You were badly torn, and the stitches we gave you will need to come out in about a week." She looks at me with a frown and a head tilt and I want to accept the kindness and also to slap her.

I don't know you, I think. *Just hurry up. I don't want sympathy.* The look the nurse casts at me changes who I am, makes me smaller, someone people will feel sorry for before they feel anything else. For years to come I will see the same look when describing each ugly detail of what happened this night: two men, a knife, a blindfold, bound and gagged, raped repeatedly in full darkness, my only introduction to the male body. It is a look of fear mixed with sadness, and it will be my lifelong torment. I can never again be a person who does not have this story chasing me. I can never make it go away, or the look it brings to people's faces. This is something I learn this very moment in the ER as I look at my examiner.

What I'd like is a magical reset button, and I don't think she has one of those. Instead, she hands me a blow-up donut and tells me I should sit on it if I'm sore. I take it, planning to throw it away when she isn't looking. "Is there anything else?" the woman who supplied the donut asks. "Do you have any questions? Anything else I can do for you? And, again, we are all so sorry."

"Do you have any clothes?" I ask. She murmurs something to a person standing next to her who then runs off, reappearing with some folded gray sweatpants and a sweatshirt. The clothes are large but will do.

"We have a lost and found and launder the clothes so we have something when people need them." The woman continues on. "Here, keep them. Please. It's quiet tonight. Stay as long as you want." And then, in a flash, she is gone.

The room is empty, and Laura and I are alone. We stare at each other, not sure what to do next or where to go.

As we sit, I hear a clatter stampede in the hallway. There is the squeak, squeak, squeak of sneakers and the thump, thump, thump of muscular legs landing hard, trying to navigate the slippery linoleum without falling. I already know it's my housemate Lise, running and peeking into rooms searching for me. Her boyfriend, Grant, who looks like a beardless Jesus with his shoulder-length hair parted in the middle and sad blue eyes, is at least fifty feet behind her frantic pace. She races back and forth past my room a few times and I watch her go, hoping she can run off some worry before she finds me. Then she is gone, and the noise stops.

A too-gentle voice intrudes, Lise almost jumping over her to see me. "Your friend is here, darling," the nurse says, and Lise has already pushed past her before her entrance can be further announced.

"Oh God. What can I do? What can I do? Why wasn't I home with you?" She has the same look in her eyes as the nurse did, but Lise's is also mixed with love and worry, so I can stand to look back at her. "Can I hug you?" she says, hugging me.

"I'm glad you weren't there. What would that have done but made them more scared? We'd probably both be dead. Let's have just that one little thing to be grateful for," I say as she sobs into her hands. "You know I'm right." Laura and Grant both stare down at the floor.

I turn to him. "Can you do me a favor? I can't leave here without my glasses; I can't see a thing. Will you go back and see if you can find them?" He nods and leaves so quickly I wonder if he'd been here at all.

"Do you mind staying while I maybe close my eyes for a few minutes?" I ask Lise. "They must have given me something. And please don't leave me if I fall asleep." Laura motions for Lise to sit in her chair so I can stretch out on the exam table. Lise puts a piece of exam paper over me like a blanket. They talk, and Laura is suddenly gone, too.

Grant returns after some time with my glasses and breakfast from Deli King, the diner near our apartment. "They were under the futon frame," he whispers to Lise, handing them to me along with the foil package of food. The eggs are sunny-side up, not scrambled the way I like them, so I do my best not to pierce the runny yolks while eating the whites around them, as well as the home fries, bacon, and toast. I am surprised at my hunger and find that being able to see only puts my fear into focus. I can't fully catch my breath, as though I've sprinted in a race.

Grant fills us in on several facts: The police are still in the apartment; the other roommates are now home. The landlord has been informed of what's happened. The police want to talk to me; they won't let anyone put the apartment back in order yet. Someone is heading to the hardware store to get a new phone cord, and eventually the police will let us make calls once the phone is dusted for prints.

"Is there anyone I can call now or something else I can do?" Grant asks.

But I'm partially resting in a twilight doze. The warmth of Lise's hand in mine has allowed my body to give in to exhaustion, and I'm in no rush to go back to the place that used to be home.

—

And so this brand-new crisis takes up residence inside me as we finish our time at the emergency room. This night has changed my future forever. I am at greater risk than I was twenty-four hours earlier for interruptions in my career and education, intimacy challenges, and mental health conditions like a substance use disorder, anxiety, depression, and post-traumatic stress disorder, including a form of PTSD that is chronic.[11] I survived the lightning bolt, but its full impact is, as yet, uncertain.

For now, I am physically compromised. My brain is barely processing information; I've been given several medicines to take, and the words on the bottles make no sense to me. Soon, I'll have to start telling family and friends what happened, and I have no words to explain something I do not yet grasp myself. I'm not sure where I'll be sleeping tonight or many nights into the future, and I'm unclear how I will ever get myself to work again.

My friends will do everything they can to be supportive, but they are temporarily homeless as well, no longer feeling safe in a place we all had loved just one night ago. While they will try to help me as the identified victim, they too are traumatized. This fact is undeniable. Someone they're close to has been violently assaulted; their apartment ransacked; their private things invaded, tossed about, or taken—and it was by chance none of them were home. Perhaps they or someone they love have experienced sexual assault in the past, making this even more difficult to process. Feelings of terror, guilt, and relief will weigh on them while preoccupied with their friend's unending needs. Even though they'll find a way to offer much despite their own pain, they'll need help, too.

Secondary trauma has its own ripple effects: sleeplessness, nightmares, anger, and depression, among others. Studies of law enforcement personnel, mental health care workers, and medical professionals show that these symptoms have potential impact on a person's ability to be an effective caretaker or first responder.[12] Rates of suicidal ideation, depression, and PTSD are higher in police officers than in the general population, as is stigma for help seeking. Writing about the impact of PTSD on critical decision making, a retired NYPD police officer notes, "Professionals working with the victims or offenders of crimes that result in trauma have the potential to be deeply affected by the stories and the images they are exposed to during their work."[13] Secondary trauma manifests through avoidance, irritability, and many other ways. An officer may have intrusive thoughts about someone they love being hurt like the victims they encounter or may already know someone who has been sexually assaulted. Given how prevalent sexual assault is in our society, the odds are significant. When trauma is not acknowledged, the behaviors associated with it can be acted out on victims, making their experience with law enforcement negative. Psychological trauma in law enforcement personnel is a possible contributing factor to, but does not excuse, the minimization of rape complaints.

With so many practical and emotional issues to address and the experience of trauma overwhelming, victims can rarely push for an investigation and hold detectives accountable, nor is it their job to do so. They offer their stories to the police and attempt to move on with their lives, trusting law enforcement to move forward with their complaint. The reality in many cases is not what the rape survivor imagined. I know that was true for me.

I didn't think much about the police in those early days. Sure, I would have liked the perpetrators caught simply to have prevented further victimization of others, but the enormity of dealing with daily tasks and the many crises that were about to emerge in my life took every bit of my time and energy. I left the emergency room that night, talked to the police the next day, and waited. When I heard nothing and nothing and nothing, I assumed they must have tried as hard as they could to catch the men who broke into my home and had come up short.

It was only much later that I took notice of the lack of contact or concern from the Boston police and wondered about it. When I first started telling people about the rapes years after they happened, the first thing everyone asked was, "Did they ever catch them?" I remember being surprised by this question and why it never occurred to me to ask it. It became clear that what the police did or did not do on my behalf was a major factor in how pervasively this life-changing experience affected me.

Two

Because I called the police the night of the break-in, my case was assigned to a detective and a manila police folder was created with my name across the top. When I held it in my hand thirty years later, I felt its thinness. The address of the "incident" was noted and the evidence collected kept along with my statement. There had been a spate of break-ins and rapes in the greater Boston area, and the police were under pressure to solve them. I could have delayed the interview with the detective who was assigned to my case until I'd recovered a bit, but I didn't, feeling a sense of urgency to protect others from what I'd experienced.

A 1994 report from the National Institute of Justice describes the initial creation of "special units" in some cities, which were intended to improve their response to rape victims or "to send a message to the community that the department is deeply committed to solving sex crimes cases." According to the report, "Law enforcement agencies do not appear to rely on objective guidelines for the formation of specialized units. Instead, they tend to establish specialized units when that organizational structure best suits their needs."[1]

This community-facing message that law enforcement is taking special care to address and solve sex crimes by creating special victims units means little when not accompanied by substantive information about officer training or how the success of these units is assessed. If such units are not held accountable with data showing their efficacy in improving the experiences of survivors reporting to them and in collecting more information, investigating more sex crimes, and solving more cases, then it strikes me that they are more of a public relations strategy than a vehicle for actionable change.

—

It's been less than twenty-four hours since the attack in my home, but it feels like I haven't lived there for years. I call Emmy, my dear friend and mentor, soon after Lise and I return from the hospital, our phone now cleared by the police for use. Emmy and I first became close in college when she lived in my residential area as quad director. I need only to spit out a few words before she summons me. "Come over now, sweetie. Get out of there. We'll figure out what to do next together." I put down the phone and walk out; a policeman is still dusting my room for fingerprints, and my roommates are walking around wide-eyed and afraid to talk to me.

"I'll be back," I tell them, but it would be the last time I ever walked over that threshold.

I arrive at Emmy's and she pulls me to her. It feels like barbs piercing my skin, but I trusted her before the rapes, and so my body allows an exception to its new aversion to being touched. Someone from my old apartment had called her while I walked fifteen minutes down Harvard Avenue from Allston into Brookline. They said two detectives had shown up wanting to speak with me. "Send them here," Emmy had said. "Tell them to please give us a little time to get our bearings."

Two detectives sit across from me in Emmy's living room. "We'd like you to go to the police station as soon as possible after we've finished taking your statement," one of them says. It's downtown, simple to get to by T—take the Green Line to the Orange Line and then walk up the street. I'm supposed to look for a big brick building with a lot of police cars parked in front. "It's pretty hard to miss, Miss," one of them says with a slight smile.

They want my fingerprints.

"It might help," the other one says, and I feel a hitch in my chest. What could it possibly help with? I think. At the time, it seemed utterly beside the point whether they catch the men who broke into my home; it wouldn't undo a thing. But I decide I will get the fingerprints taken anyway. Something about them tells me I should do whatever they say. Why should today be any different than last night? Doing as I was told saved my life. I figure it's my strategy for the immediate future.

The detectives look like twins. Both are rotund and have short crew cuts. The tops of their heads are so flat they could carry whole trays of food on them without spilling a drop. *They have come here to help,* I struggle to convince myself. *Try to give them a chance.*

I offer the detectives a seat, and they both take a moment to balance before plopping down into a couple of overstuffed antique chairs. The chairs are at least one hundred years old. Emmy had them reupholstered after picking them up at an antique show last fall. "They have good bones," she'd told me the first time I saw them. "With some new upholstery, my great-grandchildren will be able to make use of them."

Emmy offers the men coffee and both say yes with enthusi-
asm. "Regular, ma'am, that means cream and sugar, please," says
one speaking for both of them.

"I'm from New York," Emmy says proudly, "but I've been in
New England long enough to learn that term. Frankly, I see nothing 'regular' about spoiling a good cup of black coffee."

The men chuckle. I stay put—feeling guilty I'm not helping
serve our guests. The detectives have identical spiral pads that
are almost too small for their large hands. "Do you have a pen,
by any chance?" one of them asks. His partner hands him one
from inside his suit coat. He swirls it around on the paper to get it
working and tears the first few pages as he pushes down hard. He
looks up at his partner, chagrined.

It's only paper, I think. *What a baby.*

We begin to discuss the break-in.

"What time was it?"

"Did you see anything at all that could help?"

"What did they take?"

"Where were your roommates?"

One of the detectives reaches into his duffle bag and pulls out
a see-through gallon-size baggie with a large serrated knife in it.
He pushes it toward me and asks, "Do you know what this is?"

My tongue expands in my throat. So they did have a knife. I
thought I'd seen it for an instant before I was blindfolded, and
then forgot. There was too much else to attend to.

"It's a knife," I consider saying to the detective, but stare back
closed-mouthed, and he returns the silence. Finally, I say, "Did
you find that in my bedroom?" And the detective holding the baggie nods, staring at his partner. I start to worry. Was that somehow
the wrong question?

"It might have fingerprints on it," he continues, still holding it
up near me so I can get a better look. The baggie is blocking his

face, and it's hard to hear what he's saying. I think about getting up to push his hand down, but don't want to get that close to him or the knife.

I begin to float again and time feels like a toasted marshmallow—gooey, stretched, and hot. A silent movie of another way the night might have gone plays before my eyes. One of the rapists is raising that very knife and plunging it into me, while the other looks on completely bored. How long will this take? he wonders.

One of the detectives coughs deeply into his hand and wipes the wetness onto his tan slacks, leaving a palm print, and I am jarred back into Emmy's living room. My eyes can see that the knife is still in the baggie rather than thrust into me. Still, I can't breathe and start to wonder if it's possible these detectives plan on hurting me. Emmy and I are locked in the house with them and they probably have guns under their suit jackets, along with the bagged knife. The thought that this interview could get very bad very quickly passes through my mind and I try to remember if they showed us their badges when they arrived.

Where is Emmy with the fucking coffee? I think.

I am close to running out of the room and locking myself in the kitchen with my friend. *Don't act crazy,* I say to myself. They're mad enough already I can't describe the rapists. This is a waste of their time.

While plotting my escape from the detectives with the giant kitchen knife, Emmy returns with two steaming mugs. The drinks are so light they look like melted coffee ice cream and the one detective puts the baggie down to take the cup from her.

"Your room was full of fingerprints, and if we can get a set of yours, we might be able to tell which ones belong to the assailants. Can you give us a description?" I sit mute with the knife still in plain sight, now resting on the detective's lap while he gingerly sips the hot coffee. The fingerprints won't be much help if the rapists' aren't already on file for some other crime. We don't discuss the evidence gathered at the hospital. It will still be over a decade before the FBI has its national DNA database fully operational. The DNA technology that is available now is much more limited, able to link perpetrators to crimes but only if one has a suspect to consider.[2] DNA technology eventually advanced, but this did not prevent rape cases from going uninvestigated and rape kits from being shelved in warehouses, police departments, and crime labs without forensic testing.

I sit staring at the knife in a baggie, wondering why my attackers had left me alive. I wonder, too, who might have used the knife last in the kitchen. Maybe I had held it in my hands just a few hours before the break-in, using it to slice the crusty rye bread Lise had baked from scratch.

The detectives use the term "assailants" repeatedly. Maybe it is considered more polite than *rapists, maniacs,* or *drug-crazed lunatics*.

Your language choice is rather interesting, I say in my head.

"Like I said, I cannot give a description of the knife or much of anything since I was blindfolded during the entire attack. They put something on my head the second they came through the bedroom door." I pause while they write my words down in their notepads. "Maybe it was a T-shirt or a scarf. I really don't know; I didn't see a thing."

The detective asks again, "Does the knife look familiar?" and I fantasize grabbing it out of his hands and stabbing him.

"I suppose it could be a knife from my kitchen. But didn't you say that the screen door on the back porch was slashed open?" I lean forward, imitating a lawyer making a point with a difficult witness. "That makes it sound like maybe they had it when they broke in. Our silverware is a hodgepodge of stuff we brought with us. I don't have each item memorized." I try to get a view of their coffee mugs, hoping it might be time for a refill. This time, I will get it for them and make it very light and very sweet.

How much longer will this go on? I've hardly slept since the night before last and there's a twin bed all made up down the hall in the guest room Steve, Emmy's husband, uses as his study. He handed me two Benadryl before he went to work and made me take them in front of him.

"You need to sleep," he said.

I swallowed them both over an hour ago, before I knew the detectives were coming, and am still wide awake. *How many of them can you take and be safe?* I wonder. *Where does he keep the bottle?*

Emmy and Steve live in a second-floor apartment on Beacon Street. The apartment is old, like the antiques that adorn it, with mahogany wood trim and polished hardwood floors. Their place is rent-controlled, and they pay less for it than I do for mine, even though it's so much nicer. Their marble landing has two heavy doors at the apartment entrance, each needing a separate key. I'll have to ask them how one finds a rent-controlled apartment, since I can't stay with them forever.

Emmy is ten years older than I am, well out of her twenties and fully on with her life, writing a novel and married to a man with an actual career path; he's a doctor, recently graduated from medical school. He tolerates my friendship with his wife, which consists of my sitting at her feet and worshipping her. Because of the demands of his pediatrics residency, Steve is gone most of the time. This fact works well for me if I need to stay with them for a while. Emmy and I can pretend that I am keeping her company rather than that she is watching over me as I ride on a Tilt-a-Whirl that's come completely off its hinges. Steve doesn't seem at all threatened by me or my sexuality or how much I love his wife. I am grateful, because I don't know what I would have done or where I would have gone if Emmy had not insisted.

"Come here. Come right now. Come here. Come right now," she had chanted over my refusals. My friends provided both immediate and long-lasting support. I didn't yet understand how essential it would be—how long this devastation would last and how much their concern would contrast with what law enforcement offered.

I decide to go to the police station after the detectives leave. A few more questions, another cup of coffee for each of them, and it's over. The detective with the knife returns it to his briefcase. "Thank you for your time," he says. The other man hands Emmy their empty cups and they depart. I will never see either of them again.

"I might as well go now to do the fingerprint thing and get it over with," I say, and Emmy wants to join me.

"The washing machine broke a week ago and the new one's coming today. I tried to cancel, but I can't reach anyone. Why don't you go lie down and we'll go together later."

Her tone is quiet, almost a whisper. It makes me feel like a trapped animal being spoken to kindly so it won't pounce. I'm surprised at the sudden lack of influence she has on me. Although I am hungry both for that small bed down the hall and for her approval, I know I won't be able to rest and have to get out of the house. The pills Steve gave me might as well have been placebos.

I lie easily. "Don't worry, Emmy. I'm sure I can get one of my roommates to go with me, and I have to stop by the apartment anyway. I want to know what's going on and if anyone is planning to stay there." I try and rush out of her apartment before she can make me promise not to go alone. As I head toward the door, Emmy hands me a spare key, pulling me toward her and kissing me. She is barely my height, and yet the kiss touches the crown of my head. I feel very small, as if I had swallowed Alice's "drink me" potion.

Despite the showers I've taken, I wonder if Emmy can smell the rapists, or the fear that is radiating out of my every pore. I squeeze her briefly and pat her back, trying to loosen her grip. I will scream soon if she doesn't let go.

A thought begins to take shape that I try to shoo away. At some point today, I should call my mother and let her know why she won't be able to reach me at my old phone number anymore. I can easily picture the pain and fear on her face as she begs me to reassure her that I am okay.

We have no plans for her to visit anytime soon. Maybe I can just say I decided to move in with Emmy. My mother doesn't like where I'm living anyway—first floor, run-down, a half block from a giant liquor store. I know she hasn't adjusted to how much I've changed: I meet a bunch of lesbians in college, come out, and now seem to relish living in squalor. I had taken care of my mother emotionally over the last few years as her second marriage failed and she and I were alone in the house after my sister, Judy, went to college. Her deep love goes hand in hand with how terrified she is of anything happening to my sister or me, something she's expressed for years after losing her husband to cancer when she was barely thirty-three and being left with two little girls to raise on her own. She would cry if one of us had a high fever, thinking it signaled a deadly disease. Telling her this and facing her reaction isn't something I can fathom.

—

When I think back to this moment in the apartment that will be my home for the next several months, I remember being terrified of the police and have spent years wondering why. They were there to interview me as a witness to see if the crime they had been assigned could be solved. I suppose I wanted them to solve it too if they could, but I needed something else as well—an acknowledgment that this experience had been life-changing and they understood the impact violence has on the human psyche. There was no line from them like, "We've got to go get to work on this and stop them from doing it again." They seemed more interested in how Emmy made coffee than in the gravity of the severe crime they were there to investigate—a crime I hadn't begun to process and wasn't even sure I had survived.

If only they had told me that they had seen a lot of things that were hard but that, with time and support, this horrific thing would not destroy me. But they focused only on questions about the crime scene, and I failed them because I had been sightless and would be of no help. My perception of them might have altered had they made it clear that the challenges this case presented were not my fault. We should have felt like allies, working toward the same goal. Instead, I felt like a criminal being interrogated and they held all the power. The more frustrated they seemed, the more they frightened me. It reminded me of what had just happened the night before. It felt like an intense comparison at the time and still does as I recount it now, but real. I was an object to them, a case, an assignment, and a difficult one at that. I didn't feel optimistic when they departed.

The overwhelming experience of being raped and of expecting to be murdered all night left me utterly undone. I felt as if I had been pushed into a dark ocean in the middle of a starless night—and I don't know how to swim—so I was sinking. Calling the police had been my lifeline; I was reaching my hand up to them from the cold ocean before death could draw me under. I was a helpless child trying not to drown. That perspective changed within just a few hours.

—

I reported my rape. A file was started; detectives questioned me; my apartment was examined for evidence. Many rape cases never even go this far. Some people never report; some never tell their family or friends. The reasons are complex and vary depending on the survivor's age, economic situation, internalized self-blame and shame, and whether it is safe to report the crime at the most basic level. Approximately 80 percent of victims know their attacker,[3] which can complicate reporting if the perpetrator controls the household finances, is a family member and the victim is underage, or is otherwise in a position of power at work, school, church, or elsewhere. Decisions on whether to report are heavily socially informed—victims worry that the rape will not be considered important, that they will not be safe, that they won't be believed, that the crime won't be followed up on, and sometimes they see keeping the perpetrator out of trouble as self-preservation.

When rape survivors don't report the crimes they experienced at the time they occurred but disclose years later, their claims are judged by others as unimportant because of the delay.[4] This mischaracterization often serves to excuse the perpetrator. In fact, there are many reasons why individuals wait to report crimes, including the disturbing statistic that more than 30 percent of victims are between the ages of eleven and seventeen at the time they were raped[5]—when the impact of the trauma is even more severe and telling an adult may be unsafe or impossible. Sometimes, a victim can only make a claim years later, when they are in a safe environment and have had time to heal from the trauma.

Victims should not be blamed for cases that don't get investigated because they are unreported or that don't get solved because of a delay in reporting. Instead, critics should focus on

evaluating the law enforcement options available to victims. I felt
so inadequate in my brief interaction with the detectives who interviewed me and with the officer who fingerprinted me. Instead
of wondering why the reporting of sex crimes is still so low, we
should require a shift in how these crimes are handled. Victims
risk additional trauma if they enter the criminal justice system.
Low reporting numbers also reflect, in part, increased awareness
that reporting sexual assault so rarely leads to an investigation,
arrest, or conviction and that many experience their interactions
with law enforcement as additionally traumatizing. Survivors talk;
they write; they use social media. Word gets around—sentiments
and experiences get shared that reporting made things worse, that
the interview felt like an interrogation, and that the case never
moved forward.[6]

Our focus should be on improving the experience of seeking
justice rather than asking victims to enter a flawed and harmful process. Professionals interviewing rape survivors should be
trained to understand that the vast majority of rape reports are
valid. Cases should not get closed before an investigation. And rape
cases that do proceed through the criminal justice system should
be given the same attention as other felony crimes.

—

I leave Emmy's house, my brain humming with nothingness. My
goal is to comply with whatever the police tell me to do, trying to
be a good witness. At this moment, I am unaware of just how problematic and additionally traumatizing seeking justice has been for
other victims of sex crimes.

I take the T as the detectives instructed, realizing when I
emerge that I could have walked. Although I see familiar restaurants, I both recognize my surroundings and feel like everything

is new and strange. I am disoriented by exhaustion and trauma. I arrive at the police station and go to the front desk. A woman behind the counter in a low chair senses my presence and looks up without speaking. I stare at her, not sure how to start.

"Can I help you?" she finally says.

The phone rings and she picks it up. "Can I help you?" she says into the receiver, using the same intonation she just used with me. After a quick "just a minute, I'll transfer you," she is off the phone and staring at me again.

"Is there something I can help you with?"

"I was sent here," I begin. "You may not be expecting me. I'm supposed to give my fingerprints."

I think about adding, "Don't worry, I'm not a criminal," but don't think I can achieve the proper tone of levity.

"And exactly why are you supposed to be leaving your fingerprints?" she asks. Responding to that question requires me to say words I cannot yet utter. I manage to take the detective's card out of my pocket and push it across the counter toward her.

She looks down at it. "Honey, what's this card for? Are you supposed to see this detective? Why are you here?"

"My apartment was broken into and this detective, the one on the card here, said he wanted my fingerprints to figure out which ones were mine and which ones were the robbers'."

She pushes a form at me with her long, pink-painted fingernails. "Fill it out. Put in as many details as you can, especially your exact address and the date and time of the event. That's all we'll need to match it to the crime scene."

At this reference to my home as a crime scene my body stiffens, and I stare at the paper with its blank boxes. I have no idea what day it is; I'm still not sure I can remember my name. Mundane tasks feel insurmountable: brushing my teeth, eating, sleeping.

While struggling with the form, I spy the date from a day

calendar on the counter. I hope it's accurate. There are a lot of questions for me to answer. Do I have fingerprints already on file? Have I ever been arrested? I fill it out quickly, since the answer to all the questions is no.

I push the form in the clerk's general direction and clear my throat when she doesn't look up. She points her finger toward a wooden bench near the front door and says, "Wait over there," and I obey, plopping myself down. The wood is cold on my thighs, although the room itself is sweltering. My scalp feels sweaty through my big bush of black hair. Police officers walk back and forth between the back room and outside. Some of them have their hands placed firmly on the arms of people who seem to be in some sort of trouble. I wonder what people think I am doing there, or if they see me at all.

After a while, a man in a short-sleeved shirt and clip-on tie calls out my name and gestures for me to join him at the desk. He has an ink pad and is looking at my filled-out form. He begins reciting it back to me.

"Is your name . . . ?"

"Was your apartment broken into on the night of . . . ?"

"Do you live at . . . ?"

I nod yes to each one.

"It says you have roommates. Is that correct? Could they come over and give their fingerprints?"

After we confirm that I am indeed the person who filled out the form, he opens the ink pad. "All right," he says, "put your arm on the counter and let me do the rest." He grabs my hand and separates my fingers, taking each one and turning it fully to get the ink on them, then places each finger on the corresponding spot on the paper. My heart races as I watch my hand disappear under his flesh as he presses and turns. He smells of cigarettes.

When he's done, he pushes a roll of paper towels in my general direction, but the ink has already dried and won't come off. It seems the stains on my fingers will be there for a while, and I wonder if anyone will think I'm coming out of the police station having been "booked" for committing a crime. Then I realize I don't care. So what if I did?

I fuss with the dry paper towels thinking I should look for a bathroom when I become aware of a noise hitting my ears. It's a sound I know, but it's out of place. There is a dog barking somewhere inside the police station. It goes on for several minutes—three short loud woofs, a pause, and then three more. The detective who took my fingerprints has situated himself behind a typewriter. The dog barks louder and louder. I hear voices in another room yelling, "Shut up for God's sake. Be quiet, you dumb dog."

I catch the police officer's eye. "You're all set. You can leave anytime," he says. The dog barks again, and he drops his pen. He looks in the direction of the noise and then at me. "Just like a woman, can't keep her mouth shut."

He smiles broadly at his joke.

I stare at him, feeling the immediate need to escape. I wonder if anyone would block the exit if I ran for my life. The officer ponders his joke and laughs to himself.

A week ago, a former version of me would have gotten up and effortlessly engaged this man in a discussion about misogyny, power, and politics. A week ago, I might have spent some time wondering about the woman this police officer was married to and whether she was afraid of him. Or why he picked a job where he is supposed to protect people when he seems rather menacing himself.

While an undergraduate at Brandeis University and immersed in feminist politics, I had studied rape's political context—rape as power, rape as misogyny, rape as weapon of war—but not its significant impact on individuals. During my senior year, a student was raped at the train stop near campus. A campus police bulletin warned students to be careful because "something happened" near the railroad tracks. They couldn't even say the word, a word too ugly and frightening to acknowledge in writing. The victim approached my friend group, upset by the headline, and we discussed the word choice sitting in the Women's Coalition office one night after dinner.

"Why can't they say it?" the woman asked. "How will everyone know to take it seriously?" Her hands shook with a slight tremor, and I wanted to warm them with my own, but held back.

"'Something happened' could mean anything. Someone saw a coyote; they were mooned by some kids driving by," I said, regretting the latter example as too lighthearted.

"When people make the word unspeakable, it makes victims feel like they shouldn't talk about it. If even the police can't say it in a bulletin, what does that tell us?" my friend Julie said.

We worked, with the survivor's permission, to rewrite the statement in a story for the student paper, with the boldfaced headline SOMETHING HAPPENED—IT WAS RAPE. Julie and I wrote and edited it, showing it to the survivor so she could vet every single word. Then we bulk mailed the newspaper home to parents, using the Women's Coalition budget for the huge postage charges. This action wound us up in the office of the dean of students, where it seemed like we might get into trouble until we argued about free speech and shamed him about the school's reluctance to tell the truth in the first place. "Why was it so hard to write the word 'rape' in the bulletin? Rape isn't a 'something.' People can't evaluate their risk when you're so vague. What about that word scares you so much?" We shouted at the dean over one another, and he let us go without even a warning.

Another time, one of our professors suggested we invite Linda Lovelace to speak about how she had been forced to be in the film

Deep Throat and had been exploited sexually and financially for years by her manager. I thought of rape then only theoretically, as a symbol of men's power over women, as a representation of patriarchy. I never once considered the psychological impact that extreme violence might have on one's sense of self and ability to function over years.

As I leave the police station, though, I am so far away from that strong, self-assured woman of just a few days ago. I feel like she died a lifetime before. I miss her all of a sudden—her spunk and youthful hubris disguised as wisdom. I miss her self-confidence and her ease.

I miss her so much it aches.

Unlike that dog in the police station that can't seem to shut up, I am rendered mute. I consider whether I have the courage to ask the officer if I can see my fingerprints for a minute, take the paper, rip it into tiny pieces, and throw it in his face. Instead, I just walk out the door.

I am now certain they will never find the men who raped me. They probably won't even look. As rattled as my thinking is, I still recognize disregard when I see it. What can I possibly say that would make a difference to a person who would make a joke like that to someone who had just been raped—a joke that categorizes all women as loud and annoying, unaware of the space we take up and effortlessly compared to dogs? How dare we be so noisy! How dare we have a voice!

I wander outside and search for a place to buy a pack of cigarettes, the only comfort I can think of at the moment.

I know how to take care of myself, I know how to take care of myself, I know how to take care of myself, I repeat silently as I walk.

—

This moment stays with me still—more potent than the memory of the actual rapes. While I never excused the rapists for what they did, I often thought about them with unanswered questions more than simple rage or hatred. Were they really breaking into houses for the money, as they had said? Did they just happen to find a naked young woman sleeping on a hot night and they hadn't planned what happened in advance? I'm not certain whether any of that would have mattered to me, if it were true, but I can't deny I thought about it.

They said they wouldn't kill me and they didn't. Maybe their lives were hard, I tried telling myself. Maybe they had families who were hungry. This was the lens I most often turned on them in the early days as I struggled. I thought understanding them in some way would help me more than unprocessed fury and disbelief. Even years later—when I wondered why I seemed so stuck—those hours of being raped and fearing for my life weren't what ultimately crushed me. Rather, it was the experience at the police station offering my fingertips to law enforcement, hoping it would help them in their investigation. I expected more from them, and I needed more from them. I went to the "good guys" to help get the "bad guys," and there was no help to be found.

A few days after my attack, Boston's mayor, Raymond J. Flynn, announced the creation of the Boston Sexual Assault Unit, stating that the goal was to "ensure Boston will be an open, peaceful city where women won't have to walk in fear" and to "educate women about protecting themselves from these crimes."[7] He made no specific remarks on how the unit might work to prevent perpetration or solve crimes. A friend of mine, who now teaches women and gender studies at a midwestern college, was present at the forum and offered her thoughts on what she had just heard: "What we need to do is get the city of Boston to provide more education to men to get them to start thinking about what violence against women really is."[7]

I hadn't read the paper that week and wasn't watching the news. And there was no further contact with anyone in law enforcement that would lead me to believe these summer break-ins were their highest priority. The mayor's grand gesture was lost on me then and it seemed lost on the detectives assigned to my case as well.

—

Several years ago, I was asked to participate in a police training video commissioned by the Boston Area Rape Crisis Center and the Municipal Police Institute.[8] I said yes immediately and showed up at the BARCC office in Cambridge for filming. The video's purpose was to help police respond more effectively to rape victims. As the tape rolled, I told the story about my fingerprinting experience and how frightened I felt while being interviewed by the police. My goal in participating was to encourage police to expand their thinking about responding to survivors of rape and abuse and to investigate claims rather than dismiss them. The problems begin when police see the victim first as a "case" rather than as a human being who's been violently harmed during a felony. They know the same statistics the rest of us do: that sexual assault cases rarely make it to court and, when they do, rarely result in conviction. Given that, officers may consider their efforts to investigate rape futile and it's not surprising how many rape reports are dismissed before an investigation even takes place. Although not every police officer dismisses rape charges outright, it's important to emphasize that some do. If law enforcement officers believe their job is to *solve* crimes, rape cases will continue to frustrate them and victims will experience that frustration and reluctance to fully engage. If they believe their jobs are to *investigate* sex crimes, not only will more rape cases likely be solved but also victims' experience engaging with law enforcement will improve.

I pleaded to the camera, imagining the officers who might see the training video, "Communicate what steps you took on the victim's behalf even if you came up short. Investigate; do your job; update victims and check in with them. Don't hide from them because you haven't yet solved their cases."

If sexual assault survivors don't feel seen or believed by those whose job it is to serve and protect citizens and investigate crimes, they will conclude the crimes committed against them are of no import to law enforcement or anyone else, for that matter.

Three

Aunt Bar is crying on the phone. She is crying so hard that I'm worried her asthma will be triggered. This condition used to send her to the ER every few months when she was younger, and I don't want to be the cause of a hospital trip.

Come on Bar, breathe, I think. A cool breeze from Emmy's kitchen window touches the back of my sweaty neck. I need another shower.

I stare at the plants on the kitchen counter. The Christmas cactus looks dry. It's in a Guatemalan pot that has swirls of watermelon pink, mirroring the color of the single bud blooming on the cactus. *This plant is out of sync*, I think. June is six months too late for a bud. Someone needs to let this little guy look out the window at the sunshine so it can recover its timing. A couple of the shoots are shriveled and look like they need pinching off. I tug at one of them; it resists and stays stubbornly attached to the rest of the plant. My pulling turns the entire thing over, and a bit of dirt falls onto the kitchen faucet and into the sink. I turn the water on to eliminate the evidence, wanting to stay a welcome houseguest.

The phone receiver feels heavy in my hand, reminding me I am having a conversation with someone. My beloved aunt Barbara. I need to figure out what I can say to help her stop crying.

Don't worry. I'm fine is a lie.

It's okay. It wasn't so bad is also untrue.

Maybe someone could come up to Boston to check on me is stuck in my throat, since I already insisted they do not, and I look again at the poor dry Christmas cactus and want to cradle it to my breast.

It simply isn't practical.

Where would they stay? Where would they eat? What would they do?

My aunts—Barbara and Marlene—and my mother got the news from my older sister, Judy. I told Judy because I knew she'd be calm through her worry and take care of business. She calls them all, and each of them calls me within minutes of one another. Since we all live in different cities, we have only the phone to deal with family crises. My words come out sparingly those first few days, and each of them wants to talk daily. As much as I love them, I can't. Their pain and worry bury mine.

Every day is the same: I wake up; I walk; I think about what happened and float through the day. They have lives of their own, they work, there isn't room for them at Emmy's house, and hotels cost too much. Our cherished family visits consist of hanging out and catching up on all that we'd missed because of the physical distance between us. There's no place for us to do that here. My voice is limited now, hungry for silence I mistake for peace.

It takes me almost twenty-four hours after the attack to figure out how to tell them. Having Judy call my mom is crucial. I can't do it myself—the ache I know will be in her voice impossible to hear. My mother will require caretaking, and I'm not up to the task.

The calls get made. Judy does a good job, and now they all know I was raped and are distraught. I am glad they know but, as I anticipated, am having a hard time bearing witness to their pain.

"Uncle Paul told me he's going to come to Boston and kill the men who did this to you," Bar says.

"Well," I say softly, "they haven't caught them, and honestly I don't know how likely it is they will. So just how does he plan to do that?" I start tugging on a thread fraying my shorts. "Maybe he should wait until the police find them. Or maybe he shouldn't kill them at all because then he'd be guilty of murder. You'd have to visit him in jail up in Boston and you hate the cold."

"He just loves you so much and feels helpless." Her voice breaks. "Isn't there something, anything, we can do?" she pleads.

"There is," I say. "Keep my mom busy. She can't come here and pace around the apartment all day. It just doesn't seem fair to Emmy and Steve to throw her into the mix when they're already putting me up. Just call her a lot, okay?"

"Okay, honey; that's easy. I'll do that, of course. And, I'll call you tomorrow," she says.

So many people need updates and check-ins on how I'm doing and what they can do to help. Emmy and I come up with a plan—one call a day from a friend or family member, and only if I nod yes. "Oh, hi, Amy, you want to talk to Mich?" she says to a friend, staring right at me. "Let me see if she's around." If I take the call, that's my limit for the day. She will tell the next person that I'm resting and doing as well as can be expected and to call back tomorrow. Emmy always adds a modicum of reassurance to soften the rejection: that she and Steve have their eyes on me, that anyone going through this would need time.

The multiple daily calls slow within a few weeks, and I'm again able to concentrate on the massive effort it takes to wake up each morning.

—

I remember my uncle Paul's revenge fantasies clearly and recognize them now for what they were: an effort to regain control and do something to help. But I didn't want to be treated like a tender flower that needed retribution. The idea that hurting someone—even if they had hurt someone else—could be seen as helpful or healing is misguided. Victims of violence generally do not desire additional violence to feel better. I resisted any caretaking that only added to my feelings of powerlessness.

It's important for men to work to understand the impact of sexual assault, but too often these efforts are superficial. One organization, called Walk a Mile in Her Shoes, organizes fund-raisers in cities across the country, where men don a pair of red high heels and, according to the group's website, walk to "help men better understand and appreciate women's experiences . . . decreasing the potential for violence" and showing "that men are willing and able to be courageous partners with women in making the world a safer place."[1]

Walking in high heels—a stereotypical symbol of female attire—will not help men understand the high risk of experiencing violence that women face over their lifetimes or its impact. It will not help them understand sexual violence or abuse experienced by other men, transgender persons, or children. Yet for almost twenty years, these walks have occurred in multiple cities, often sponsored by police departments and universities. It may not be harmful, but it's not effective.

The Obama White House's It's on Us campaign addressed sexual assault on college campuses and encouraged young people to "take the pledge" to stop sexual violence.[2] At the 2015 Grammy Awards, Obama said, "Nearly one in five women in America has experienced rape or attempted rape and more than one in four women have experienced some form of domestic violence. It's not okay and it has to stop." These astounding rates of felony violence merit more than a statement that "it's not okay" and deserve a more specific plan than "it has to stop."[3] A cameo at the Grammys allowed only a sound bite and nothing more serious. Different media sites referred to his words as "powerful,"[4] "important, inspiring"[5] and "intense,"[6] as if the act of naming sexual violence and domestic abuse as "not okay" was so astonishing that a U.S. president deserved praise for mentioning it at all.

—

I found it complicated in those early days to figure out how to separate the entire male species from male perpetration. I looked to find men out there in the world whom I could trust not to hurt me. Movies helped, since there was a comfortable distance between me and the people on the screen. I watched *It's a Wonderful Life* during the holidays and wished the angel would visit me with his kind smile and twinkly eyes. I sobbed over Sidney Poitier's portrayal of a teacher in *To Sir with Love*; his character reminded me of my father, who had worked in an underresourced school in Chicago. I both craved and feared male companionship. It wasn't practical to hide from half the population, and I needed a reminder of men's potential for kindness beyond Emmy's husband—sweet, gentle Steve—whom I considered an anomaly.

I found myself invoking the memory of my dad, someone I had loved and with whom I'd felt safe. He died of cancer when I was barely seven years old, and my memories had faded over the many years since his passing. He became etched in my child's mind as a mythic figure, larger than life and not very real. When I thought about him, I saw him as ten feet tall, scooping me up onto his shoulders until I was as high as the highest skyscraper in Chicago. His shoulders were so broad and I so small that I could practically walk around on them without fear of falling. He had me and I was safe. He was the moon landing; he was the Beatles; he was a Cubs World Series sure to come soon.

After I am attacked in my home, I dream of him most nights and crave his return. I plan on buying a ticket to Chicago just to sit near his grave. One day, just when I feel as if I can't get through another moment of my new life without him, he comes to me.

Looking at me patiently, he waits.

The world looks very different now than it did to my dad in the late sixties, when he left it. But he inhabits it without complaint or hesitation, for my sake and my sake alone. I see his handsome face and kind eyes and feel him grabbing my hand and holding me tight, his embrace one I can bear, as he does anything he can to try and make me feel safe. I don't feel much safer, but I am beyond grateful for the effort. Because he is dead, he can't help much with the practical issues I face, like collecting my things at my old apartment or managing daily living needs that now feel overwhelming. Still, I conjure him to simply be with me in my hurt, to love me and ask for very little in return save the relief of providing a moment of ease.

I breathe in the smell of his skin as I walk the streets of Boston, trying to survive the day ahead of me. He smells like roses. His skin is smooth flannel. His hair is soft sand. His smile is crooked, warm, and wise. I talk to him often as I walk, from morning till night.

"You're the only person I know who knew you were going to

die," I say out loud to him, remembering my mom telling me how scared he had been after being told of his grim prognosis. "You had months to worry about dying, and I only had a couple of hours, but there's really nothing else quite like it, is there? You wait and hope; then you give up and then hope again. You think about the people you love. You try to remember if you believe in miracles." I shift and look into his sad eyes. "Even with the disbelief and terror you feel, somehow you worry more about the people you'll leave behind than what's happening to you."

I had this same conversation with my dad every day. I only had to think of him if I needed to cry, and when my tears came he sat right down next to me, never moving from my side. Sometimes he held me tight. Sometimes he buried his face in his hands and we cried together.

There was one other man I spent time with after the rapes, a college friend named Isaac. I felt like his frequent phone calls, all expressing an urgency to see me, were to reassure himself I was okay. But later I learned that he held something inside he needed to share, and it mattered when he did.

Back when he first came into my life, I was a sophomore at Brandeis. He was loud and contrary and picked fights, perhaps an odd choice of a friend. Our little group of radical lesbian feminists probably should have confronted him about his behavior, but he intimidated us into silence. "With Isaac, my values go out the window," I said to Julie after he argued with a friend at dinner. "There's some sort of sadness under the anger, and I guess I'm just a sucker for that."

"That's no excuse," Julie said. "We shouldn't just give him a pass for rudeness."

Isaac was a big man in both directions: six feet tall and close to three hundred pounds. He had a large scar on his forehead that gave him the appearance of a unicorn with the horn penetrating his eyebrow. When his lip curled and his left shoulder rose, I knew Isaac was about to pounce.

Once, he and I were eating lunch at a diner when our waitress arrived. "There's a great pasta dish as the special today, and it's a nice portion, too."

Isaac smiled, his lip taking on the telltale curl. "Oh, a nice portion, is it? I must look like someone who needs a lot of food. Do you think that's a polite thing to say to a fat man?"

The waitress took a step back. "I was talking to both of you. The portion sizes are big here. It's a fact for both of you to consider."

"Do you think my little friend here, who weighs about a hundred pounds, is looking for a really big serving? Wow, your lie came so easily." He gave an angry little laugh and I stared down at the menu.

Isaac called incessantly to make plans after he learned I was raped, and I had no idea how to say a simple no to him.

After agreeing to hang out, we sat on a stoop waiting for a bookstore to open. "Isaac, can we talk?" I squeaked out. He had been unpleasant to Emmy when he picked me up, accusing her of not giving me his phone messages, and I planned to tell him he needed to stop insulting my friends or I wasn't going to see him anymore. The thought of making this man angry terrified me.

Isaac looked at me and I sensed he knew what was coming. He sighed and, with some effort, reached around to his back pocket and pulled out his wallet, opening it to show me a picture of a beautiful young man. The boy was thin, with trimmed black hair and a clear forehead, no scar. He looked around eighteen, a high school yearbook headshot of a smiling stranger.

"Who is that?"

"It's me," he finally said, in a soft voice.

"In my last year of high school, around the holidays, I started getting headaches. Sometimes, the pain was so bad, I would cry." I listened, trying to picture him when he was that boy in the wallet. "I had a brain tumor, and the doctors told my parents I was most likely going to die." He wiped his face with his hands, never taking his eyes off the photo. "I had brain surgery and spent months getting treatments. This scar is partly from the radiation and partly from surgery," he continued. "Well, obviously, I lived. My family was so happy to have me back, after months trying to prepare for my death. As far as they were concerned, it was over.

"But it wasn't over for me. I had no idea how to live after waiting to die. I gained a bunch of weight and pushed my family and their relief as far away as possible."

The pain in his face warmed him.

"Not dying kind of ruined my life."

"I think I . . ." my voice trailed off.

"Take a lesson from me. Do whatever you can to feel better. You're just too nice to get lost in what happened to you. You've had quite a blow." He leaned into me and I let him.

"You're alive even if you may not always believe that. I see you, I get it, and I understand. Don't let it destroy you. It can, and it would make sense if it did, but don't let it."

Isaac put the picture away and eased into a soft, gentle smile.

If I hadn't worried that he would somehow misconstrue the gesture, I would have grabbed his hand, stroked his face, and walked silently around Boston with him all day and all night long. He was an unlikely guardian angel, but there he stood. The darkness that weighted him down now held a morsel of light—a small sliver of hope. I felt myself reaching for it.

Spending time with this often angry man gave me more than I could have ever imagined. After that soft and vulnerable moment on the stoop, he went back to having unpleasant interactions with strangers, and eventually we parted ways. Still, I thought of him often when I felt like I should surrender rather than live this unfamiliar life, watching with envy and bafflement as my friends moved on to the futures we had dreamed of together. Then I'd think of that boy in the worn photo and find it in myself to look ahead and hope for a time where some optimism might still reside. I thought, given the generosity it must have taken to tell me his story, I owed Isaac at least that much.

—

Finding help and deciding from whom to get it felt urgent and yet confusing. In some ways, since I didn't feel like me anymore, strangers were easier to deal with than those with whom I had loving and deep relationships, who seemed constantly alarmed by this new person in front of them. I talked a few times with someone at the Boston Area Rape Crisis Center, the second oldest rape crisis center in the nation, formed in 1973 and still in existence today. According to Janet Yassen, a Boston therapist and one of the founders of BARCC, "Everything in the gender based violence movement was created by the grassroots/ground up. From the beginning, BARCC always had a social justice mission; working on law reform, public health policy and social action to raise awareness and to confront the myths about interpersonal sexual violence."[7] Their work in Boston has expanded and grown over the forty-plus years they've been in existence.

The center was housed in Cambridge, a short T ride away. They offered a twenty-four-hour hotline and counseling at no charge. I called the hotline the day after the break-in because Lise told me I should. "Maybe they can help," she said, handing me a scrap of paper. I looked at the phone number and name scribbled there. *Hmm, rape is apparently a crisis*, I thought. The validation provided by the center's very name helped me make the call.

Rape is a crisis. I'm in a crisis. This is one big mess of a crisis.

The woman I met had a short haircut with bangs and looked even younger than I was. She had the biggest round eyes I had ever seen. They made her face look like she was surprised all the time, whether I was recounting a detail about the rapes or a small unrelated detail about my week. In the immediate aftermath of the attack, I didn't find talking all that useful. *Nothing will undo this* was my constant internal refrain.

I stopped going to BARCC after a few meetings with the big-eyed counselor and then found a rape victims' support group that met, of all places, at Beth Israel Hospital. Beth Israel was one of the first hospitals in the nation to develop rape crisis services in the 1970s, along with Boston City Hospital a few miles down the road. The support group met once a week in the main hospital building, far away from the emergency room, or I wouldn't have gone. I was the only one in the group who had been raped by a stranger, let alone two. This fact left me feeling freakish and angry. *This is not my peer group,* I thought as I left every week. What do I have in common with women who were raped by abusive boyfriends and husbands they've been trying to leave for years? My values had flown out the window. I was in too much pain to see how much we had in common, and self-pity trumped any empathy.

I left the hospital every week reciting in my head why I didn't belong there:

Two men.

Tied up, blindfolded, gagged.

Lesbian.

Younger than these women by half.

Still, I went to the group without fail every week for months, cataloging my grievances as I walked home: *I don't really like any of them. I can't believe the group is at Beth Israel. Why is everyone else so much older than me?* When I look back now, I remember how concerned the group members were about me. They'd ask me questions when I was silent and made sure I didn't make rash decisions about work, shelter, relationships, and my own personal safety. "You still take walks at night? Maybe go with a friend once in a while. We worry about you; do it for us." One of them would say some version of this to me every week when the sessions ended. Another might make a slight gesture of physical contact if I was nearby—a brush of my shoulder I could somehow tolerate without shuddering. Something kept me going there.

The stories of the other group members were ugly—tales of bad men who didn't care or understand the emotional and physical scars they were inflicting. Most of the group members were terrified of their perpetrators; many had been hospitalized and badly hurt. "So my sister said I should move in with her and just stop blaming myself," said one. And another, "My daughter has been great, although I feel guilty involving her. The man I have the restraining order on is her father."

During this time, I never once juxtaposed the support I received from these victims of violence and the utter silence from the police. There had been an article written four days after our break-in, "A Series of Rapes Alarms Allston-Brighton."[8] In it, Lise describes the break-in and talks about the assailants. She points out, "[They] weren't afraid. They left fingerprints all over the place." Someone described as "a high ranking official in the police department" acknowledged an "alarming citywide increase in rape." I anticipated hearing something soon—an arrest, an update, a call to see if I remembered anything else now that I had more distance. But there had been none of that. Only silence. So instead I found this support group and focused on feeling heard, cared about, and understood. I'd deal with the rest when I had the strength.

Once in a while, I talked to the group about my friends and family. My sister was having a medical work-up for a constellation of unusual symptoms, and she called to say the doctors thought she might have lupus. I love my sister very much and was really concerned about her. Still, I spent one group complaining about how my mother seemed so worried about Judy and yet so uncomfortable asking me how I was doing.

I recounted this phone call to the group. "Are my walls that impenetrable? Is rape that scary?"

"Try not to make it so hard for someone to be let in on what you're going through," one of the group members had said.

"How are you doing, honey?" my mom had asked during a different phone call. "Emmy said you weren't sleeping that well."

"I'm getting by," I said. "Emmy's pregnant and Steve's been offered a job in California at a new lab. They're moving in a few months." I knew I should have been happy for my dear friends, but instead I felt crushed. I had no idea how I'd survive without them or where I would go.

"That's so wonderful," my mother said, her voice rising in pleasure. Please tell them how happy I am."

When I relayed this conversation to the support group, they were silent for so long the leader had to step in. "Can anyone relate? Offer their thoughts?"

The woman next to me said, "Maybe you just need to be mad at her for a while, but I want to say this and I hope you can hear me. Your mom is most certainly devastated and doesn't know what to do. It seems you want her to know without you saying so and that's completely fair given the circumstances." I looked down. "Try telling *us*. Tell us over time. We're old. We're moms. Try telling us. We won't break."

That night I saw that we weren't so different after all. We all needed something, and learning to trust again was a big part of that. And as much as I hated walking anywhere near Beth Israel Hospital, I returned week after week.

I told them how I felt, in pieces, over time. And they didn't break. And neither did I.

—

I finally saw my mother in September, having purchased a flight for my high school reunion several months earlier, before the rapes. I had no intention of going to the reunion anymore but decided to use the ticket to visit home. It felt as if I had lived several lifetimes in the last few months, all without her. She was my mother. It would have been reasonable if I looked to her to help repair my shattered soul, or at least to help with the myriad of practical issues I faced, like finding a new apartment. But I hadn't been able to reach for her hand across that phone line.

Maybe I said, "No, don't come, really." Maybe it was, "Let's wait until I know where I'm staying." I must have been convincing, and she complied.

The second after the rapists left my apartment, my thoughts turned to my mother. My death would have killed her; I was grateful she was spared. As for me and how I was going to process the extreme violence I had just experienced—that was less clear. It was the strangest thing, really. Any rational person could tell me that the terrible danger had passed. The rapists were gone. The task ahead was to focus on getting well, adorning myself with the label "survivor."

"In cases like this, miss, where there's more than one perpetrator and a weapon—we often find a body. You don't know how lucky you are," the officer who had dusted our house for fingerprints had said the morning after.

I found it baffling this police officer could see things so differently than I did. From his perspective, I could have been murdered but wasn't. There was something fortunate about that, which we should celebrate.

For months after the attack, my body was wholly unaware that the danger had passed. From the second I had realized the light coming into my room was created by two unpredictable strangers with a knife, I had been overrun by fear. Small electric shocks on each of thousands of nerve endings went off in my body all day and all night long. There was not a thing I felt lucky about, having been humiliated and violently sexually violated as I begged for my life.

It would never be over for me.

Even if something horrible could have been worse, it does not erase how bad it actually was or make a person lucky. This point is especially poignant when a law enforcement official says it to the victim of a crime historically underresponded to by his profession. The crime I was lucky to not have been the victim of—murder— would have been considered a legitimate crime. But the crime I experienced was not, and it left an indelible mark, despite the officer's assertion that it could have been worse. While nothing would undo the deep impact of this trauma, some acknowledgment by the officer of the gravity of the crime I experienced might have helped me make sense of the pain I felt for years. His message did not feel hopeful or optimistic, but deeply dismissive of the experience of sexual violence.

My mother had also expressed relief I hadn't been killed, and I worried this had clouded her ability to see what I might need emotionally from her. In my fog, I believed having my mom come to Boston in the immediate aftermath would have been my taking care of her. So I said don't come, and I meant it.

At least I thought I did.

Many years later, I was introduced to the Persian word *tarof*.

Tarof describes a common practice in Iran, layered with subtext.[9] A first assertion is understood as a gesture of politeness that must be refused and haggled over. A typical example used to explain *tarof* is a taxi ride. The passenger asks the driver what he owes. The taxi driver emphatically says, "I couldn't possibly charge you. The pleasure of your company and our pleasant conversation was all the payment I require."

The passenger knows the rejection of money is not genuine but simple politeness that must also be refused. "But of course I must pay. I couldn't possibly accept such generosity."

Much back-and-forth occurs.

Finally, the passenger convinces the taxi driver he should accept the fare. "Fine," the driver says, "but only because you insist." Both understand at the outset that the driver must be paid, but participate in *tarof* since it is integral to the cultural exchange. If the passenger had left the cab without paying, the driver would then have demanded his money. *Tarof* exists only if both parties understand what is supposed to happen up to the point when the exchange is properly concluded.

My grandfather was a Persian Jew who left Iran around 1920 and settled in Chicago. He married and fathered four children, whom he supported by working multiple jobs, when there was work to be had. He didn't talk much about his homeland and had moved on by necessity. They were all Americans now.

My mother, half Iranian and first-generation American born, knew almost nothing about her heritage, save the Persian meals her father cooked on holidays. I do wish that she had absorbed the cultural legacy of *tarof*. I needed her to come, despite my insistence that I was fine without her, but she was too afraid to do so without being sure that she was welcome.

Had she come despite my saying no, I might have been more confident in her ability to take charge, to ignore the first words spoken by a daughter so overcome that she may not have known what she needed. But she took me at my word.

The wisdom of *tarof* and its virtues were lost on both of us. When I said "don't come," she was supposed to argue; I would continue to protest, and then she was supposed to insist some more. Then, just maybe, I would have relented. My younger self never forgave her for following my instruction.

That is, until I understood why.

My sister and I talked about this when we were both in our forties, when my mother was dying in a hospital in Cleveland from a brain bleed resulting from a stroke. Judy and I were in her car after a challenging visit to the hospital, where we'd sat for hours holding our mother's hand, listening to beeping monitors, and telling her it was okay to let go. She had not accepted our guidance and stubbornly held on for a while longer.

As we reviewed the moments in our lives when our mother had been at both her best and most challenging, this moment emerged. Judy brought it up, and I acknowledged pain I hadn't let go of fully.

"How could she not have come?" I looked at Judy driving, thinking how much she meant to me and how infrequently we'd been in the same city for much of the past twenty years. "Can you imagine if one of our daughters went through something like that? Could anything have stopped us from jumping in a car and driving a hundred miles an hour to get to her?"

"I can tell you what happened," Judy said. She had been in a high school chorus ensemble that won a number of state competitions. Her voice was so soothing, carrying the undertones of a melody, no matter if the subject was pleasant or difficult. "Mom was frantically calling the airlines trying to get a plane ticket, and you had just insisted you weren't ready for a visit. So I called a rape crisis center to ask them what we should do."

"You did?" The signs on the highway blurred; Judy was driving too fast, and I reflexively started watching out for police cars.

"I did," she replied. "And the person I spoke with said there was nothing more important than letting you have control after an event where you didn't have any. She was emphatic that whether we liked it or not, we had to listen to you and have your permission to come visit."

"Wow," I said, not knowing how to respond. "Wow," I said again, needing more time to consider what she'd just told me. "That's astonishing. I wish I had known this years ago so Mom and I could have talked about it. I wonder why she never mentioned it." The impending loss of my mother became overlaid with the unexpected prospect of forgiveness, a possibility I hadn't considered. Judy had sought help from professionals, and they told her the family had to put my needs first. Whether they liked it or not, I needed to consent to the visit.

"You know, I think that rape crisis person might have been wrong," I finally said. "But so was I when I said don't come." Judy pulled over into a mall parking lot, turned off the car, and shifted in her seat to look at me. "What I should have said to her was, 'I need you to come, but I'm unable to do anything to help figure out the details—the plane, the hotel, the rental car, how long you should stay, whether you should come alone or bring everyone.'"

Judy nodded. "Mom was confusing that way. She loved us both so much but sometimes couldn't put her feelings into actions without some direction." I noticed Judy was talking about her in the past tense and remembered we had several difficult days ahead.

I talked to Emmy—with whom I had remained close—later that day to let her know the seriousness of my mother's condition. "I thought for years she didn't care enough," I said. "I assumed she'd felt relieved she didn't have to come and take care of me. It helps a little to know she thought she was doing the right thing, that she was doing what she was told."

That day, my sister had given me a gift I had not expected. I felt so grateful that she had seen the wisdom of providing it, even in her own grief during our shared moment of impending loss. It opened my heart and, in forgiving my mother, allowed me to heal a bit myself.

—

My plane lands in Ohio, two days before the high school reunion I won't attend. The Cleveland airport is almost ninety miles from Ashtabula, and my mom sits curbside waiting in a white Ford I don't recognize. She must have needed a car after my stepfather moved out. I wonder what the house will feel like without him, whether the ever-present smell of Terry's stale alcoholic sweat will have dissipated now that he's gone. It had been several years since he'd had a drink, but when I last saw him at my college gradua-tion, his pores still exuded that briny, damp barrel smell of pro-cessed whiskey. He and I have not spoken for about a year, and I am stunned that he has not been in touch since the assault.

"Mom, you married him when I was eleven; he raised me for over ten years and hasn't even called me. I almost died. He di-vorced you, not me," I say in the car, easier words to utter with us both staring straight ahead.

"He asks about you and asked me for your number when it happened. I don't know what to say. You know he loves you." Her voice carries a squeak of humiliation.

"Don't defend him." I cradle my face with both hands. "Every single one of my roommates' parents called me that very week, and it wasn't easy to find me. He's my stepfather."

I look at my mother, and instead of the shared rage about Ter-ry's behavior I hope for, it is her shame that stares back at me. *Why did I marry him? Why did it take me so long to leave him?* The familiar plaintive cries are etched in every line of her face as we drive.

I'd written Terry a letter but never sent it. Julie had stopped by Emmy's to visit, and I'd asked her to listen to it. "If you're writing to get something off your chest, send it," she'd said when I finished reading. "Otherwise, don't bother. Not calling you after what happened tells you everything you need to know." Now, I'm in the same city as my mother and stepfather and am ready for a fight.

She and I have settled in the living room of her ranch house. "I can't even express how wonderful it is to see you." She clasps her hands together. "I can't believe you're here. How are you doing, love?"

"I'm okay. Emmy and Steve leave for San Diego soon, so I'm looking for a place. There's a program Lise just told me about called victim compensation to help with rent and my other bills."

Her face darkens. By mistake, I have given permission to dis-cuss the attack.

"Thank God you weren't killed. I can't even consider what could have happened; I don't think I could have survived it," she says, and with no warning, every bit of rage I've been holding explodes.

"Well, that is better for you, but the jury is out on whether I think that was better for me."

She grabs her waist, hugging herself. "What are you saying? What do you mean?"

"I mean exactly what I said."

"What do you mean?" she repeats. "You can't be saying you're sorry to be alive? Do you wish they killed you? My God!"

"What I'm saying is that you can't always make lemonade out of lemons, Mom!" I'm yelling. I'll know this fact later because my throat will hurt no matter how much water I drink leaning at her kitchen sink. "There is nothing to be grateful for when this shouldn't have happened at all, and I am not okay just because I look like I am alive!"

The officer's words become a refrain in my head: *lucky, lucky, lucky, lucky we didn't find a body, so gosh darn lucky, lucky, lucky.*

She jumps up from the couch and runs around in circles like a child playing musical chairs, sobbing. "What have I done? What have I said? What did I do? What have I done? What have I said?"

I let her wear herself out. She runs and runs, mumbling no longer at me, "What have I done? What did I say wrong?"

Finally, she slows down, and when she's near enough, I reach up and grab her arm, pulling her down next to me. "Mom, stop it. Here's what I need you to do—stop trying to find a way to make it not so bad. It was really bad, and it still is bad. It's a fact we can't change by looking on the bright side. I wasn't saying I'm going to hurt myself, but please don't try and tell me that it could've been worse, because it absolutely could not have been worse. I know you're glad I am alive." She thinks I've forgiven her and collapses in my arms.

I hold her like a child, rocking her as a gesture of comfort. I don't realize that I am sobbing now, too, and she is holding me as well.

"I know it was bad, honey, of course I do." She rubs my knotted black curls. "You just cry. It's okay. I know it was bad. I do. I know it was. I got you. I'm so sorry."

Four

The attack occurs on a Thursday night, and on Friday morning someone calls my workplace saying I won't be in. On Monday I am still in pain, barely verbal, and not ready to face anyone. Emmy leaves a message for my employer, which I overhear: "This is a friend of Michelle's. Please call me back. I don't mean to shock you, but did you see the news this weekend about the home invasion in Allston? We need to talk." I close the door to the spare room and take a six-hour nap.

After graduation, I worked for two years in jobs that paid my rent but had nothing to do with my interest in writing. At the time of the break-in, I had been working as an assistant editor for a magazine in Boston with national distribution—a fact I told everyone, even strangers. "I am so glad this turkey is on sale because I want to bring lunch to my new job at a magazine," I remarked at more than one supermarket counter. The job made me feel so proud and hopeful about my career prospects. Then, the break-in happened before I'd even worked there a full year.

I am preoccupied and overwhelmed after the attack but worry about work piling up. When I return to the office one week later, I can't get anything done.

Joe, my boss, acts as if I'd taken an unapproved vacation. He points to a pile of articles. "Can you get to these first; we're behind schedule." He must not know what to say, I think, feeling just as glad. There'd been quite enough sympathy and sad looks during the past week to last forever. Still, he makes it clear I am expected to perform as I did a week ago, which is going to be a problem.

"Karen," he shouts to the only other worker in the office. "Have you firmed up the ads for this month? We're supposed to send everything to print by Friday."

"It's okay. He's just mad he had to do any work. We'll take it one day at a time." Karen pulls me aside and holds both my hands in hers. "I wanted to call you, but I didn't know where you were," she says. "I'm so very sorry. We're all set for this issue. Take it slow and try to ignore him."

I try reading articles and can't make sense of them. My lunch sits untouched. Police sirens make my heart race. I notice myself wiping tears off my cheeks, unaware that I'm feeling anything at all.

Two weeks after my return to work, I go into Joe's office. He gestures toward an empty chair. "Have a seat."

"I'm not doing great," I say, looking past his shoulder out a window with a direct view of the Boston Citgo sign near Fenway Park. "Maybe I should take a short leave of absence. I was thinking a month. I'm not getting as much work done as I'd like." Joe sits listening, hands in his lap. "I'm hoping you'll let me do it—take the time off, I mean. If I were quitting, it would take at least a month to find someone else. Why not just give me that month, and I'll come back in better shape?" I try so hard to keep the pleading out of my voice, to sound confident and sure of my worth, even though I just laid bare my vulnerability.

"I already gave you that first week off and paid it as sick time," he replies quickly, as if my request comes as no surprise. "If I give you the month off, what's to say you won't need more time, or quit then? It would put us way behind schedule if I had to fill the position after waiting for a whole month for you to return. I'll get back to you." I had planned to shake his hand but find my arm glued to my side.

A few days later, Joe calls me into his office. "I thought about your request and can't do it. It's too risky." I wait, thinking he might have more to say. My face feels red-hot, and I eye an open soda can on his desk, thinking I might grab it and run.

I wasn't really asking, I say to myself. *You can't make me stay.*

"Then I'm giving my notice."

The trajectory of my career changed inalterably and for the remainder of my work life when I walked out of the building, leaving my magazine job behind. For the next four years, work would be a thing I did to survive, a thing I did when I could manage it, for the sole purpose of making enough money to pay my bills and buy food. At the time, this reality didn't feel like the consequence of a brutal crime but a personal failure. And how could I have thought otherwise? For me, as for so many other survivors of sexual assault, there were no external signals that what happened was not my fault. The inability to function at work is a common reaction among those who have experienced rape and sexual assault.

Rape survivor Helena Lazaro, an advocate I met during my first foray into activism on untested rape kits, wrote about the meaning of work for her: "Before the abduction, I had dreams about who I wanted to be—a teacher, a writer, an actor. Afterwards, plans were out of the question. Believing your life may end at any moment makes envisioning a future practically impossible. I was only able to work in bursts—a few months at a time—before the symptoms of PTSD and depression made it impossible, losing the momentum necessary to sustain a meaningful professional trajectory. That's one of the hardest things for me to come to terms with: the lost time, the lost life and career—my lost self."[1]

Lavinia Masters, whom I met at the same event where I first met Helena, explains how her assault impacted her career aspirations: "Since I was a child when I was raped, it did not impact my work per se but my education. I was a rebellious and spiteful teenager demanding attention for pain I did not understand. I never completed my degree and it shattered my childhood dreams of becoming an attorney."[2]

The estimated lifetime cost of being raped is over $120,000 per victim, a cumulative economic burden of nearly $3.1 trillion in the United States.[3] A study looking at the long-term economic consequences of rape for victims found that "sexual assault and the related trauma response can disrupt survivors' employment in several ways, including time off, diminished performance, job loss, and inability to work."[4] Every state in the United States has a victim compensation fund meant to help individuals who have experienced rape, homicide, or assault, and money for lost wages is one of the available benefits listed. Assuming victims learn that these funds even exist, they must apply for them, requiring the wherewithal to request and fill out forms. Coverage and amounts vary by state. In order to qualify, most states require victims to report their crime to the police, cooperate with the investigation, submit the application within a certain time frame, and have no insurance or other means to cover the costs.[5]

Requiring victims to report a crime in order to receive compensation is a serious barrier for those in need of funds to survive. Dozens of articles are available that would give anyone considering reporting a rape concern: for example, "Where Police Failed Rape Victims," the lede of which notes, "They Pressured Victims. They Didn't Interview Suspects. Then They Destroyed

Rape Kits . . . [and] Used 'Disturbing' Practices";[6] "How Police Still Fail Rape Victims: A New Justice Department Report Exposes How the Baltimore P.D. Isn't Doing Enough for Victims of Sexual Assault—But They're Not the Only Ones";[7] and an article on inadequate police training and staffing with a lede that declares, "High Turnover, Thin Staffing and Poor Training Plague Police Departments' Investigations of Rapes and Other Sexual Assaults."[8] Until we make training police to respond effectively to rape victims a national imperative, it is unjust to make crucial financial resources available only to victims who report crimes. Those responsible for disbursing victim compensation funds should consider alternative ways to confirm the need, including a therapist's note that the patient is in treatment, documentation of a rape exam done at a hospital, and a statement from the survivor for the reasons they have not reported their assault to law enforcement.

There has to be a process for disbursement of victim compensation monies, but the system is not set up to respect and honor the victims' experiences and, instead, places the responsibility on them to seek financial protections and get their needs met at a most basic level. The first line on the application for victims applying to receive funding from the Massachusetts victim compensation fund states, "I understand that the Victim Compensation Fund is a fund of last resort."[9] For many victims, this funding is essential at a time when work may be impossible, going home unsafe, finding shelter critical, and addressing trauma with a professional expensive. The accessibility of this resource is key to many people's economic and emotional survival.

I learned about the victim compensation from a friend, not from the detectives I met with in Emmy's apartment. I received one payment early on, a couple thousand dollars. It was invaluable. It helped me pay for some initial therapy and a security deposit on an apartment. It never occurred to me to reapply, nor would I have felt comfortable approaching the victim compensation fund a few years later, when I was suffering just as much and still underemployed as a direct result of the trauma that held me by the throat most days.

In those first few years of underemployment, frequent moves, and unabated post-traumatic stress, I continued to hear nothing from the Boston police. I had called my detective once, a few months after the attack. The conversation lasted two minutes at most. I remember the words, but mostly his tone. I'd done something wrong, broken a rule. What a nuisance, what a bother.

"Hi, Detective, it's Michelle Bowdler from that Glenville Avenue break-in in Allston at the end of June," I said, hoping I didn't need to be any more specific; I couldn't yet say the word "rape" out loud. It took me years to add an "s" at the end of that word to describe what happened accurately—the rapes. "I'll be moving soon and I don't have a new phone number yet, and wondered if I should call you when I do so you'll be able to find me when you have some information or maybe a lead in the case." The phone was so wet with my anxious sweat I had to hold it with a paper towel. "While I have you on the line, do you have any updates? Have there been any more break-ins in the area?"

"We're the police," he said, ignoring my questions. "We know how to find people; that's what we do. Didn't I say I'd call you if we knew anything? And I haven't, so that means I don't have anything."

"That makes sense," I squeaked out. "It's just that I'll be moving into an apartment where the phone is already in someone else's last name, so I didn't know how you would find me. So, you're saying you don't need me to call you back when I get the number?"

"We'll find you if we need you," he reiterated.

I hung up. How, exactly, would he be able to find me if my name wasn't on a lease, I wasn't listed in the phone book, and my driver's license still had my old address on it? I wondered. He said he could do it, but he didn't explain how, and I wasn't going to call back for clarification. Eventually, I lost his card on my third or fourth move. This was our last conversation.

There must not have been any news.

For almost four years after leaving the magazine, I worked as a secretary for a temp agency, the most I could manage. The important part of my work life was the key phrase "temp," which defined my situation as short-lived, meaning not forever, I hoped. "This is just for now," I said to myself, as the weeks turned into months, and the months to years.

The question of when I would feel better no longer took up space in my brain. Fretting about graduate school or when I might be able to concentrate enough to read a book again exhausted me. Most of the time I could convince myself I was only working to support myself while I expanded the editing and writing services I offered through tear-off sheets on utility poles around the city.

I am a writer; I am an editor, I told myself.

I got called once or twice a month to edit something. My few customers had no idea these transactions helped me hold on to whatever self-esteem I still retained. I was connected by an inky thread to the person I used to be and considered making my services free to garner more business. More important, I had a ready answer if I ran into a college acquaintance who asked me what I'd been doing since we graduated: "I'm editing and writing some. It'll be a full-time gig soon."

As I sat answering phones in a series of random offices where I'd been assigned by my temp agency for the week, I wondered if I might ever have some dreams again someday, but I'd lost all sense of optimism and possibility. Quite often, a sense of dread would overtake me and I'd make up an excuse to leave work in the middle of the day.

I wasn't even thinking about what came next. I had a modest paycheck and something to do on the days I could manage to do anything at all, needing the rest of my attention to focus on making certain I was breathing, eating, sleeping, and bathing. Deep inside, I was convinced I'd be doing exactly this for the rest of my life. And even though the answer was appallingly obvious, I still asked myself every single day, "How did I get here; how did this happen?"

No one explained to me, neither the people at Beth Israel or at BARCC, nor the multitude of therapists I saw, how common work disruption is after being the victim of a trauma. In fairness, I never brought it up to ask if this kind of stall was normal. Instead, I felt my humiliation in silence, experiencing it as my own failure. I didn't hear from the police at all. I didn't hear the gravity in their voices when speaking with me about the crime they were investigating. Instead, my intense reactions felt alien and outside the norm—my own self-imposed catastrophe.

—

A few years in, when I was able to work a full week without quitting, I took a longer-term placement, not quite sure whether it could be a sign of something about to change. When the temp agency first sent me to his lab, Dr. Judah Folkman noticed the editing business listed on my résumé. "I'm writing a book," he said. "I'll show you what I have so far and you can help me write the rest." He turned to his office manager. "Call the agency and tell them we're keeping this one."

Shelly, the office manager, had blond curly hair and wore tailored business suits, even though she was surrounded by postdocs in jeans and sneakers. She and I shared an office, giving her a clear view of this not-writing-a-book dance that had been going on between Dr. Folkman and me since I arrived. We kept trying to find a time to meet, but he inevitably got called away to attend to something else and canceled.

"He's been trying to write this book for years. I'm not optimistic." Shelly rolled her eyes and took a sip of the herbal tea she made every morning. She had several things on her desk that marked good self-care: a day calendar with positive affirmations she'd read to me every morning and her own mug so she wouldn't have to use the paper cups in the coffee area.

"I want this to work out with him," I said. "Maybe I could offer to meet on the weekends." I had spent a year typing, filing, and not helping write a book.

"I want to talk to you out of the office," Shelly said. "Don't bring your lunch tomorrow."

"Okay," I said, and wrote her invitation down on a notepad, not trusting myself to remember. I didn't know much about Shelly other than that she did her job, kept to herself, and neither offered details about her personal life nor asked me much about mine. This style—one today I'd call having good boundaries—appealed to me. I was working to hide in plain view, and she allowed me that courtesy.

The next day at noon, we walked to a nearby food court, and Shelly insisted on paying. Today would be the day she moved aside her boundaries, and I hoped I was ready for it.

"I love having you around, but don't you have a college degree? Is everything okay?" She leaned forward, placing her lovely suited elbows on a crumb-laden table. It was a direct question that required a direct answer. So I took a deep breath, and the words followed. I offered her the basics: a break-in, two men, a weapon; friends took me in; I couldn't work. She listened without interruption. I looked down at my sandwich through much of it— turkey on whole wheat with a soggy tomato and wilted lettuce. My heart beat steadily, quickening only when I described leaving the magazine. "I loved that job. It was everything to me. When I think about it now, it feels like a hundred years ago. I couldn't work right after it happened and eventually signed up for temp work so I could pay my rent." I had only uttered a few sentences and the telling exhausted me. I considered throwing my sandwich to the floor and using my Styrofoam plate as a pillow.

Shelly spoke softly. "Here's how I see it. You never take a day off and you do a great job, but I can tell you're bored. Maybe you're more ready than you realize. When we get back to work, we're going to look at the want ads. I really like having you around. I like it so much I'm going to help you leave." She stood up and placed her hand on my shoulder. "Come on, let's go."

"Okay," I said. "But do you have any idea where we should start?"

"We are going to start by starting. I've often found that's the only way."

I imagined saying goodbye and trying to find words to convey my gratitude for a kindness I might never be able to repay. I wondered if we would stay in touch through the years, if I would remember her name or the color of her favorite dress, blazer, and shoes.

They were yellow.

—

The North Charles Institute for the Addictions was a rather extravagant name for the methadone clinic I applied to for my first full-time job since quitting the magazine. By now, I was closer to thirty than twenty, and the great future I had once counted on had melted away like the ice caps. Whether this situation was due to circumstances beyond my control seemed more irrelevant the longer it continued. I no longer bragged to anyone that I had been my high school valedictorian and voted Most Likely to Succeed. Those were secrets I held even closer than the overwhelming fear and anxiety I felt at the beginning and end of each day. I considered burning my high school yearbook in the small hibachi grill that sat unused on my porch deck to hide the evidence of the expectations it held.

The job opening advertised was for a career counselor. This seemed easy enough, except I had no background in either careers or counseling. I had experience, though, at the art of résumé amplification, making my tiny editing business sound almost like a full-time job. To have me offer career assistance to the underemployed seemed like an ironic joke the universe had decided to play. I imagined myself moving from one chair to the next, offering advice one minute and then hopping over to the empty seat across the room to receive my own guidance in a cruel game of musical chairs with only one participant.

"Most importantly, you must be respectful of the clients," my soon-to-be boss Leslie said during our interview as she marched me through the dim waiting room that smelled like an ashtray. "Many of them have spotty work records and feel great shame. These folks have hit some bumps in the road, and this clinic is helping them get their lives back. Work is such an important part of self-worth."

I stared at the spot above Leslie's head, where a picture of a giant sunflower hung, slightly off-kilter in its frame. Would this be my office, I wondered, a place where I could bring a coffee mug and knickknack of my own, like Shelly? Would someone call me from the reception area to say my client had arrived, a job I would have done for someone else only weeks ago?

The waiting room seats were all full. I noticed a couple with

twins, a man with a graying beard and a woman in a red business
suit. They looked just like anyone else, waiting for any kind of
appointment.

I wondered how they got here, and whether their stories were
like mine.

Leslie called to offer me the job that evening.

"We have an addictions fellowship program that's part of the
package through the psychiatry department at Harvard," Leslie
said. "It's a big draw for the folks who work here."

"Can I have some time to think about it?" I choked out, having
been told by a few friends not to seem too eager.

I called the front desk the next morning. "Hi, Jenny, may I
leave a message for Leslie?" I'd asked Jenny her name after my
interview on my way out. I knew what it felt like to be just the
bridge to the person someone really wanted to speak with, someone known most often as only "miss" or "ma'am" or with no name
at all.

It was the late 1980s, when drug counseling was often done
by people in recovery. Because of this, the want ads for these
jobs did not require any formal education, which might be why
I was hired with no relevant experience and years of only short-
term job placements. The new job gave me a twinge of hope. I'd
be a career counselor while learning about the field of addiction
and maybe figure out a way forward. Julie was well on her way to
finishing her Ph.D. at Stanford; Sara had earned her law degree
and soon would take a civil rights job that would have her arguing
cases before the Supreme Court; and Lise was in graduate school
in California following her passion to dance. These were the peers
to whom I compared myself.

I was beyond happy just to feel taken seriously somewhere but,
in truth, had applied only because Shelly pointed her painted fingernail at the job ad and said, "Here, try this one." And I did, to

get away from something but not to go toward something—an aftermath of the attack that created a tangle of shame so difficult to unravel—believing I'd never be able to have the future I once envisioned.

Time passed, and my friends suggested that I begin looking for a magazine or editing job again before too much time went by. But I couldn't. A job rebuff would have felt like confirmation that I'd lost whatever it was I had "before" and that it would never return. Maybe my job-searching clients at the addiction treatment center felt the same way.

College had made me feel unstoppable. I had walked into numerous events with my big hair and straight back and listened to Angela Davis, Grace Paley, Adrienne Rich, and so many other famous writers and activists in auditoriums packed with students. I can recall my resolve listening to those giants. *I have a voice. I can help shift the conversation in a flawed world. Let's see what this life holds for me.*

After the rapes, I was no longer that young woman, and I felt fully accountable for my situation. I didn't blame the rapists or the police for my unrecognizable life; I blamed myself. A few years later, the psychiatrist Dr. Judith Herman published *Trauma and Recovery,* a groundbreaking book that analyzes the long-term effects of post-traumatic stress disorder. It transformed our understanding of the experiences of sexual assault survivors. Herman likens rape survivors' experiences to torture and their trauma response to victims of war or those in concentration camps. Her work, which combines research, historical analysis, and patient vignettes, validates trauma victims' experience as overwhelming and explains why society's tendency to blame victims is prevalent. She writes, "It is very tempting to take the side of the perpetrator. All the perpetrator asks is that the bystander do nothing. He appeals to the universal desire to see, hear and speak no evil. The victim, on the contrary, asks the bystander to share the burden of pain. The victim demands action, engagement and remembering."[10]

I first read Herman's book around 2010, when my post-traumatic stress had been retriggered and someone had lent me their copy. I had known since my college days that rape was generally misunderstood and minimized, but reading about the impact on victims made me sob every few pages. I bought my own copy so I could highlight salient passages, but after spending a couple of hours reading, I realized that more was underlined than not and put down my pen. While I was relieved to feel seen and understood, I wondered how this book could have existed since 1992 when everything the author wrote about then was still relevant decades later. One line punched me in the gut: "In order to escape accountability for his crimes, the perpetrator does everything in his power to promote forgetting. If secrecy fails, the perpetrator attacks the credibility of his victim. If he cannot silence her absolutely, he tries to make sure no one listens."[11] I read and reread this sentence. Something about it nagged at me. I read it again, this time substituting *society* each time *perpetrator* was used. Then I tried it with *law enforcement*. Then I use *those in power.*

What will it take before things change? I asked myself aloud, putting the book down on the table. Emotion welled in my body, and I needed a moment. I then thought, *I hope I survive the impact of these crimes and can eventually make a meaningful life for myself.*

Five

At the end of my first year at North Charles, I received a small diploma. It wasn't an advanced degree but a certificate with HARVARD MEDICAL SCHOOL–DEPARTMENT OF PSYCHIATRY emblazoned across the top—a certificate in Addiction Studies. I couldn't wait to hold it in my hands, add it to my résumé, and boast of this modest accomplishment. It felt like tangible evidence that maybe, just maybe, I could move on.

One of the other students in the training program had been a nurse named Mary. She looked like a teenager with her short hair, scrubs, and backpack. "I'm a medical nurse at Beth Israel Hospital," she'd said with a wide smile, showing a one-sided dimple. "I'm in training to work with addicted patients on the medical units." Beyond the mention of working at Beth Israel, a place I still carried an aversion to, I didn't pay her much mind.

A few months into the program, we were scheduled for the same morning at the dosing clinic. Mary dispensed the methadone while I checked people in and took their blood pressure if they seemed high. She and I had already begun to get to know each other in the office break room. She packed her own lunch; I bought mine at the sandwich place down the street. She loved coffee; so did I. She was a runner; I barely moved. She came from a big family—one of eleven children—and worked her way through nursing school. Unlike me, she had confidence working with clients and had the ability to be direct and empathic. And she made me laugh.

Often, over coffee, I'd put my hand up like a stop sign while she told a story so I could swallow and not spit out my food. One lunch hour, she described confronting a patient who was using cocaine. Mary had been firm when the client said the urine test must have been wrong.

"When she knew I wasn't going to be convinced, she said, 'No offense, Mary, but I really hate your fucking guts.'"

"What did you say back?" I asked, horrified.

"No offense taken."

This led to our first real conversation—how we grew up, the lessons we learned from the experiences we had. She had a genuineness about her. You didn't have to guess what she thought or felt, and, as the interaction with the client showed me, she wasn't easily offended. My skin was still so thin—even the wind blowing too hard made my body hurt and sometimes brought tears to my eyes. Someone more in command of her emotions was appealing, and a bit seductive.

"How do you like our program so far?" Mary asked during a lull in dosing.

"I like it; I'm learning a lot." A handful of patients walked in, cutting our conversation short. When the clinic closed, I locked the door and waited for Mary to finish her count. The amount of methadone she gave patients had to be reconciled perfectly before she could leave.

"Right on target," she said after ten minutes, smiling my way.

"See you back at the main building then." I held the door open for her as she juggled several notebooks.

"Hey," she said, "do you like basketball? I split Celtics tickets with a group from work, and I have a game coming up. Want to go?"

"Sure," I said. Basketball wasn't my favorite sport, but I'd never been to the Boston Garden, and at this time, the late eighties, the Celtics were making history, winning one conference title after another and a few championships. *What the heck*, I thought.

Throughout the day, I started wondering if this might be a date. We had been seeking each other out more lately, for a walk around the block or an afternoon break over coffee. She had a great dimple. She was funny. She was straightforward. And she liked coffee! I was lonely, but not sure I'd be a great companion.

When I got home, my new roommate was making dinner and offered me some. "I'm going to the Celtics game next week with a woman from work," I said as I sat down. "I'm not sure if it's a date. How would I know? I'm not even sure she's gay."

"Don't ask her; that would be awkward. You'll be able to figure it out somehow."

Mary picked me up at my apartment wearing jeans and a turtleneck under a down jacket. "What a great location you live in; it's a ten-minute walk to Beth Israel."

"I know," I replied, trying not to frown.

"The Brookline Village T stop is closer than Longfellow. We'll get to the Garden in fifteen minutes." We stepped out of my apartment and Mary walked briskly toward the train.

"Slow down," I said to her back.

"Oops, sorry," she replied and slackened her pace.

Mary's seats were on one end of the court, high up. I watched the game, ate the snacks she had in her backpack, and stared at her with a side eye so she couldn't tell I was looking.

I thought, *Is this a date? And so what if it is?* During the lull
I'd had in dating over the last few years, I'd considered trying to
hook up with a man, but my only motivation was to change the
disquieting fact that my only experience with men had been rape,
and it felt wrong to use someone that way. There was a woman on
my softball team I'd had a crush on over the summer, but she had
taken none of my hints and I was too shy to ask her out. So now
here I sat with this Mary person who walked fast, liked basketball,
and was thoughtful enough to hide some great snacks in her backpack for both of us.

In the immediate aftermath of the attack, I mistakenly thought
that sex might somehow erase the rapes from my mind and body.
It's no surprise to me now what an utter failure that was. At the
time, I yearned for solace and proof of life. I needed confirmation
that my ability to feel anything had not been stolen from me. The
act of sex, where trust and release bring pleasure, beckoned. It
was a concrete way to be in my body, to feel alive and successful
at something. Rape is not sex, and I never thought it was, understanding it to be a crime of violence and, at its center, about power
and control. At the time, however, it certainly seemed like some
kind of sex—unwanted and forced by someone else, but sex nonetheless. And I simply could not let it stand.

—

I had my first brief sexual encounter with Chelsea. She was also
a victim of the break-ins and rapes that summer, her apartment
about three miles away from mine. A citywide crisis meeting four
days after my attack was held at a nearby church following the
Globe story of yet another break-in, ours. Chairs creaked. Arms
waved. Voices screeched. The room smelled like old pastries. I
wanted to run out of the hall before anyone figured out I was the

one the most recent news coverage had been referring to as "the city's most recent victim of a home invasion."

Unacceptable. Investigate. Do something!

After the event, my former roommates and I drank tea in a café. Lise mentioned Chelsea had hoped to get in touch with me. We knew each other casually from our lesbian softball league. I coached a team called the Rude Girls and she played for the competition.

Chelsea was about ten years older than me and worked as a medical assistant. We met for coffee. I arrived a few minutes late, and she was sitting in a booth with a glass of water in front of her, waiting until I arrived to order. That small courtesy dislodged the thick lump in my throat.

"I woke up to a man in my apartment," Chelsea said, pouring a stream of sugar into her black coffee. "He pretended to have a gun in the pocket of his sweatshirt. It looked like his hand, but I didn't want to find out.

"Honestly, he seemed terrified. He was a skinny little guy and shook the whole time. After he took my money, he came nearer and started to finger me. I begged him to stop, and he did. Then he left out the window. It was horrible."

This is a huge mistake, I thought.

My toe tapped on the uneven floor of the diner. I felt my own story disappear somewhere deep inside my body. "I don't know. It doesn't really sound the same. Maybe there are a bunch of different rapists running around the city, the publicity creating copycats."

Chelsea talked about her friend's reactions, her family's. Words intruded in my head as she chatted, those same words that felt like my new mantra: *blindfold, knife, phone cord, scarf.*

Her hair was dirty blond and curly and her mouth wide.

Blindfold, knife, phone cord, scarf.

My reaction embarrassed me. I know I shouldn't have been mad at her just because the details of our attacks were different, but I couldn't shake it.

"Did I hear there were two men? Michelle, were there two?" I hadn't heard a word she'd just said. I stared at her mouth moving while I tried to remember what position she played in softball. She looked like a catcher with her strong arms and wide thighs.

"My ex-lover is coming to Boston in a few weeks," I finally said, changing the subject. "We had a tough breakup, but we're close again, especially after this. I feel like I need to have sex to feel normal again. Maybe it's stupid."

"I'll have sex with you," Chelsea said. "The normal rules don't seem to apply anymore."

Now I had a decision to make. This woman across the table was almost a stranger to me, and I felt no attraction to her. I missed my ex, Sara, so much, and wanted to feel her arms around me. That feeling of being held by her was really what I'd been wanting, and I had considered taking the bus to New York to see her. My flashbacks were incessant. Several times a day, I relived that night, but in my fractured brain, the scarf went around my neck rather than my mouth and I couldn't breathe; I felt as if I was screaming through much of my day and didn't understand why no one seemed to notice.

"Okay," I said, because in that moment I would do anything to prick at the feeling of being terrified, all day and all night, without end.

Somehow, we found a place to go. We had some kind of intimate experience together. I felt warm skin against a crisp sheet. I was touched and didn't break. And while I didn't exactly feel alive, I did feel a tiny bit less dead. My heart pounded in my chest from a gentle brush of a hand rather than from fear. And when I fell asleep and she reached over me with her arm, I pretended it was Sara and I ached for her visit even more.

Sara came up from New York two weeks later. "I wish you'd let me come sooner," she said. "I've been so worried." She hugged me and I didn't want her to let go.

"I needed time before I felt comfortable asking Emmy and Steve if they minded me having company." Emmy had been mad at Sara since we broke up, no matter how many times I told her it wasn't her fault. Still, Emmy threw her arms around Sara when she arrived and understood we would be sharing my room. Mostly, Sara and I just held hands or sat together on the couch leaning into each other. We made love a couple of times over the course of the weekend, but it didn't soothe my pain as I'd hoped. Over time, I learned this marathon had to be run step by step, then back to the starting line to try again, and then once more, and then again.

"How are you doing?" she asked as we lay in the twin bed in Steve's study.

"I have no idea," I replied, and she nodded.

We walked down Harvard Street, stopping at the Paperback Booksmith to browse. Sara concentrated on a shelf of staff picks, and I remembered the last time we did the same thing in New York City a couple of years ago. We had just heard Audre Lorde read in a small venue uptown that Sara had found hunting through the *Village Voice*. When it was over, we walked into the first bookstore we could find and went straight to the poetry section to buy books we couldn't afford.

Back then, I browsed too. Back then, I chose books from the shelves and enjoyed familiar words on the page, but not anymore. I watched Sara tilt her head up and down, searching. She reached, read, and put several back, finally choosing three. I was about to ask if we could leave when she pulled out her wallet and walked to the front. As soon as we got out the door, she took a book out of her bag.

"Please, take this. You know how much I love Adrienne Rich. I have to leave you with something."

I accepted the offering, *Diving into the Wreck*, her favorite and an apt title for what felt like my task ahead. "Thank you," I said, hugging the book, hoping its wisdom would enter my body.

It was dusk, and as we walked back to the apartment, we were talking about safety in Manhattan. I'm the one who brought it up, worried she's living alone in a new neighborhood.

"I've lived in New York my whole life. You learn how to protect yourself," she said. "You have to know how to look at people if they meet your eye. You can't look scared." And she glowered at me to demonstrate, wrinkling her brow and setting her jaw.

A memory of a slice of light hitting my sleeping eyes took hold.

"It helps not to look intimidated."

Blindfold, knife, phone cord, scarf.

I said nothing.

She saw the look and audibly gasped. "It's not the same thing, love. Not at all. Not in any way. There is absolutely no comparison. None. How about we change this unfortunate topic and forget the last five minutes."

"I knew you weren't . . ."

"Shhh . . ." She reached for my hand and walked me home— lucky for me, since I'd forgotten the way.

While Sara understood the shame I carried and sought to reassure me, my story created a door other people sometimes walked through uninvited. What happened to me scared them, and they thought themselves wily enough to protect themselves from harm.

Walk with purpose. Lock your doors.

Someone isn't safe, I considered saying, because they avoid a place where something bad happened; really, who knows where the next bad thing might be lurking? These people do not understand that there are wolves about who aren't avoided so easily. And I hope they never have to find out.

After Sara went home, we decided we did better as friends and would continue as such. Several months later, when I moved out of Emmy and Steve's apartment, I had a short but intense relationship with a hairdresser in the next apartment I'd moved into, which I moved out of to get away from the pain of it not working out. After that, I didn't date anyone for years.

—

This time, if Mary and I were on a date and did start seeing each other, I had the feeling I wouldn't just be experiencing sex but intimacy and vulnerability as well. All of this scared me. Maybe this basketball game date–not date thing was a very bad idea.

"How about we leave now?" I suggested with ten minutes left on the game clock. "The trains will be packed, and we both have work tomorrow."

"We can't leave before it's over; they might still win," Mary said, and I sat back in my tiny wooden seat, rebuffed. With less than five minutes to go, the Celtics scored over a dozen unanswered points and took the lead. "Impressive," I said. They had pulled off the victory, and Mary had spoken up for what she wanted. We took the T home, and I invited her in for coffee. My roommate was home. "This is Mary," I said, introducing her as quickly as I could before ushering her into my bedroom down the hall from the kitchen in our railroad-style apartment. I carried two seltzers from the refrigerator and an unopened bag of pretzels; I hadn't bothered to open the bag first and put them in a bowl. There was only the bed to sit on, so I gestured toward the floor and we both sat down facing each other with the pretzel bag between us.

I don't remember what we talked about, but I remember laughing a lot about nothing important: the way the guy across from us on the T sat with his legs so spread out he took up enough room for three people, the happy look on my face when I realized Mary had hidden some almonds in her backpack. We never opened the pretzels, and she wound up staying over. In the morning, I confirmed with my roommate that, yes, it had been a date.

—

Maybe precisely because I had a clear separation between my single experience with the male body and with women, whose bodies I never associated with pain, I could let myself feel pleasure in this new relationship. There were never any moments with Mary where I had a flashback and needed to stop in order to collect myself. But I did have trouble with intimacy, those moments when you share secret emotional spaces with another person, knowing both of you can tolerate and accept what is being shared. I felt happy and blessed in one moment and then unsure and critical of Mary the next. As Judith Herman writes, "Over time as most people fail the survivor's exacting test of trustworthiness, she tends to withdraw from relationships. The isolation of the survivor thus persists even after she is free."[1]

Mary was unaware she cohabitated with a panther looking to pounce at any error and watching for any reason to run away. About once a week she irritated me about one thing or another. She'd forget something I told her, like coming home with dill pickles when I said I liked sweet. Or she'd get distracted in the middle of my telling a story: "Oh, look, there's that cardinal I told you about; he's on the fence post right now!" she had shouted, when I was telling her for the first time about my stepfather making me buy beer at a store he knew wouldn't ask me for an ID. "I was listening; I just didn't want you to miss the bird. It was a matter of timing," she explained. Mary's "transgressions" should have told me more about me and my state of mind than about her. Still, I held them close so I could tolerate my vulnerability as we grew closer.

I knew I loved Mary; I just wasn't sure how to cope with all that it brought up. When I think back to the early days, to keep myself from running I focused on external things—something she said, something she did. I fumbled through my discomfort with intimacy until I didn't have to anymore. Slowly, Mary and I nested into our new life.

We kept separate apartments for one year but spent every night together in one of them. I adjusted to a nurse's schedule—twelve-hour weekend shifts meant days off midweek, and I'd take a day off occasionally so we could spend time together. If a nurse called in sick when Mary was working, she'd have to cover the shift. "Couldn't you tell them you were tired?" I'd ask, sad to miss her warm body in bed.

"It doesn't work that way," she explained. "Nurses are essential personnel."

"You're essential to me," I wanted to say, but could hear in my head how needy that sounded.

When Mary got together with other nurses, their stories and laughter filled the room. These hospital tales had everything—patient health crises and deaths, challenging family members, and patients who returned repeatedly to the unit and became legendary. I'd listen as they shared, cringing at their laughter about situations that, to me, seemed tragic.

"Someone like me, someone from the outside, might think

you're making fun of them," I said once after we hosted her friends.

"You have to do this work to understand," Mary said as we cleaned up. "We loved these patients. We knew them and their families for years. Humor is how nurses sometimes cope. No one could stand so much loss otherwise."

"In my family, when someone dies, you're never supposed to get over it or you didn't really love them."

"This is a little different," she said. "But that way of coping isn't exactly the healthiest either. People die. It's a fact. It doesn't change how much we cared about them if we let ourselves have happy memories."

"Mary . . ." I paused, unable to ask the next question.

"No one would have made fun of you," she said, grabbing my hand. "There was not a single thing about you or that night that anyone taking care of you would ever crack a smile over. People generally aren't that cruel and thinking they are only hurts you. I see how much it hurts you."

"Okay." I felt tears in my eyes as the suspicious panther inside me retreated.

"Come here," she said, waving me toward her open arms, and I complied.

There was another story she told that night, after the laughter settled and a few nurses remained. It was about a beloved patient she had attended to for many years. This small anecdote offered me something that simple encouragement to be patient with myself never could. There seemed some magic or grace to be found in the fact that the hospital I went to on the worst day of my life also held the person who would hold my hand through the rest of it.

Mary was a medical nurse working seven floors above the emergency room the night I arrived there, years before we would meet at the drug clinic and fall in love—she, with abandon; I, slowly and with caution. But on this dreadful night we were strangers. I picture her there now, doing rounds and checking on her patients. Sadie was an elderly woman Mary had gotten to know well through several hospitalizations. This time, she was recovering from a heart procedure. Mary came into her room, hoping to get Sadie up and walking to aid her recovery, despite Sadie's protests to stay in bed.

Sadie had survived much in her long life—a war that took dozens of friends and family, a new country that seemed at times to hate her as much as the one she fled. She resisted help with suspicion.

She asked, "Why do you treat me this way, Mary? Why must you torture me so? Is it because I am a Jew?"

Mary, smiling and helping Sadie sit up, held on to one of her arms and placed the other onto the small of her back. She reminded Sadie where she was. "You are at Beth Israel Hospital. No one will hurt you, I promise. You're safe here. *You are safe.*" Mary tried again. "You've had a big surgery and you have to walk to get better."

"If I have to walk to get better, I'd rather just die. Go home and bother your husband a little, but leave me alone already."

Mary kept her voice steady. "I don't have a husband, so you're stuck with me tonight. Just a few steps."

Sadie got up reluctantly, moaning and swearing in Yiddish under her breath.

The next day, this conversation was forgotten and Sadie started her evening by accusing Mary of hating her because she was a Jew. Mary was kind and patient in return.

Learning that Mary worked at the same hospital where I spent my most horrible night, a sweet stranger showing basic kindness just above the ER where I had lain torn apart, grounded me. I saw her and the hope in her eyes, which made it seem easy to believe that the world is good, that a person can fight to feel better simply by holding fast to someone who loves them and offers their hand.

Mary reached out to Sadie, and she grabbed on. Sadie didn't want to, and yet she took the hand when it was extended. Eventually, I would too.

Sadie is my companion in arms. She and I, old phantom friends. We both chose hope from the same well, albeit reluctantly. It is how we both survived the hard work we had ahead.

Six

Mary returned full-time to Beth Israel and I stayed on at North Charles when our addictions fellowship ended. We celebrated graduation by buying a house together, a tiny condo in a suburb west of Boston. This might have been a big step for anyone, but for me, it was the first place I considered home since the attack—*home,* a word I had almost forgotten, the meaning and value of which I thought had been destroyed for me forever.

My three former roommates and I had each found a place to sleep the night after the break-in; friends took us in, eager to help with a sofa to sleep on and arms to fall into. One of our friends called the landlord on our behalf and asked for our last month's rent and security deposit back so we would have money to move. Since it was late June and we couldn't give a month's notice, he said he'd use the last month's rent to cover July and allow us to break the lease if he found someone to rent the place. The detectives who interviewed me asked if I knew whether the apartment building had been a frequent target of burglars, which I had never considered. Maybe the previous tenants had left quickly as well for similar reasons. We never found out. When Mary and I bought our condo, it had been almost five years and several apartment moves since I knew what it meant to belong somewhere.

I was not alone in this feeling. Almost half of sexual assaults occur in or near the survivor's home, and following the assault many have no choice but to flee.[1] For rape victims, "home" can be a complicated concept, especially if the perpetrator is a family member or if the attack(s) occurred at home. Not everyone has the option or financial ability to move, and yet after experiencing a rape in one's home, a person's relationship to it is forever altered. One rape survivor, Debbie Smith, a friend I made during a focus group session in Washington, D.C., was abducted from her home and raped in nearby woods. She conveyed the mixed emotions of being attacked where one lives: "I struggled for years about my decision to sell my house or to stay. Not wanting him to take any more from me than he already had, I finally made the decision to stay. It was not until we moved years later that I realized just how much peace I had forfeited. Upon returning to our *new* home for the first time after a few days away, I was overcome with feelings of joy and regret. The joy was the new peace in returning to this home and regret that I had forgotten what it had felt like to want to go home."[2]

"Shouldn't we rent before we buy?" Mary asked when I said that I wanted to call a real estate agent in the hope that we might find something we could afford. "We haven't even officially lived together yet."

"No," I said, louder than I intended. I didn't know what I would do if she disagreed. "I want something that's ours that no one can take away, or make us move out of before *we* decide. Trust me on this; I so often don't know how I feel or what I want, but on this I am absolutely certain. I need you to do this for me. I'm sorry if I seem bossy, but I really need this."

She nodded. "I understand. Let's do this." And she grabbed the Sunday paper from our recycle pile to look at the real estate section.

Mary's kindness buoyed me, and I'd seek to emulate it as I healed. After one year together, she probably saw buying a house with me as a risk, but her ability to defer when it mattered made it possible for me to move ahead in the relationship at all.

My job at North Charles changed again when I became the HIV education coordinator, and I felt deeply engaged in the work, believing my job had value. It was the late 1980s, and AIDS was a national health crisis: over one hundred thousand cases had been diagnosed, and the numbers were rising. Infection rates for IV drug users were among the highest, and they were growing. I considered whether it was time to really invest in this line of work as a career and whether the decision to work at North Charles hadn't been as random as I'd first thought.

While monitoring the dosing clinic one morning, I saw a job advertised at a new HIV clinic at a nearby hospital. "I'm going to apply," I told Mary. "I like the idea of doing similar work in a new environment." I had a great interview but didn't get the job. They chose someone with less work experience and a master's degree. "You were a strong candidate and maybe something will open up here in the future," the head nurse said when she called.

"They made the wrong choice," Mary said at dinner. "And I'm really sorry."

"Maybe it's time for me to go to graduate school. If I can't get jobs I want because I don't have the credentials, I may be stuck at North Charles forever." I paused, hoping my next words were true. "I think I'm ready."

My focus on choosing a graduate program had shifted. I no

longer considered publishing, writing, or women's studies as options. I was a different person, a drug counselor in a methadone clinic, my former aspirations belonging to someone else. My love of language and the beauty of words had no place in my life anymore, and I barely read, since my ability to concentrate failed me when I tried. Without knowing much about public health except that work colleagues told me it sounded like something I should investigate when I described my interests, I applied to Harvard and was accepted.

I could once again speak without shame about my career. Another dusty layer of disappointment became overlaid with hope. Not that it was that simple. Going back to school felt both exciting and fear-inducing. Maybe the work would be harder than I thought and I'd fail. Maybe I'd be much older than most of my classmates and feel out of place. All I knew was that I was moving toward something—something that resembled the future I'd once dreamed of.

Mary arrived for dinner late one night with a plastic bag from the Harvard Coop containing a sweatshirt with the name of my new school embossed on the front. "Put it on," she said, smiling. Inside the plastic bag that held the sweatshirt was another smaller one containing a pencil case with twelve yellow pencils inside. Mary explained that even when her family's resources were limited, she looked forward to receiving a pack of pencils from her mother every fall, an affordable token showing both the promise of education and the thrill of a shiny new start.

A new home, graduate school, and a commitment to stay together. I was working on trusting Mary, knowing there remained something I hadn't yet shared fully with her, for which I hoped I could finally find words.

—

As I began to feel more solid and built a new home and a new life, I thought back, remembering the pride my former roommates and I had had before we fled our apartment in Allston. That apartment held dear and important memories of our development as independent young adults. We wanted to share our joy with family members we'd previously been dependent on—and invited all our mothers and grandmothers for Mother's Day.

"Sounds good, I'm in," I said when Lise first brought up the idea, not sure my mom would feel like she had the money to fly. Still, it had been a year since we'd seen each other, and I knew she was curious about the apartment.

"What's the place like? Do the windows lock?" she'd asked when I first called to say we'd found a four-bedroom in Allston.

My mother was often silent and would never have said she didn't like my choices, but I learned her signals over time. I no longer asked her if she was hungry, for example, because she always said, "No, that's okay, not really," waiting for me to say when I was ready to eat. Her own preferences disappeared over many years and a thousand little instances. I can't recall the one singular moment when she lost her voice. Maybe it started after my dad died. My mother was there with my sister and me in our collective grief, but I thought if I lifted my hand up to her, it might pass straight through her body like I'd seen in a *Casper the Friendly Ghost* episode. She didn't get mad or sad anymore as far as we could tell; she just hung out with whomever she was with, content to be in their presence, but so achingly quiet. I missed her terribly, mostly when she was right in front of me. She reminded me of John Singer in *The Heart Is a Lonely Hunter,* one of my favorite books. Almost every character reveres the deaf mute man and feels understood by him. Since he doesn't talk during the one-way conversations others have with him, he is exactly who they need him to be in his silence. Ultimately, though, his loneliness and alienation are revealed.

As to the Mother's Day invitation, I was almost certain my mother would say yes when I asked her to come, whether she could afford the ticket or not, so I fretted about asking her at all. I finally did, and the rest of my roommates asked their mothers, and within a week we had received a spate of affirmatives.

"You can stay with me," I told my mom. My family didn't believe in hotels if an alternative free space could be arranged. I had a full-size futon. We would both fit. It might not be fancy or comfortable, but it would most certainly do.

I looked around my bedroom, trying to see it through her eyes. There was the futon, whose cheap wooden frame could be pushed and pulled with effort to become a couch of sorts, a desk the previous owner had left behind, and a variety of milk crates. One served as my bedside table and the others were stacked as a makeshift dresser. Best of all, there was a handwritten sign over my desk that Lise had made for me that said, "A Room of One's Own." I was the happiest I had ever been living with my friends in that apartment.

My mother flew in on a Friday afternoon. I unlocked the front door and made a sweeping gesture with my hand. "Welcome to the Waldorf," I said and she giggled. The night before, I had borrowed a second pillow from one of my roommates and washed my bedsheets at the Laundromat down the block. I had no memory of when I changed them last.

I grabbed a photo album I'd borrowed from home during my last visit and led my mother into the kitchen. "Let's look," I said.

It contained pictures of me from high school that I'd wanted to show my friends. I was at least twenty pounds heavier then, with thick-framed plastic glasses and short curly black hair. I looked closer to forty than barely sixteen. The sweater vest, pearls, and makeup in my senior-year photo cemented the impression of me as a depressed midwestern housewife. My current lesbian hipness was stunning by contrast. I was thin and muscular with a giant head of frizzy hair like Abbie Hoffman's—depending on how recently I'd washed it. I wanted to share these with my friends, show them the person I was back then: someone who longed to leave rural Ohio and who had an outward identity that didn't match how I felt inside.

The album was covered with sun-worn green cloth. My mom and I sat side by side, staring together at one picture showing my three-year-old sister leaning into my mom with her upper body, my mom's arms fully occupied with me as a tiny baby. She looked weary, her eyes at half-mast.

"If you had been born first, you would have been an only child," my mom said as she sipped her Dunkin' Donuts coffee and looked down at the photo.

A ray of sunlight came through the kitchen window and caught the plastic sheet on the photo album just so, and my mother squinted. I jumped up to pull the shade down, afraid if she got up to find her sunglasses the moment would pass. I pointed to the picture. "You were saying?"

I leaned forward, my hand on my chin with my finger crooked like a question mark.

"You cried nonstop. No matter what I did, you cried. I used to wake up in the morning and hear you screeching, and I'd start crying myself thinking, I have no idea how I'm going to get through another day with her."

I touched the cuff of her sweater. "Maybe I had colic. Did you take me to the doctor?"

"Babies cry. I wasn't going to bother the doctor with that."

"Well, if there *was* something wrong, he could have fixed it and then you wouldn't have had to suffer so much," I said.

"Suffer? You and Judy are the best things that ever happened to me." Her eyes teared up as she skillfully took back what she just said. "You've never given me anything but joy."

Mother's Day weekend was a success. On the day of the brunch, we all crowded into the kitchen. The moms helped make the salad—there were cherry tomatoes to cut in half, cucumbers to slice, feta cheese to crumble. Lise made a four-layer chocolate-raspberry cake and my mom frosted it with a double batch of homemade whipped cream.

The pictures we took of that day sit in another photo album I now keep in a bookcase in our living room. In one, Lise's mother is smoking a cigarette while Lise stands behind her frowning. Julie stands in another, squeezed between her mother and grandmother, arms wrapped around them both. In all the photos of my mother, she is laughing, her black eyes sparkling and her cheekbones stretched by her wide smile. I am captured in one photo as well, just staring at her, thrilled in that moment at her ability to laugh fully, enjoying my home and the memories I invited her to share with me in a city I chose to make my own.

I don't notice the grime on the walls or the mismatched chairs in the pictures. I don't see the three worn tablecloths we used because we didn't have one that was big enough. All I see is the joy on our faces: we had hosted a fabulous time, with two older generations graciously allowing their children and grandchildren to be the grown-ups in the space we created together—our home, my home.

There would be only one shared Mother's Day celebration in our apartment on Glenville Avenue. A little over a year later, it was broken into on that terrible night, and we scattered, leaving behind our memories, the fond ones along with the ones that devastated. Somehow, the green worn photo album found its way back to me. I have no memory of how; someone must have grabbed it for me, and I carry it still.

When I look at those photos from Mother's Day, I see a young girl who was brash and full of life. For years after my attack, I searched for her, the young girl I knew was still inside me somewhere, perhaps waylaid by circumstance but in there nonetheless. I looked long and hard for the key that could unlock the sense of promise she once carried, and my gaze often fell upon the photos of our shared life in that apartment "before." That young woman was vibrant, loud, and fearless. How could she really be gone before her adult life had barely begun? She and I worked hard to move forward, hoping together not to share the fate of John Singer or my mother, beloved yet, somehow, unknown. It would take time to recalibrate—more than either of us could have imagined—but we were determined. We were determined to become one being again, to find a sense of home and place that no one else would ever again have the power to unmoor.

As I felt myself healing—recovering parts of who I once was—it was often the gesture, the small kindness, the feeling of simply being seen that helped me the most and, I believe, helps others. I remember a woman named Kathy who lived on my floor freshman year. Midway through our time at college, she confided in me and another friend that a professor had been sexually harassing her. She was a very private person, and telling us must not have been easy. We did our best to listen; we were angry on her behalf; we asked if we could help. Years later, when I didn't even know she still lived in Boston, she was the person who found me an apartment after Emmy and Steve moved. I don't even know how she knew about what had happened to me. But she called Julie to say that she had seen an advertisement for a place in Brookline she thought I might like. Kathy explained the circumstances briefly to the people looking for a roommate, got me an interview, and told me when to show up. Every detail she took care of meant one less mountain I had to climb that day.

I'm not sure how you become a person who knows exactly what to do when someone needs you. I still get it wrong a lot. But because of Kathy and the small gesture she made that was so large to me, as well as Mary's ability to both see me through my trauma and listen when it counts, learning how to get that right is, and will continue to be, a central goal for the rest of my life.

Seven

Mary had the perfect imperfection: a small space in between her two front teeth, like Lauren Hutton. It was exactly what I needed at first, a flaw, to help me focus my fear of feeling happy. Happy felt like another solar system—a curious and desired, yet unwelcome, destination. Nothing good could come of wanting something because everything was always taken away. I was not at ease but hid it well. Mary's optimism was deep enough to hold us both while I adjusted to loving and being loved.

So there sat that small space. I could try my hardest to see the beautiful smile that held it. Or I could just see the space. We bought a house, made financial decisions about each of our graduate programs, and then had kids. As I allowed happiness in, I'd carefully collected all the imagined imperfections and held them in my hand like a snow globe, shaking it about wildly, the flaws overtaking the scene and then settling down, harmless.

When Mary was in her forties, she decided to close up the space by wearing invisible braces for a year. She said she was tired of wearing her childhood poverty on her face. By then, I didn't worry what I would do without it. It had served us both rather well in a life we built together in spite of the odds.

In those early days, I was still unsure about what might come next and always expected something bad around the next corner, but worked hard with Mary to construct our brand-new life, slowly and with intention. Part of that life necessitated a telling, a telling I'd kept to myself over the last few years, as if silence might scrub it away. It didn't. Instead, I tried looking at it again through the prism of the person I loved.

I looked at Mary once and then looked away. We were in bed. I'd told her over the last few months that things were hard in the years before we met: there was a break-in; I was attacked; it got me off track. This vagueness may have worked on casual friends, but Mary was having none of it. Instead of saying, "Why don't you trust me?" a subtle demand to prove I cared for her, she murmured, "Unburden yourself when you're ready. I'll wait. Let it live outside of you a bit. I won't break and neither will you." Then she was quiet and reached for my hand.

I didn't want to be touched. "How can you be so sure?" I said, imagining racing through details I was uncertain I could still say aloud.

"I'm sure and I'm listening," she said.

—

On the night that changed everything, I go to bed naked in a steamy apartment. It is the first night of summer, and the thought of anything on my body is intolerable, although I prefer a T-shirt and underwear most of the time. Tall buildings block all air movement. If we walk up the street to where the one-story markets and restaurants are, the air feels at least ten degrees cooler. We have no air-conditioning, so we crack our windows and use a small fan in our empty living room to move hot air around, trying for a cross-breeze.

During dinner, Lise suggests we all go topless. "If we were men, no one would think twice about it. It's stupid that we have to wear shirts in ninety-five-degree weather." She bangs the kitchen table for emphasis, and the forks go flying. I smile, unpersuaded.

"I don't think I can do it, especially since we have no shades. I'm not that brave," I say. Lise yanks her sleeveless shirt over her head and walks down the hall. I smile at her naked back, remembering the time she took off her shirt in college, yelling "Divest now!" on top of a table in the cafeteria to protest the university's investments in apartheid-era South Africa. "Best double entendre of 'divest' I've ever heard," I'd remarked to her then, laughing and taking a bow.

Our roommate Susan takes a spray bottle to bed with her and spritzes herself like a houseplant whenever she feels hot. The rest of us take cool showers and run to our rooms trying not to leave gallons of water trailing behind on the bare hardwood floors. We sweat; we smell. We try to look forward to the summer ahead, knowing it promises more long days with stifling hot air and humidity that choke at every inhale.

After dinner, I do the dishes, change, and run off to meet my friend Rachel at a concert. The event is dull, featuring an assortment of feminist musicians singing original material. "If I hear one more song about depression or oppression, I'm going to scream. I haven't seen one of them smile all night," I whisper. Since the hall is air-conditioned, we stay. Otherwise, we might have left at intermission.

At some point, an old friend from college comes over. "You live nearby, don't you? Have you heard that there have been a lot of rapes in the Allston-Brighton neighborhood near Commonwealth Ave.? A neighborhood watch had these posters made. Would you mind putting some up?"

"Sure, no problem," I say. "I'll put them up in the morning." We don't get the newspaper at our apartment and our TV is broken. I feel a bit out of touch as I grab a big handful of flyers, more than I need and more than I can possibly put up, even if I put aside an entire day for the task.

When I get home that night from the concert, I put the flyers on the kitchen table and go to bed. None of my roommates are home, and this is unusual. Our place is the designated boyfriend or girlfriend sleepover spot, and I often wake up to a houseful of guests. I hope my roommates see the posters when they come home. Maybe they'll help me put some up. I picture women being chased as they get off the subway and make their way down the streets of Boston. *We'll have to be more careful*, I think to myself as I fall asleep, never even thinking that I should close the windows or check the lock on the back door leading to our porch. My sense of safety is impenetrable and doesn't change as I look at the words on the flyer. I go to bed.

When I feel my bedroom door open later that night, I think it's Lise coming in to say goodnight. I'm fast asleep, but she has an open invitation. Lately, she comes in at bedtime and we talk, hold hands, and share a few moments. Sometimes, we give each other a goodnight kiss that lingers. We are cautious, though. She has a boyfriend for now, and it seems too complicated. We do much better as friends.

I am looking forward to showing Lise how brave I am, sleeping naked despite the lack of shades in our first-floor apartment. Screw modesty! It's hot out there. I know she will be pleased and surprised by my sudden audacity. There we will be, naked warriors—two Emma Goldmans fighting the heat as if it's our political enemy. We have no fear; we will not be beat, even by the stifling hot summer that lies before us.

—

I leaned over to Mary. "Maybe it's enough to stop here," I said, hopeful she'll agree.

"Oh love, oh darling," she said, stroking my arm lightly. "It's your choice, of course, but it might help. It scares you more than it does anyone else; it breaks my heart for you, but it's nothing I can't hear. I promise. It's so apparent how keeping silent doesn't serve you."

There was nothing but love looking back at me. I sighed and began.

—

A flash of brightness hits my eyes as the bedroom door opens. There is not a sound on the street outside my bedroom window. It is the stillness of a city tucked in bed, the few short hours of night when the trains cease and when even those who stir late retire for a few hours of slumber before dawn. I lift my head and look at the gleaming streak of light, expecting my dear friend at the end of it asking, "Mind if I come in for a few minutes?" She'll be tentative, worried about waking me. I'll gesture for her to come in and wait to feel her easy plop on the side of my bed to tell me of the day's escapades—why she's home so late, where she's been and with whom. I want to know every single unfiltered detail, anticipating tales of misadventure and gossip.

Instead, there are two male voices talking to each other, not to me. It is the sound of intrusion, like gravel hitting pavement. They are insistence. They are fear. They are the hum of anxiety.

In an instant, two strangers are at the side of my bed.

"Don't talk or yell. Be very quiet."

"Put this over your head," one of them says. It is a cloth of some sort. I do as instructed. The darkness helps me focus my vibrating senses; it is a relief. I am unclear about all that is happening and fully at attention.

"Is anyone else here?" one of them barks.

"I don't think so."

I feel a hand pull my necklace off without undoing the clasp. The tug breaks the chain. It holds a small silver Star of David that belonged to my dad, one of the few things I still have of his. The hand is rough; it is the first touch.

I do not resist, explain, or say, *He died when I was seven; please let me keep it.* Speak when spoken to, I decide right then, not realizing I'm deciding anything. The dry hand reaches for mine and pulls off my ring. It is platinum with a tiny diamond in the center; my stepfather gave it to me a few years ago for no occasion in particular. *Take it,* I think.

One of them seems to come and go while the other stays with me and chats. "We don't kill people; we've been doing this for seven years. It's the economy. We need the money. Stop shaking. We won't hurt you."

And I believe him. They won't hurt me as long as I give them nothing to be scared of.

After what seems like hours, the other one comes back into the room. "What else you got around here? Anything worth anything?"

The one who has been staying with me touches the sheet where I lie and suddenly becomes urgent. He is fumbling and moving toward me, the sheet no longer covering my naked body. Until this moment, I thought I might escape this. Maybe they were really just here to rob me, as they said. They needed the money; they promised. Maybe they weren't the men from the posters on the kitchen table.

He climbs on top of me; his shirt remains on. My hands need to go somewhere, and in that moment, they move to grip the fabric. It feels thin, with small holes that bring air through and release sweat on a steamy hot night. The shirt is damp, and I imagine it is striped, purple and green with a collar, a shirt he is fond of, his favorite for an outing or special occasion. It pleased him when his mother brought it home from the store for him although she had gone to buy herself a new nightie. "I got you something; try it on," she says, smiling. It fits just right; he can wear it to hang out with friends or maybe to church with dress pants.

Later, when I remembered this moment, I wondered if he thought of me when he wore it. Did he remember that night and my hands on his back? Did he think I was embracing him? Did he think of me at all?

I feel nothing. I am not there. He tries to enter me and gets angry. "Come on, help me. What's the problem?"

I have a thought that he'll be mad if I say I've only been with women, so I mumble something like, "It's been awhile."

I hear the second voice. He is back. "Just have her give you a blow job. Come on, man. We have to hurry; it will be light soon."

"No, man, I want some pussy."

How can I describe the rest when I am no longer here? My body floats to the ceiling. I can't describe physical pain because I don't feel any. I feel nothing, over and over again. I feel nothing when he finishes and then moves me over to his partner and shoves my face onto his penis. I feel nothing as that man moves me away after a while. I feel nothing when the first man then moves my head toward his penis for a brief time and then gets on top of me and rapes me again. *How long? How many times?* I think vaguely. At some point, he bites me hard on the neck, and I feel that. Its sharpness brings me back into the room, not completely back, but enough to be aware that I have to pay attention again.

At that moment, there is a shift. Neither one of them seems afraid anymore. The first one is happy. For a moment I think he might take a nap. The second one wants to go.

"Come on. We need to get out of here."

One of them moves me onto my stomach and tells me to put my hands behind my back. He takes a cold plastic cord and wraps it around my wrists several times. He then extends it to my ankles, ties it around them, and pulls until my knees bend and my wrists and ankles almost touch. I fall to my side, unable to move. My fitted sheet has loosened from its edges and wraps me like a cocoon, covering the lower part of my body.

"We should go before it gets any lighter outside."

"Okay, but gag her so she can't yell for help."

I don't like that they're talking about me in the third person. I don't like it at all. My goal all night has been to try as hard as I can to make myself human to them, not an object to fear and extinguish, but a person who is no trouble whatsoever.

"I never saw either of you. Please, the blindfold never moved. I couldn't identify you even if I wanted to and I don't. I promise; I don't." Tears sting my eyes. "Why would I? Like you said, you just need money. I promise; you have nothing to worry about with me."

All I can see in my mind's eye is my mother. This would break her.

For her sake, for everyone else's, I would like a different conclusion to the night than what I now expect is about to happen. There is no room for me in my thoughts; I am focused only on living a few minutes more.

"Here, take this scarf and tie it around her mouth."

I struggle to insinuate myself into the room as a person and not the thing that is a danger to their freedom.

"Can you please make sure I can breathe? My hands are tied so tightly. If you accidentally block my nose, I'll suffocate. Please, can you please be careful?" I say to the dark.

One of them moves closer and brings his hands and the scarf over my head, and I breathe freely a couple of extra breaths, waiting for his hands to place the scarf around my neck and squeeze. Instead, the scarf goes around my mouth until the skin cracks as he ties it twice and knots it. I feel the callused tip of his thumb touch my nose with his finger, making sure the scarf is not covering it. Once and then, almost imperceptibly, again.

"Hurry up," one of them says. "Just leave her and let's go. We have to get out of here."

"Okay."

And then they were gone.

—

Months after telling Mary the story that I liked to hide away, she asked me the question she hadn't asked that night.

"Did they ever catch them?"

"No," I said.

"But you said there was a crime spree that summer. Do you know if they arrested anyone for the other break-ins?" It felt as if she was asking me the plotline to a book I'd read with a conclusion I'd forgotten. This conversation seemed so much harder than what I'd shared with her about that night. I started to sweat.

"That's a lot all at once," I said, evading that there were no updates and never had been. "What would finding them do? It won't take away what I've been through."

"No, no it would not; nothing would." Mary frowned. "But I'd like to think they tried, especially since these men seemed determined to keep doing what they were doing." I tried to remember if I'd thrown out the detective's card in a moment of anger or stuffed it in a box during one of my many moves.

Why would it be my job to make them do their job? I thought.

We settled into silence. I thought about my alcoholic stepfather and how I'd hint for a week about my birthday coming up so he'd remember to buy a card. It wasn't the card I wanted; it was to help him so he wouldn't be embarrassed he forgot.

"Mary, I can't, and I don't want to," I finally replied. "The last thing I want to get involved in is being with men who haven't done what they were supposed to do on my behalf and have their disappointment in themselves boomerang back to me."

"I get it," she said. "Let's make dinner."

I watched her grab some food out of the fridge, her back facing me as she pulled out what we needed to make pasta with vegetables. *What a cute bum she has,* I thought. I did feel happy. It seemed right in this moment that I could force the past behind me if I focused hard on the present: our cozy home, our little dog, Mary's cute bum and her sweetness. Don't look back; don't look at the randomness of violence and ask why it was your bedroom they walked into. Don't obsess over the lack of police response. Shove all that away and focus on the smell of the garlic simmering, the soft fur of our dog Ruby sitting in your lap, the loving partner you chose.

This "push it all away and move on" strategy worked until it didn't, until it couldn't. I continued on with my life and my partnership. We created a home together. Some would say that I moved on, but many know that this is never truly the case. Years from this moment, I would return to the fact that the police had been silent and ask them to be accountable, not to make them feel better, but because what and who they were ignoring needed to stop being overlooked—for my sake and for thousands like me.

Part II

An Investigation

When a person knows and can't
make the others understand, what does he do?

—CARSON McCULLERS, *THE HEART IS A LONELY HUNTER*

Eight

A single article in *The Boston Globe* led me back to my rape case and changed the trajectory of my life. It was 2007. I had finished my graduate degree and started a job at a liberal arts university just outside Boston. A significant part of my role involved ensuring the medical and mental health staff responded skillfully to students who disclosed sexual assault and provided university resources to support them. The job engaged me in meaningful work, and my home life sustained and nurtured me.

From the outside, I'm sure it looked as if I had done the hard-fought work of moving on. But I suffered still. Something was gnawing at me. There remained an unfinished and unattended-to piece of my past, but I didn't know exactly what. A little over twenty years had passed since the rapes, and yet I still felt that what had happened to me lay just below the surface of my consciousness—whatever closure I had delicately hovering in the balance, waiting to be undone. I saw disregard everywhere I looked and took it personally—comments by politicians, news

stories about rape cases that went nowhere, campus responses to
sexual assault at colleges around the country, as well as where I
worked. I tried hard to understand what I needed to do to heal the
still-deep wounds, but I couldn't quite do so.

The Boston Globe headline that stunned me one day as I drank
my morning coffee read, "Crime Lab Neglected 16,000 Cases—
Evidence Was Never Analyzed, Probe Finds."[1] "Evidence samples
from thousands of crime scenes across Massachusetts, including
nearly 1,000 homicides and 6,500 sexual assaults, were never analyzed by the State Police crime lab, according to an investigation
of the lab ordered by the state," the article began. These untested
samples dated back to the 1980s and were of "crisis proportions."
The piece followed reporting several months prior regarding the
urgent need for an audit of the state crime lab: "An administrator
at the troubled State Police crime laboratory has been suspended
for failing to tell prosecutors of DNA matches in a number of
unsolved rape cases, which now cannot be pursued because the
statute of limitations has expired."[2] The audit was done, which
then led to massive numbers of additional untested samples being
reported.

As I pored over the article, my mind returned to the rape kit
that I had endured, believing it would be used as part of an investigation. I thought of the other break-ins that summer. Could any
of the victims' evidence be linked to mine? Had they been able to
connect any of our cases to the same perpetrators? Or, could the
evidence kits all have just been sitting together for two decades
in the crime lab, untested even as DNA technology improved?
Then–state attorney general Martha Coakley disputed the findings, stating there were more like two thousand untested samples.
Despite Coakley's assertions, the secretary of public safety, Kevin
Burke, stayed firm about the report's conclusions and, according

to *Boston Globe* reporting, "insisted that the study found 16,000 untested biological samples that must be processed."[3] Top state officials continued to reassure the public that they had the situation under control and to suggest that the issue was too complicated for the public to understand. Prosecutors argued in the same *Globe* article that "thousands of the untested samples are from suicides, drug overdoses, and criminal cases where other evidence or guilty pleas made the biological evidence unnecessary at trials." The latter part of this statement ignores the reality that many rapists are serial perpetrators. Deciding that available forensic material will not be tested has the potential to impact countless lives. As the National Center for Victims of Crime states, "The DNA profile derived from tested kits can be entered into the FBI's national DNA database . . . regardless of whether the statute of limitations has run. Law enforcement can then search . . . for matches or 'hits' between crime scene DNA and offender DNA. Since we know that a majority of rapes are perpetrated by repeat offenders, entering evidence from untested kits . . . will result in more hits, thereby linking offenders to more crimes."[4]

"What are you reading?" Mary asked me. "You're sitting there just shaking your head back and forth."

"Let me finish reading first and I'll explain it to you the best I can when I'm done," I said, and turned back to the paper to reread the article. This was the very first time I heard anything about vast amounts of untested rape evidence, and the article was from my city newspaper about evidence that could be relevant to a crime I was victimized by over two decades ago. The sheer number reported in the *Globe* article felt impossible to understand.

Wouldn't someone have spoken up when there were a thousand untested samples, two thousand, three thousand? The fact of the untested evidence was hard enough to comprehend, but the way in which officials minimized the report and claimed the evidence, or the cases it was tied to, didn't matter stung even more deeply.

In a few years' time, I will hear Helena Lazaro's story for the first time. Her case makes clear why it is important not to reflexively dismiss testing rape kit evidence when a perpetrator is known to the victim or has pled guilty. Helena's attacker was a long-distance trucker from Indiana whose DNA had been entered into the national database after he assaulted his wife and she had a rape kit done. Had the rapist lived in a state where law enforcement didn't test rape kits when the perpetrator's identity was not in question, he would never have been linked to Helena's attack. Still, it took *thirteen years* and an advocate from Peace Over Violence to have the match discovered.[5] While we argue over policy and nuances like whether all kits should be tested or how much money testing will cost, precious time is lost, not only in the victim's life but also in the effort to stop subsequent attacks. It shouldn't have to be this hard. We shouldn't have to get stuck debating whether examining evidence in a felony crime is worth the effort or money, and victims shouldn't be responsible for nudging detectives to follow through on investigations of felony complaints.

I didn't know anything about DNA, statute of limitations, or much beyond what I'd just read in my living room over morning coffee. But the article got me wondering if this was why I never heard more from the police. I remembered the flyers my friend had given me. *You live nearby, don't you? Have you heard that there have been a lot of rapes in the Allston-Brighton neighborhood near Commonwealth Ave.? A neighborhood watch had these posters made. Would you put mind putting some up?*

—

In 1994 the FBI was able to formalize a national DNA database for law enforcement purposes through the DNA Identification Act.[6] The national DNA database, known as the Combined DNA Index System, or CODIS, became fully operational in the late 1990s. As Dwight Adams of the FBI's laboratory division explained to the Senate Judiciary Committee in 2002, "One of the underlying concepts behind the development of CODIS was to create a database of a state's convicted offender profiles and use it to solve crimes where no suspect exists."[7] Before the creation of the larger database—and as early as the mid-1980s, when I was assaulted—there was DNA technology, but it was more limited. At that time, fingerprinting served as one of the key forensic tools for linking someone to a crime scene.

"Why is this not national news, Mary?" I said, once I'd read the *Globe* article aloud to her. "On the one hand, it doesn't seem real that there could be so many untested samples in one crime lab, but on the other it doesn't surprise me in the slightest."

"I don't even know what to say. It's not right. Could Boston be the only city where this is happening?" She stood up and wrapped her arms around me while I kept my hands on the keyboard, afraid the words in front of me would disappear.

"I have to get dressed. Let me know what else you find out." Mary scooted upstairs, and I typed different phrases into my search bar.

Untested rape kits

DNA matches on old rape kits

Victim's attackers identified when rape kits tested

When I looked up, it was 9:00 A.M. and I was late for work.

According to the few articles I found then and the hundreds more that would come within the next few years, many rape victims had been undergoing forensic exams and reporting their crimes to law enforcement for nothing. None of us would have expected that after being raped, our evidence kits were turned over by hospital personnel to the police only to be shelved like a mediocre paperback.

These stories shifted how I thought about my rapes. I'd been dealing with it as a personal crisis. But I now saw I was far from the only one and that the circumstances surrounding the aftermath of the attack were central to my reaction. It came more clearly into focus as a crime that had been committed against me for which no information or investigation had ever been communicated. This crime still held me tight, its impact firm and immovable like a boat moored by its anchor in the harbor, unable to break free. The piece that was missing was a resolution, one that I didn't have the capability to give myself.

Maybe my rape kit was sitting on a shelf in the state crime lab waiting for someone to pluck it off and unveil the treasure it held within. I assumed my attackers were in jail at this point. They had told me they'd been breaking into houses for years, and I figured someone must have arrested them by now for something. I had many fantasies but no information. But *to know*, to know their names, to know what happened to them or see their faces for the first time. I resolved to follow the story about the crime lab. I would make some calls. I was scared but determined and hoped I could handle what I might learn.

Each subsequent article I read about untested rape kits felt like a piece of yarn that wove through the decades—connecting my own experience of feeling ignored and invisible to the experiences of present-day rape victims. The problems I encountered weren't ancient history; they still existed.

I waited to see whether there would be additional reporting about a plan to address the thousands of crime lab samples. The *Boston Globe* article stated that Secretary Burke had promised to first review the evidence on homicides and rapes, triaging them based on whether they remained unsolved and whether they were still eligible for prosecution. Disappointingly, two years after the initial audit, only five hundred of the sixteen thousand had been tested, and testing only happened if a district attorney had requested it. "We are exercising triage," John Grossman, the Department of Public Safety's undersecretary of forensic science and technology, is quoted as saying in a *Boston Globe* article. "When the requests come in, we analyze; otherwise, most of those 16,000 samples will remain in cold storage." While the lab was still behind on testing, it was "no longer focused on reducing the backlog," meaning thousands of pieces of evidence would remain untouched.[8] The article stated that the crime lab's highest priority was testing the newest samples and entering them into CODIS. Those cases from years past that would receive no attention did not get old on their own. Someone put their evidence aside long ago and ignored them when it could have made a difference. And now they would be considered less important and unworthy of the state's resources.

I felt a burgeoning need to understand what had happened in my case and how it was tied to more recent cases. Had so little really changed while I'd withdrawn and rebuilt my life from scratch? I couldn't comprehend how such a progressive state could ignore rape evidence like this. The words spoken to me so long ago echoed in my head: *Can't keep her mouth shut* and *Didn't I say I'd call you if we knew anything?* What words were today's victims hearing? What results were today's investigations rendering?

I insisted on information only once I could—after I'd recovered enough to feel reasonably sure that the effort wouldn't undo the life I'd worked so hard to reclaim. I had created personal scaffolding over the years that kept the rapes from destroying my life. Paradoxically, this scaffolding allowed me to experience the crime's true weight and impact. Only then was I able to ask for more.

Nine

1991–2000

My life had shifted once again toward possibility when I started graduate school. As it does for so many, education created a space for me to develop—or, in my case, return to—a feeling of self-worth. The Harvard School of Public Health bordered the medical area near downtown Boston, and on my way to class I walked by the many hospitals I had worked in as a temp. I thought about going into the Boston Children's Hospital research building to see if Shelly still worked there but couldn't face walking into the past when I was working as hard as I could to enjoy my present life.

My program began in September 1991. Every morning, I'd drive into the Mission Hill area of Boston hours before class to find a parking space and grab breakfast in the school's atrium. There, I'd sit doing my homework, waiting to find a new friend to wave over. We'd have coffee and chatter about easy things.

How was traffic for you this morning?

I'm not used to having homework on the weekends; what an adjustment.

I love this place!

Over the aroma of my dark roast blend, the building smelled to me of hope, of an experience overdue and hard won. Could it really be me who felt so at ease, looking forward to a future I welcomed? My mom called repeatedly after the acceptance letter arrived to say, "Daddy would have been so proud of you," and I teared up every time. He had dedicated his life to education and what it offered to others' futures. I didn't know as a child that he had been accepted to Harvard to pursue his doctorate in education the summer he got sick. "We were going to move to Massachusetts when he got his diagnosis but never made it there," my mom told me during one of these phone calls. "Imagine how different our lives would have been." Maybe I survived for this reason, I thought, to honor his legacy and the dreams an early death had stolen. And because I had lived, I wanted to give this gift to the man I had once loved so.

"It's only graduate school, Mom, no big deal. It's not that hard to get into." While my voice sounded definitive, I was lying. Continuing my education felt like a very big deal.

During orientation, the dean who welcomed us told a practiced joke: "Don't worry; we double-checked everyone's admission status and I promise you that none of you are here by mistake." I laughed along with my classmates but didn't find it funny.

If another student asked what I had been doing before coming to Harvard, my answer was brief: "I did HIV education for injection drug users at a drug treatment clinic. The work got me interested in health systems and policy."

I skipped the rest.

Maybe the past can be put away. Maybe it doesn't have to chase you.

I intended to find out.

This transition marked the point in my life when I stopped telling people about the rapes. Time for a new story, I must have decided without knowing I had decided anything. I'd share a brand-new narrative, not a lie exactly, just an omission. I convinced myself I did this because a history of sexual violence wasn't something with which to open a casual conversation, but it was more than that. If all these new, exciting people saw me as one of them—just a graduate student hoping to get the skills to further her career—maybe that external lens would help me feel less damaged. Naively, I thought I could put it behind me just by ignoring the fact of its existence in my past.

A shared national moment upended my belief I could push my past aside: experiences shape you and change you; they can't be buried or forgotten, and their meaning is determined by what you do with them. Barely a month into graduate school, I read in *The Boston Globe* about a woman named Anita Hill, a law professor, who would be testifying before the Senate Judiciary Committee about the nomination of Clarence Thomas to the Supreme Court. Hill had worked with Thomas early in her career and would speak about his behavior toward her when he was her supervisor. She agreed to this reluctantly.

A search of *The Boston Globe* archives before October 6, 1991, yielded zero results for the name Anita Hill. Now, a search of her name on the internet shows close to 70 million. Unknown to the world in early October 1991, Hill's testimony under oath about the sexual harassment she endured from a man seeking a position on the nation's highest court changed her life, and our country, forever. Behavior that many women considered normative and private, a terrible burden one must tolerate too often in the workplace, was being seriously questioned in a national conversation. Many people experienced Hill's testimony with a sense of validation and relief; others denied her credibility while minimizing the impact of the behavior she described experiencing. Within a day of the announcement that Hill would testify and before she had uttered one word publicly, senators supporting Thomas's nomination were working to diminish the significance of her remarks. Senator John Danforth said the "'deplorable charge' of sexual harassment is categorically denied by Judge Thomas and predicted it would have no effect on the Senate vote."[1] Senator Dennis DeConcini said, "If you're sexually harassed, you ought to complain instead of hanging around a long time, and then all of a sudden calling up anonymously and saying . . . 'Oh, I wanna complain,' . . . I mean where is the gumption? . . . Complain!"[2] Senator Orrin Hatch accused Hill of using racial stereotypes against Thomas to turn people against him,[3] and Senator Alan K. Simpson read a statement from an anonymous source declaring that Hill was delusional.[4]

On my way home from school the day before the hearing, I stopped and picked up new VHS cassettes, since I couldn't afford to miss a whole day of classes. For the next few nights, Mary and I ate dinner in front of the TV. At times, I felt as if we were watching a silent movie, as I took note of people's expressions and movements as much as their words. I will always remember Anita Hill in a turquoise dress holding her head high when she was sworn in, whose face softened when she gestured to introduce her mother and father, and who described being the youngest of thirteen growing up on a farm in rural Oklahoma. I watched the way her mouth shaped words of ugliness and humiliation as she stumbled when asked to repeat things from her written statement, which recounted how her boss had asked her out repeatedly, mentioned a pubic hair on his Coke can, and inquired whether she had ever heard of a porn star named Long Dong Silver and his ample penis size.

"That poor woman," Mary said. "What she went through is horrifying, not to mention enduring this god-awful hearing."

"Why is Ted Kennedy just sitting there looking like a hound dog but barely talking?"

"Look at all those white men judging her; literally looking down on her from their high seats." Mary's voice rose. "Even if they believe her—and they should and probably do—they'd still have to think what he did was wrong. And why would they, when they probably do the same thing themselves?"

Mary was right. The real issue being argued wasn't, in fact, whether Hill was telling the truth but whether sexual harassment was a matter of concern to the senators on the Judiciary Committee. Had any of them ever been held accountable for how they treated women in the workplace?

"Women don't make those things up," I said, feeling a familiar tug downward. "How can anyone possibly think someone would put themselves through something like this if it weren't true?"

We had pressed the pause button, yet neither of us moved. I wanted some ice cream or cookies, thinking sugar might improve my mood. "I'm telling you right now he'll be confirmed, and they'll keep trying to make her look like she's the problem." Mary's voice rose as she stared at the frozen image of Senator Arlen Specter, from Pennsylvania, frowning. "You can see it from the questions they're asking and the looks on their faces. That one senator saying, 'Are you a scorned woman?' and the other one saying it's not really all that bad talking about women's large breasts at work. As if that's normal everyday banter and she's oversensitive. I mean, what the hell?"

That night, I cried after Mary fell asleep. I imagined sitting behind Anita Hill along with millions of women who had been impacted by violence and harassment and felt concurrently unheard and blamed. *The truth doesn't matter,* I said only in my head, so I wouldn't wake her. *How do we manage to live with that?*

I lay there, trying as hard as I could to think only about the friends I would see for coffee the next day and whether my professor had graded our papers. But sleep wouldn't come, because all I could think of was how this hearing showed the world what I already knew: women's experiences—particularly those of women of color—are invisible, our words swatted aside like nothing more than a pesky fly at a picnic. I wanted my brain to stop these negative thoughts, stop before I'd hear the words spoken by the police in my rape case, words of erasure I'd counted on this new chapter of my life erasing.

Just like a woman, can't keep her mouth shut.

Didn't I say I'd call you if we knew anything?

—

When the hearing ended with Thomas confirmed, his ascendancy wasn't enough to mollify his supporters. They continued to attack Hill's reputation, in large measure to protect Thomas as a legitimate conservative voice. A Yale-educated law scholar with a stellar reputation, Hill was humiliatingly referred to as "a little bit nutty and a little bit slutty" by the conservative writer David Brock.[5] Others who supported Thomas pressured the University of Oklahoma to revoke Hill's tenure, and she was subjected to death threats for years.[6]

I followed these stories about Hill as if they were my own, the message clear and instructive: if you challenge the status quo and question behaviors men in power enjoy and feel entitled to, they will try to squash you, unconcerned about lying or inflicting lasting damage on you. As I looked at every one of those senators,

I imagined the words, *How dare you, young lady?* etched in the lines of their faces.

After the Thomas hearing, there were thousands of buttons and T-shirts printed with the words I BELIEVE ANITA HILL, but that was never the real issue. In order to deny Thomas a seat, the senators would have to believe that the behavior Hill described warranted a man facing some consequence for his actions. In the space of male power, pretending to care about the issue of sexual harassment or sexual violence is the requirement; being committed to creating change is a whole different story.

This moment in history changed me and sharpened my resolve, something I wouldn't fully comprehend until I found my own voice on issues related to sexual violence years later. Witnessing the entrenched power structure embodied by a committee—so fully white and male—charged with overseeing the administration of justice within the federal courts provided a powerful message. Clearly, this body could not effectively represent all its constituents. I found it a particularly stunning indictment of the members of the Senate Judiciary Committee that when their colleague mentioned how common it was to talk about women's breast size at work, not one of them felt the need to counter. Instead, they moved on with their own questioning, as if Anita Hill were the one on trial.

These were our nation's lawmakers. This seat was for the highest court in our country.

Twenty-seven years after Thomas's confirmation, Brett Kavanaugh's hearing echoed the same hypocrisy. Judge Kavanaugh was accused by Dr. Christine Blasey Ford, a psychology professor and researcher, of sexually assaulting her at a party when they were both teenagers. Senator Orrin Hatch, one of the few remaining senators on the Judiciary Committee who was also present at the

Thomas hearing, is quoted as saying, "I think it would be hard for senators to not consider who the judge is today. That's the issue. Is this judge a really good man? And he is. And by any measure he is."[7] And there it is, right there. This statement is about the nominee; Hatch doesn't explain why he believes Dr. Ford was "mistaken" in her account of being sexually assaulted by Kavanaugh in high school. Kavanaugh gets a pass. The senator has judged him a good man based on standards he doesn't even feel compelled to explain. During Kavanaugh's testimony, the judge yelled at senators, asked them if they liked beer, refused to answer questions, and seemed enraged rather than wise and circumspect. But by Hatch's measure, and the others who voted to confirm him, he is a good man and qualified to serve a lifetime appointment on our nation's highest court.

Even if he did what Dr. Ford says he did, he's still a good man.

How is any rape survivor to look at the Supreme Court and have faith it can meaningfully address issues of sexual assault and rape? This most recent spectacle didn't even attempt to seriously reckon with the epidemic of rape and sexual assault in our nation and the general lack of consequences for perpetrators.

Our male-dominated systems focus their attention on who wins, who gets the prize, who ascends instead of thoughtfully and seriously addressing, for example, the damage done and the lifetime consequences of trauma for survivors, as Dr. Ford so eloquently described as being "indelible in the hippocampus."[8] We were all asked—in both 1991 and 2018—to first look at and then to judge the accuser, to wonder why she waited, to wonder if she was credible. We were further asked to collude in minimizing behaviors that, even if they occurred, would not disqualify a man from the highest court in our land, a court whose only job is to ensure that laws passed abide by the Constitution and protect all of us equally.

Where does that leave those of us who do not minimize the impact of rape and sexual assault? Is there any room for our protection, our optimism, our sense of hope that the judicial branch is separate from politics and can adjudicate issues impartially? And if there is no room and our lives and safety are therefore at stake, how can we seek reform?

—

The Thomas hearings taught me something I started to incorporate into my graduate studies—analyzing what causes a problem instead of just describing what the problem is. I'd been working on a research paper on the high rate of suicide in LGBTQ youth, focusing on the social factors and political climate that contribute to their sense of isolation, shame, and self-hatred. Each suicide has its own individual story. Yet any solution aimed at reducing rates needs to reach beyond the individual and examine how society's biases impact health outcomes and responses to them. I'd experienced this same framework in my work on AIDS; we had a health crisis in our country, but the fact that it first mainly affected gay men, IV drug users, and people of color contributed to government's slow response in funding research. Understanding the social factors affecting health outcomes is essential to public health and would be essential to me as I began to investigate my own rape case as well as the state of rape investigations in this country.

I showed Mary my paper on LGBTQ youth the night before it was due, and explained how much the Thomas hearings had impacted my thinking about analyzing a social issue. "Okay, I get your point," Mary said after reading my paper's introduction. "But maybe you could include a suggestion that we should start electing people who look more like the rest of our country or I don't think much will change."

—

In the late 1990s, Hill took a job as a professor at a school known
for its commitment to social justice. The school was named after
Louis Brandeis, the first Jewish man on the Supreme Court, who
famously said, "Sunlight is the best disinfectant." The Brandeis
University seal reads, TRUTH EVEN UNTO ITS INNERMOST PARTS. As
undergraduates, my friends and I used to joke that this awkward
phrase sounded like a truth speculum searching the world's nether
regions for what is real among competing narratives. The thing
about the truth, though, is that it is not relative, even though those
with power and influence would like us to believe it is. When I
heard Hill was teaching at Brandeis, it seemed to me an inspired
choice given its namesake's ardent defense of free speech. No
matter the cost to her personally, Anita Hill had spoken truth to
power, and her example resonated for millions of those who would
come after.

Given the stakes of the decisions made by the Supreme Court,
we must expect that those chosen to serve will have a deep understanding of and commitment to the United States Constitution
and adjudicate accordingly. Further, we should expect them to be
committed to the rights of all, not just to those who look like the
white men who first wrote the Declaration of Independence, who,
while declaring that all men are created equal, owned slaves and
denied anyone but white men the right to vote for a significant
part of our history. Thurgood Marshall, the first African American
to serve on the Supreme Court, stated, "The government they
devised was defective from the start, requiring several amend-
ments, a civil war, and major social transformations to attain the
system of constitutional government and its respect for the free-
doms and individual rights, we hold as fundamental today."[9] It is
not unpatriotic—I'd argue it is the opposite—to understand our

history and state the fact that basic rights for all Americans have never been equally applied. Liberty and justice for all remain aspirational concepts rather than reality in our nation.

Twenty years after I finished my graduate program, I had the opportunity to meet Anita Hill in person. Steve, the loving friend who had welcomed me into his and Emmy's home after the break-in, asked me to do a consultation at Brandeis on their sexual assault policy, work I was absorbed in at Tufts University, where I was now the executive director of health and wellness. Steve had become an internationally known scientist and had returned to Brandeis to assume a senior role in the administration as well as continue his laboratory research studying ion channels. We had remained close, and I felt more like a younger sister to Emmy and Steve than the baby I had perceived myself to be when I shared their Brookline apartment. After I completed my consultation, Steve invited me to consider a job at my alma mater and arranged a day of interviews for me, where I would meet his key colleagues, including Hill, with whom he worked on policy and academic affairs.

—

"Okay, Mary, tomorrow I am going to meet Anita Hill," I said. We were in our bedroom and I was grabbing handfuls of Mary's work clothes to try on since they were more professional than mine. "I'm trying to remember she's just a person who probably can't stand it when people treat her like she's an icon. I want to respect that, but I also wish I could find some way to tell her what her work has meant to me."

"I'm sure she hears it all the time." Mary took the scarf I had chosen and folded it up. "I'm sorry, honey, but you can't wear black pants, brown shoes, and a yellow scarf. Try this one instead."

"Who cares what I wear, just as long as I look dignified and not like a fangirl? I hope I can pull it off."

"I don't know what a fangirl looks like or what it even is, for that matter. Just be yourself, the one we all love so much," she said, grabbing another mismatched scarf out of my hands.

I walked into Brandeis the next morning with a list of names in my suit pocket, too nervous to enjoy being back on campus and the memories it evoked. I stopped at the reception desk in the building Steve directed me to. I unfolded the paper and read off the five names of the people I was supposed to meet, Anita's listed last.

I heard, "I'll start," and Anita emerged through an open office door. She was smiling and had her hand out to greet me. "Come in, Michelle. It's so great to meet you. Let's sit down and chat."

Her office had enough room for a desk and two chairs. We sat across from each other. I had my résumé with me and she took it and put it down near her computer. "I've heard such great things about you from Steve and so appreciate how you've been helping us look at our sexual assault policies here. It's so important," she said. "Tell me more about what you do."

At this time, I not only worked on sexual assault issues in my professional role but had been involved for about a year in nation-wide advocacy addressing untested rape evidence. It was a topic that eschewed brevity. If I said, "I've been doing work outside my job to understand how there could possibly be hundreds of thousands of rape kits untested around the country and am trying to do something to change that," the person sitting across from me would want to know more. *How could this be? What do you mean they never tested rape evidence for decades?* And then, inevitably, *How did this come to matter to you?* Even though the purpose of this interview was for Anita to learn about my skills and interests, I was reluctant to bring up this part of my life. It was certainly a job credential—being part of an effort to change the way sex crimes are handled going forward—but it was also deeply personal to me. Shyness and shame sat in my body and kept me silent.

Instead, we talked about the impact of sexual assault and harassment on students' college careers and how it seems as if the victim is the one who most often suffers, while the accused experiences few consequences. "Sometimes it feels to me like nothing has changed since you first spoke out on these issues," I blurted out and then stopped, not knowing if it was a subject I should avoid—worried bringing it up made me appear presumptuous. She nodded and said, "The work isn't done yet." And I said, "And it won't be anytime soon."

I lost track of the details of this moment even as I sat inside it. Someone else in the world—regardless of her name or history—understood the need to take allegations of sexual assault and harassment seriously and to create policies that would allow fairer outcomes to occur. I was beyond overwhelmed and grateful for that.

When our meeting was almost over, I took a deep breath and found my voice. "I hope it's okay to say thank you. I know in my own small way from some advocacy work I'm doing outside of Tufts how hard it is to be public about a personal issue." I very briefly touched on what I'd learned from my own activism and experience. I was not surprised that she focused on the issues rather than asking me personal questions. It's what I expected from her, somehow, and why I didn't want to intrude by commenting on her public face without asking.

I tried to choose my words carefully when I next spoke. "It makes a difference when we name a problem. It doesn't make it disappear, but it's a start." She smiled, and we both steered the rest of the conversation back to sexual assault on college campuses and our shared work on that front. And then she thanked me for the work I was doing and for helping Brandeis with their consult.

I'm not sure I have ever met someone as gracious as she.

I declined to take the job at Brandeis. Given how much I loved Steve and how indebted to him I still felt, I didn't want to risk changing our relationship by working for him. Knowing Anita Hill was out there, a woman who had spoken publicly about sexual harassment, helped sustain me in my own work. As my advocacy work intensified and received public attention, I'd feel conflicting emotions when getting notes of thanks from friends and strangers. They were generally kind and acknowledged my work, but I felt exposed and raw. Then I'd think of Anita and her acknowledgment of my efforts to make change, and it helped me continue on in a way that I hoped would honor her legacy and hard work.

—

The Thomas confirmation hearings had left me shaken, but I soon became immersed and distracted by the rigors of graduate school and completed my degree two years later. While I learned so much in my time there, in retrospect I couldn't recall whether any courses had been offered on the public health implications of sex crimes, including the health costs and health consequences of trauma, standard concepts in most of the classes I took. Given the number of people impacted by this critical public health concern, I wanted to confirm this memory and, if accurate, understand why it had been absent from the curricula. I found a need as I peeled back the layers of my own personal experience to examine the societal overlay as well, suspecting there was a deep connection between them. I reached out to my former advisor, Dr. David Hemenway, who is currently the director of the Harvard Injury Control Research Center and one of the "twenty most influential injury and violence professionals over the past twenty years."[10] He confirmed that, in fact, there were no courses in our program during the early 1990s on the topic of rape, sexual assault, and sexual abuse. Courses addressing violence prevention focused primarily on homicide and suicide, including the impact of youth violence within communities.

I'm proud to have attended a public health program at a time when youth violence, HIV research, and maternal and child health were critical issues being researched and taught. I did wonder, though, why conversation about sexual violence had been absent from the curricula, especially given that this was just before the passage of the Violence Against Women Act and public health data at the time showed how domestic and sexual violence and childhood sexual abuse were pervasive and serious health issues.[11] In Boston alone, the Boston Area Rape Crisis Center had been operational for almost twenty years now, Judith Herman's groundbreaking book on the PTSD of trauma survivors had just been published, and there were services specifically for victims of violence at multiple area hospitals. It seemed conspicuous by its absence in such an esteemed institution.

What is absent or slower to grab notice in the history of health and social issues is just as important as what is included and when, and this extends to our national conversation as well. We determine as a society what has value, in part by what we read, what new research studies teach us, and what valued figures in a field teach and deem important.

—

On the day I graduated from Harvard—hoping to embark on a career at the intersection of health care and social justice—I still worried that I was no match for other young professionals whose lives reflected a more linear trajectory than mine. So far, the jobs I'd applied for required more experience than I had, and I hadn't received one call back.

A few hundred students processed to a small courtyard behind the school on a brilliant day in May. My entire family and several friends came early to sit up front since I had been chosen to give the commencement address. It was 1993, and the Clinton administration was working on developing a comprehensive national health care plan. Several professors had spent time teaching about what impact universal health care would have on our country if passed, some of them consulting with the White House on different models. I hoped to make a clear connection to health care as a basic human right and my father's lessons to me as a young child that education was also a human right and great equalizer. Mary had heard me practice the speech several times, and Emmy had edited it. "You're ready," they'd both said after hearing the final draft.

"My father was the principal of a school on the west side of Chicago," I began. He had cared passionately about the students he served and wanted their lives to be buoyed by a decent education and recognized the impact poverty had on their dreams, if they dreamed at all. He had taught me in the seven years I shared with him on this planet that everyone should have access to a decent education, economic opportunity, and health care—items that speak to basic dignity and fairness. And that we should stand up for values that championed fundamental rights and access to basic needs. Fifty years after his death, I still hear from his former students, who well up talking about his impact as a teacher and principal.

I finished my remarks and took my seat onstage next to the surgeon general of the United States, Joycelyn Elders, the keynote speaker. She leaned over and whispered, "Nice job," but I was looking at my mother, who cried her way through the speech and was blowing kisses in my direction. After the ceremony, a favorite professor would introduce me to Dr. Jeanne J. Taylor, who ran one of the largest community health centers in Boston, and this introduction would lead to my first postgraduate job. I felt I understood public health and the way it related to my father's beliefs about opportunity and access. The field I'd chosen could help me find a way to honor his legacy and make a difference. I felt proud; I felt hopeful. In that one moment, I experienced a sense of agency return to me that had been taken a decade earlier.

—

I have only three memories of me and my father together. They are distinct and cemented.

In one, he's holding the back of my bicycle as it races down an incline on two wheels. It's going too fast and he's running full out, and I'm certain he won't let go, which keeps my terror under control. Each bump on the concrete raises my forty-pound frame two inches off the seat, and I feel his fingertips lightly touch my back so that I know he is there as I fly.

In the second, I see him picking up my plastic toy clock from the floor to teach my friend's older sister how to tell time. "I'll be right back," he yells as he lopes across the postage-stamp-size backyard to our neighbor's townhouse. Even though I'm only five, I know that my dad's attention will make the little girl feel special rather than slow. When he returns, he gives me back my clock and we play.

In the third one, I feel his lean body sitting next to me in the hot sun surrounded by piles of rocks. My father squints as he looks them over and chooses one. He studies it for a moment before he splits it open with a tap from a screwdriver, finding the fossil he knew would be inside. He rubs my fingertips over a small, perfect skeleton that looks like a willow leaf. The rock is warm as I stroke it, looking at the image set in stone. I know at that moment this man is in touch with miracles and that I am safe.

I noticed a change in the rhythm of our lives in late May, a busy time for a high school principal as the academic year concludes. My father stopped working and his short-sleeved T-shirt hung a little looser over his once-athletic chest. A few months later, he disappeared from the house, inpatient full-time in a downtown Chicago hospital. Two months later, he died. Bone cancer. My mother kept my sister and me from the funeral, knowing my Hungarian grandmother—a woman who'd just lost her baby boy—would wail, a terrifying, ear-splitting guttural screech of pain that would last throughout the service. She thought she was protecting us, but I never had a chance to say goodbye.

Grief hardened me and created a belief that good men came around rarely and that when they did, they couldn't stay. I would be safe from harm if I never loved anyone as much ever again, a childhood belief that took years to unravel. After being sexually violated and confused and disappointed by the silence from the police, I built a small, quiet world inhabited almost entirely by women with whom I could manage to share some emotional and physical intimacy.

After graduation, the frank memories and sleepless nights receded; my days were no longer spent feeling shame or yearning only for all I had lost. I enjoyed a happy relationship, had graduated at the very top of my class, and now had a job I never thought my lean résumé would have garnered. Mary and I soon turned to the possibility of adding to our family beyond just the two of us and our beloved dogs.

Parenting had been something I planned to skip altogether.

Back when I came out, motherhood as a theoretical concept felt contrary to my lesbian identity, pregnancy impossible to imagine. Considering this step with Mary gave me access to memories I thought I'd put away for good. As I now allowed joy and love into my life, I still wasn't sure I could take the kind of risk that sends you tightrope walking over a canyon with jagged rocks waiting below. And what is the risk of loving a child if not that?

For months, I wanted no part of parenting and Mary tried to understand. "It started in college when the idea of motherhood didn't fit with my identity," I said, knowing it sounded weak. "Back then, I thought raising children was something the patriarchal structure invented to subjugate women and reduce their power."

"Did you ever consider revisiting that notion over the last fifteen years?" Mary asked. "Has anything changed your thinking since then, like having a partner who loves you dearly and isn't part of the patriarchy as far as I can tell?" She sat with her hands in her lap, letting me get it all out.

"Childrearing perpetuates economic injustice. Women are pushed out of the work world to reproduce the species."

"Is the idea completely closed for you?" Mary asked.

"No, I'm just telling you how I feel." I finished my rant. "Go ahead. I'll listen."

"We would be such good parents. There's so much love to give right here," she said, waving her hands around our small condo. "You love being around children. It's one of the only times your eyes reliably sparkle. And I'll get pregnant; I don't mind."

Some part of me understood my thoughts were fear-based. As Judith Herman writes about parenting after sexual assault, "The survivor's overriding fear is a repetition of the trauma; her goal is to prevent a repetition at all costs."[12] If I'd had the words, I might have said, "I'm scared to death to care so much." I tried to imagine what it might be like to have my nerve endings living outside my skin again, this time for something life-affirming, if I could only manage my terror.

Then, one day in a moment of grace, I took Mary's hand and said, "Okay."

—

We'd spent over a year trying by doing the insemination at home. Every month, a dry-ice-encased tank appeared on our porch, delivered from a lesbian-owned California cryobank recommended by friends. After wheeling it into the house on a dolly, it took muscle to open the hatch and extract the half-inch-tall cylinder and put it directly into the refrigerator. After several failed attempts, we relented and had the sperm delivered to a fertility clinic, where an intrauterine insemination resulted in Mary's getting pregnant right away. We went to the ob-gyn clinic together for a routine ultrasound about halfway through the pregnancy.

The technologist brought us into an exam room, and Mary lifted her shirt, exposing her belly. I stood next to her, staring at the screen as bluish jelly was squeezed onto her middle and the wand moved back and forth. The familiar swishing sound filled the room.

"There's the heartbeat, and it sounds great. Look, there's the outline of the spine, the head, the feet." The technician pointed at each as she named the parts, avoiding pronouns.

"Do you want to know the sex? Because if you look at the screen for a few seconds, it's pretty obvious."

And it was. There, along with fingers and toes, head and spine, sat a body part I was pretty unfamiliar with, representing a gender completely remote to me. Sometimes I imagined men as alien beings I knew were out there in the world but whom I had banished for self-preservation—from my home, my bed, my heart. How was I going to do it? This little being would be my son soon and for the rest of my life. There would be boy clothes and underwear and boy needs stretching me as a new parent, and I had no idea how to do any of it. Someday, there would be a young man living with us, who would need me to parent him and help him learn how to become an adult in this world, a gentle and loving person—a man who asks permission, who understands he can't just take what he wants without asking. Maybe, just maybe, he would be like the one who taught me how to ride a bike and open a fossil. I thought of my father and begged him to help me push away my fears and simply love this child with everything I had, the way he had once loved me. Seeing that tiny, vulnerable body on that screen softened my defenses. Familiar or not, I was going all in, already in love with him.

"Can we name him Benjamin Gilbert?" I asked Mary, still staring at his floating impression. "It's my dad's name backwards. Instead of Gilbert Benowitz, he'll be Benjamin Gilbert. It would make me so happy and so much less scared, somehow. Do you mind?"

"There is not one single thing about that request I mind in the slightest." She smiled up at me. "You are going to be a great parent to Ben." She said his name for the first time, and I couldn't imagine having to wait another several months to meet him. "All this baby needs is your love, and I know from experience what an amazing gift that is."

The terror I felt when I first saw Benjamin on the ultrasound was replaced with something else—unambivalent joy. I had to try on this unfamiliar feeling; it felt great.

The day we brought Benjamin home from the hospital he was so tiny, wearing a yellow knitted cap and swaddled in a matching blanket. The three of us were exhausted by 7:00 P.M., and we'd been told by experienced parents to sleep whenever the baby sleeps to survive the first few weeks. We raced to bed.

Ben would stay in our bedroom, in a little wooden cradle we borrowed from friends. He was right next to my side of the bed, less than an arm's length away. Mary was slumbering the instant her head hit the pillow, and Benjamin was sleeping as well. I got into bed, realizing there was no way I could sleep. I touched Mary's shoulder gently, thinking about shaking it hard if she didn't wake up.

"What if something happens to him in the middle of the night?" I said. "What were we thinking?"

"Okay," she said, struggling to sit up. "He's going to be okay, but here's what we'll do. Let's put up a little prayer into the universe and see if that helps. It doesn't matter if you believe or not. Do it anyway." I held her hand, not arguing.

"God, Goddess, Buddha, Mother Earth or whatever spirit might be in the universe," she said, "thank you so much for bringing this wonderful, sweet, beautiful child into our lives. We pray that nothing happens to him and you keep him safe, but if it does, thank you so much for even these few days you've given us. Nothing will ever undo the joy we've had with him. Now, we really need to get some rest so that we can take care of this little baby. Please help Michy put her fears away for tonight so we can all get some sleep."

Mary looked right at me. "We really do need to sleep," she said, touching my arm. "Do you want to say anything?"

I repeated her sentiment. "We wouldn't trade these days for anything so, thank you and, I guess, we need to try and sleep." My voice was quiet, and I felt so small. "Can you please help us keep him safe?" I said to no one in particular.

Two years later, our daughter, Rebecca, was born. She too is spectacular—an unexpected redhead whose eyes twinkle like

Mary's and whose smile filled me with such love I was overcome. In those days of early parenting, my joy was occasionally inter-rupted by the residue of trauma. But mostly, when I looked at both our children, my body thrummed—a ballet dancer in midair, exultant and unafraid in a moment of flight. My heart opened to every possibility I thought I'd buried. It felt like a minor miracle that I could let myself take the risk of caring this much again, of chancing something so precious and so fragile. It was this ability to care once again and love deeply that drove me to look into my cold case. I wanted a different world for my children and, most of all, to be a parent who showed them that injustice and the harm it does cannot stand, that self-regard can help you find what you once believed was lost.

Ten

2008–12

I started to make a few inquiries about my cold case several months after reading the *Globe* piece about the state crime lab. I wrote a letter to the attorney general's office saying I'd been a victim of a stranger rape in the mid-1980s and had never heard back from the police. I asked whether there was a process in place for victims to learn if their rape kit was among the thousands of untested samples that had been reported in the paper.

The attorney general's office responded with a phone call from someone who identified herself as a client advocate. "What were you hoping we could help you with?" she asked.

I experienced what I imagine a bad witness feels like on the stand. I couldn't be specific and felt I might be wasting her time. Finally, I found my voice. "Is there a process in place for victims to get more information about the untested samples and who they belong to? I mean, I don't expect a list of names, obviously; I just want to know if my name or my evidence is logged anywhere."

"I'd call the District Attorney in whatever jurisdiction the crime occurred and see if they know more about this."

"Why would I do that? There was no trial."

"I'd give them a try," she said again. "Maybe they'd have a record of your original case."

I hung up, knowing it would take me weeks or months to feel ready to take that step—to write another letter, to make another call, to wait for a response, to have a confused or frustrated person on the other end of the phone wonder exactly what I wanted.

I met with Saundra, a senior staff member at the Boston Area Rape Crisis Center, curious whether other survivors had reached out to her agency after the *Globe* article about the untested crime-lab samples. She seemed much less intimidating than an official in a government office.

I explained to her my shock in reading the state crime lab had decades-old samples from rape cases. "Has anyone reached out to you about that at BARCC? I can't be the only one who read that article."

"We really aren't getting calls that I'm aware of about that," she said. We were at a coffee shop between my office and hers. Saundra's voice was soft. "Say more," she invited.

"Have you requested a briefing from the state executive office for public safety?" I asked, thinking those responsible for the crime lab would have done damage control with key constituencies. She said she'd heard they disputed the number of untested samples—which I'd read in the original article as well—but also recalled the investigator's adamancy that the numbers were accurate. She further explained that BARCC's core mission was to help survivors, and, given the overwhelming number of people who use their services, this type of investigation was not a central part of their mission. I looked at her, feeling ashamed for taking her time. It wasn't her priority and it wasn't the attorney general's priority and maybe it was no one's priority but mine. Unsure what to say next, I just stared at her and wondered what it would be like working for years at a rape crisis center hearing story after story. Saundra had the same big brown mane of hair I did and eyes that held patience.

Maybe because she seemed so kind and maybe because I felt safe letting out some frustration, I said, "If the crime lab had tested those samples that had been sitting around for decades and identified serial perpetrators, maybe there'd be fewer rape victims who needed help." As soon as I said it, I felt frightened I'd gone too far. I don't know what I would have done without BARCC all those years ago. I admired the work they did. But it came tumbling out of my mouth, and I couldn't take it back.

Saundra smiled at me and nodded. Maybe she was used to people getting rattled; she didn't seem to personalize my distress. "I hear you. I'll look into this some more, see if there's something we can do to be helpful."

I called the Victim Rights Law Center, a nationally known and also widely respected pro bono legal organization, to see what they might think about the untested samples in the crime lab being of "crisis proportions." They put me through to a lawyer who thought I wanted representation in a lawsuit. "I'm sorry, but you don't have a case," she said to a question I hadn't asked. "The statute of limitations would have expired before the CODIS database was even in wide use. It was only ten years back then."

She explained that it was hard, if not impossible, to file a civil action against someone in law enforcement, since they are legally protected from being sued by civilians over which cases should be investigated—often their own. This concept is known as "qualified immunity."[1] Police are given these protections, in theory, because they have challenging and dangerous jobs, and it would inhibit them from being effective if they had to constantly worry about lawsuits. Other professions doing their best to save lives are not afforded such vast protections—most notably, perhaps, medical professionals.

"I'm not calling about my individual case and I don't want to sue," I said, trying to squelch my frustration. It had crossed my mind that this wholesale disregard of evidence in crimes overwhelmingly impacting women, children, people of color, and other marginalized populations had the makings of a great class action suit. "I'm trying to find out more information about how your agency is thinking about the massive numbers nationwide of untested rape evidence from a legal perspective." I had looked up their number on my computer and sat staring at their website as she talked. There was a DONATE button, an EXIT SITE button, a HOW CAN WE HELP button.

"I can ask around, but I don't think we're involved in anything like that yet." She paused, waiting to see if I had more questions. I couldn't think of what to say next. "People who call us usually want us to represent them in a legal matter. It's less often someone calls asking for our opinions on something they read in the paper. I'd need to spend more time researching before I felt comfortable answering you."

"Okay, thanks." I hung up, thinking I had wasted her time.

Saundra from BARCC put me in touch with one of her staff members. Jennifer was a lawyer who had a good working relationship with local police departments. "Saundra told me you had questions about your rape kit possibly being in the state crime-lab backlog. Can I help you with that? I'd be more than happy to make some inquiries," she'd said during our phone call.

"Let me think about it," I'd replied. Even with all the calls I'd made and the emails I'd sent searching for answers, having a lifeline to information on my case frightened me.

It had been almost fifteen years from the experience some rape survivors refer to as "soul murder," a term used by the psychologist Leonard Shengold initially to describe the experience of sexually abused children being robbed of their joy as well as their childhoods. Survivors and trauma therapists began using the term as a way to describe a broader phenomenon: the innocence or lightness that dies after sexual assault at any age.[2] For a good part of the last several years, my thoughts of the rapes had only emerged in June, the attack's anniversary. As Mary and I ceremoniously turned over the calendar page when the month of May concluded and those four ugly letters were revealed—JUNE—I smelled sweat, saw darkness, tasted blood, and lived with an overlay of dread until the first day of summer concluded.

We had subtle hints June approached as the day's light grew longer and short-sleeved shirts were needed to survive the heat. Mary and I often planned a seaside vacation to distract ourselves. The crashing sound of the waves soothed me, the cold water in southern Maine providing a tingle of pleasure to my bare feet. The kids spent hours digging in the sand, running in circles on the beach when low tide left an endless playground of seaweed, shells, and scampering crabs to chase. We spent time at a nearby amusement park where locals competed in sand-art competitions, and we procured tickets to watch minor league baseball games fifteen minutes from our beach house rental.

A friend of ours with Turkish ancestry taught me the expression "may it pass," and this mantra carried me through these difficult days each year.

May it pass. May it pass. May it pass.

The memories now bled beyond the isolated anniversary month, triggered by unwelcome health news a few years back. A noncancerous fibroid had taken up residence in my body and grown large enough that it was pressing on a number of organs, squishing them together like a pig pile at dinnertime. A two-pound weight gain on my five-foot frame felt like twenty pounds might on someone taller, and my naked body showed a small protrusion that could be mistaken for a budding pregnancy.

"It has to come out," the doctor said during a phone call after a recent ultrasound showed the growth now about the size of a grapefruit. My work phone sat silently in its cradle after I hung up on her with a brisk send-off. "I'm at work. I'll talk to Mary and get back to you." A grapefruit really isn't that large, I decided— much smaller than a cantaloupe, maybe just slightly larger than a navel orange. I knew my produce, having watched my step-father buy and sell it by the crate to local supermarkets during my teenage years. In the scheme of things, grapefruits could be managed.

Since the rapes, I had been in a hospital only when Mary gave birth to our two children, which was not comparable in any way. The thought of this operation walked my nervous system directly to the top of a tall building, and I looked for something to grab on to to keep from tumbling. Rape survivors experience body memories often. Trauma experts talk about "triggers"—events, places, smells, sensations—that somehow stimulate a traumatic memory and, in the most extreme form, give a survivor the sense that the danger they experienced years ago is once again immi-nent, present, and impossible to evade. If asked to explain the full terror this surgery held for me, there was first the anticipation of bodily intrusion, the pain from being cut, and the physical vul-nerability during a long recovery. Further, I'd be unconscious in a room of strangers and at their mercy. My nervous system was ablaze: I couldn't sleep; I couldn't breathe. I was positive some-thing would go wrong and I would die. My unbridled terror mor-tified me, but there it was—insistent and cruel.

I did not want the surgery.

To pile a bit more onto my already frantic nervous system, my doctor's admitting privileges required the surgery be performed at Beth Israel, the hospital I now referred to in my head as "that fucking place." It didn't matter how expertly and kindly the clinicians had treated me there so many years ago; I would've been happy if a sinkhole opened up in the Longwood Medical Area and it disappeared. Sometimes, in the state between sleep and wakening, I'd hear those soft, careful voices taking a deep breath before speaking to me. I hated their lilting tones—full of unbearable empathy asking unimaginable questions.

Did they ejaculate into your body?

Is it okay if I take a better look at that bite on your neck?

I need to ask what body parts they entered of yours and with what body parts of theirs so I don't miss anything.

After every sentence, one of them would say, "I'm sorry" or "I'll do this as quickly as I can," offering their words through pursed lips. Their kindness just elongated the difference between us, one that did not exist mere hours before.

The question of surgery had been discussed for weeks, following a routine appointment to check on the fibroid's size. "I think we're to the point where we should remove the uterus. I don't think you plan on getting pregnant," said my doctor. "Isn't that Mary's job?"

I ignored the joke. "Look, Ben and Becca are only two and four years old. We're exhausted as it is now with both of us fully functioning," I pleaded. "The only problem right now is I look like I ate a whole pie. I don't mind if people think I'm getting fat."

She countered. "It's going to have to come out eventually and it doesn't make sense to wait while it gets bigger and more complicated to remove." The control I had nurtured for the last fifteen years imploded. I knew she was right; it had to be done, but there would be a cost to my mental well-being. The knife held a few inches away from my blindfolded eyes had returned. I could feel the blade's warmth; I was in a lot of trouble.

For years now, the violence surrounding that night felt like it was something that had happened to me in the distant past, tucked away in a box and taped over with an inordinate amount of duct tape. Still, Mary and I were careful. We paid attention to books and movies that found their way into our home. "I wouldn't read this if I were you," she cautioned after finishing a novel she relished.

"I'll think about it," was my standard response, grabbing the book to read the jacket, then putting it aside next to the many unopened ones at my bedside. I appreciated the warnings—like the sign that says: proceed with caution. Some people read those signs and continue anyway; others know to turn around. I didn't mind crime dramas on TV, but if the victim was tied up or gagged, I would hand the clicker over to Mary without a word and she would change the channel, no matter how engrossed in the story we were.

When memories encroached, I would catalog the gifts in my present-day life: wonderful relationship, two gorgeous kids, life-long friends, great job.

I am safe; I am alive; I am loved; people depend on me; I survived for a reason.

My thinking about rape and sexual assault had begun to evolve—I no longer thought about it in terms of my personal pain but its larger impact on society. All I could do at this moment, though, was work to cope with a body memory of a young girl tied up on a bed waiting to be strangled. It left little room for anything else. The larger meaning of how sex crimes are dealt with in the wider world took up no space in my rattled brain. I blamed myself for this unbearable resurgence of terror. I thought I was weak and a little crazy, like so many other victims do.

I looked to Mary for reassurance; I needed a life raft, and she was mine. "Did you know they put a tube down your throat and you don't breathe on your own when you have surgery?" I had forgotten she had been a nurse for nearly twenty years. "The anesthesia *literally* stops you from breathing!" My voice moved up an octave. "They're going to cut me while I'm unconscious. I could die with the slightest mistake."

Mary stayed quiet and I was ready to scream, "Say something!" I could see the concern in her eyes, but the quiet allowed my brain to continue its spin and I filled the space with more ranting.

"I must have drowned in a past life. I don't know why, but that's the worst part for me. I feel dizzy just thinking about it."

"It wasn't in a past life, love bug," Mary finally said, and she drew me to her. I laid my head in her lap, and she stroked my body from head to foot.

Later, when I'd settled down from the gentle petting, she added, "This isn't what happened to you before, but I know it feels like it is. Your whole body—your nervous system—is activated by trauma. We can't outthink it; it's going to take some time. Let's get the surgery done and then try and figure out together what you might need to get through this rough patch. I won't let anything happen to you. We all need you way too much."

I recovered from the surgery physically within two months, but the trauma memories had implanted solidly in my brain much as I tried extricating them. Mary helped me find a therapist who had worked for almost twenty years at the Victims of Violence program in Cambridge with Dr. Judith Herman. I needed to speak with someone who would understand that my responses were normal, though they felt anything but. Being activated by triggers that brought forward a trauma response was like being in the witness protection program. Those who interacted with me in the present day noticed nothing unusual and accepted the self

I put out to them as genuine. But I carried a past life experience and identity I was afraid to share for my own safety and sanity. PTSD is more severe and likely to recur if, during the original event, the violence experienced is extreme, the victim believes death is imminent, and the response from others in the immediate aftermath is insufficient.

As I worked to understand and settle my trauma response, the memories of that violent event included what happened after it as well as all that did not. I found myself thinking and talking more about the aftermath of the assault with this new therapist, including how very little I knew about my case. And the more I talked, the more I wondered.

I began considering more seriously whether the absence of a response from law enforcement was part of my continued pain. Victims of sex crimes are familiar with having their own behavior and choices critiqued, analyzed, and commented upon. We are blamed for being alluring, not fighting hard enough, taking chances by walking in poorly lit areas, having too much to drink and not being able to fight someone off, staying with someone who exhibits violent behavior, living on a first floor and not checking if the windows are locked on a hot summer night. It is too often victims' behaviors that are dissected, not the people breaking the law or those charged with investigating the crimes. This injustice causes self-blame and hopelessness that a fair resolution will be found, feelings too many survivors have experienced for far too long.

The need to minimize rape is all too prevalent, and a false equivalency is drawn between the suffering of victims and perpetrators. In this world, being accused of a crime is supposedly as bad as or worse than being the victim of violence. Someone's life will be "ruined" if a credible accusation makes the person lose any power to which they are entitled. And in this same world, where

82 percent of all juvenile sexual assault victims and 90 percent of adult rape victims are female and those in power still overwhelmingly male, this frame puts the lives and safety of over half our country at risk.[3]

If most of the people who either write or are charged with enforcing our laws equate rape with sex rather than violence and sex is considered a male need and not to be challenged, then rape and sexual assault will continue being crimes for which there are few consequences. Instead, rape and sexual assault are framed as accidents, misunderstandings, and the fantasies of women (and children) who don't understand the rules they must live by, including the rule that the perpetrator must be given a pass. If men in power see themselves and their past behavior reflected in accusations of sexual assault, they will be strongly motivated not to frame those accusations as anything other than what they are: felony sex crimes. Not an accident. Not a misunderstanding. Not a confused woman who changed her mind. Not mixed messages. Not inevitable. Not "as old as time," as someone once described rape to me with a shrug after learning about my story.

I understood all this intellectually. I studied it; it was my life's work; I could articulate it in front of audiences and around a conference table with colleagues, and yet the strength I needed to take action on my own behalf eluded me. As I tried to recover from the current bout of PTSD the surgery had shaken loose, I took baby steps toward the ultimate goal of uniting my intellectual understanding of rape and of the societal constructions that support silencing and diminishing it with my personal story. To do that, I still had some work left to do.

And then one day at work, in the middle of completing a task, I saw Jennifer's number at the top of one of my paper piles and reached for it. "If the offer still holds, I'd very much like you to see what you can find out about my case," I said to her when she

picked up. "And thank you." Then, I waited. I had been so vulnerable for so long that I was exhausted and resigned it might never
abate. I had to hope that pursuing something to get some answers
would provide relief rather than make me feel worse.

About a month passed before she called me back. "Michelle—
this is what we know today," Jennifer reported. "Your evidence
is not at the state crime lab where the backlogged evidence was
reported by *The Boston Globe*. Boston cases are processed in Boston. They don't have a backlog; they're caught up. I spoke to both
the head of the sexual assault unit and the lead scientist in the
forensic lab. They can't currently locate your rape kit but were
clear it would have gone to them, not the state."

"Maybe it's just me but I don't believe a word they say. If they
can't find it, maybe it accidentally got sent to the state lab and it
is in that backlog. Maybe the hospital made a mistake. How can
we be sure?"

"I asked and they don't think that's possible, especially because
they did say they found your file. I wish I had better news."

I would need to contact the Boston Sexual Assault Unit if I
wanted to take this quest any further. Jennifer had provided me
with the names, phone numbers, and emails of the people to contact. "They're ready to talk with you if you want," she said. "Take
your time and call me anytime if I can help in any way."

Eleven

The Boston Sexual Assault Unit—a division of the Boston police force—was started on July 1, 1984, just one week after the assault that changed the course of my life. I don't find out about its history until 2013, when I meet the lead detective at the unit and he fills me in on it. While I was struggling to navigate potential homelessness, job loss, and nightmares as well as trying to recover both physically and mentally, the Boston police put in operation a unit intended to assist with the coordination efforts needed to solve crimes of rape, including mine.

Before the unit's existence, individual officers were assigned cases in their own jurisdiction, even if similar cases were occurring within blocks of one another. Now, these cases were to be turned over to the sexual assault unit to see if there were important clues that might be connected.

I reviewed whatever I could find in *The Boston Globe* archives about the early years of the sexual assault unit to determine whether they achieved their goals—to make the city safer, to solve crimes, and to reduce rates of rape and sexual assault. At the time, I had not heard anything of their existence, despite being the victim of the series of crimes that led to their creation.

In May 1984, Mayor Raymond Flynn announced that the new unit would begin its operation in July. "You read about it in the newspapers every day," he said, "You see it on your TV news every night. Whether it's because there is an increase in such attacks or an increase in reporting them—sexual assaults are the crimes of the day."[1] According to Flynn, who acknowledged that only a small percentage of rapes are reported, the city had 404 reported rapes or attempted rapes the year before.

Five days after my rape, a *Globe* article described our home invasion in detail.

> Lise Brody, whose roommate on Saturday became the latest in a number of rape victims in Allston Brighton this year described the attack yesterday at a meeting on rape prevention. Two men climbed onto the raised first floor porch at 27 Glenville Avenue at 4:30 am, opened the window, took a knife from the kitchen and ransacked the apartment. . . . Deputy Supt. Paul F. Evans, who addressed the meeting, said the recent rapes in Allston Brighton reflects an "alarming" city wide increase in rape this year. . . . Brody, near tears, told the group her roommate's assailants "weren't afraid. They left fingerprints all over the place. If these two heard about rapists being jailed for life, maybe they would be more scared. I want rapists to be as scared as the victim." . . . Evans said victims in Allston have at times been reluctant to prosecute. "There's a large number of students, maybe it's the end of the school year, they're moving, their parents feel it's in their best interest to forget the whole thing."[2]

Paul F. Evans would go on to serve as the police commissioner of Boston in ten years' time. In responding here to a series of horrific rapes in the city he would later represent as its chief law enforcement officer, he comments on low reporting numbers and holds victims and their families largely accountable. I did not see mention of his thoughts on how the new unit will make reporting easier and why.

Two days after the article about the home invasion on Glenville Avenue, Mayor Flynn holds another press conference to introduce the unit officially. He highlights that the unit will operate twenty-four hours a day and will consist of six female and six male officers. Mayor Flynn is quoted as saying, "This task force will make Boston a model city in dealing with violence against women."[3] Again, there is no explanation of how this will happen.

Two months later, in early September, a headline in the *Globe* states, "Felonies Overall Are Down 13.5% In Boston; Murders Up Sharply." The police commissioner, reporting on this crime data, said, "Since the Sexual Assault Unit began operating July 1 . . . people feel more comfortable in dealing with its members and have the confidence to come in and report the crime."[4] I am not sure how he knows this information only two months into the unit's existence or that this statement accurately reflects victims' experiences. There is no mention of surveying those who reported their rape and assessing their comfort level.

About nine months after the unit's creation, a headline reads, "As Rates Climb, Boston Seeks Ways to Fight Rape." The article reports figures from the police department showing Boston has a rate of rape higher than New York or Washington, D.C., and that "so far, the unit has had little success in improving the rape arrest rate," with a 14 percent increase in arrests compared to reported rapes up by 50 percent.[5]

Four years later, in February 1989, two articles in one week cite problems with the sexual assault unit. In one, victim advocates fear the unit is being phased out, with the number of officers shrinking and the "impending elimination of a counseling program for rape victims at Boston City Hospital."[6] Police officials denied the assertion that the unit was being neglected and "vowed" the counseling program would continue even with staff reductions. By this time, the original twelve officers had shrunk to six, even though hundreds of police officers had been added to the force in the last few years, according to the article. The chief superintendent of detectives stated that many more officers would be trained in sexual assault response, adding it to the other work they did.

Less than a month later, in March 1989, the intense criticism and negative publicity surrounding the changes in the sexual assault unit led the Boston PD to backtrack. As the *Globe* headline read, "Bowing to Protests, Boston Police to Restore Staff of Sexual Assault Unit." Mayor Flynn is quoted as saying, "Despite the budget problems we face because of state cutbacks, the sexual assault unit will receive highest priority. It's been tremendously effective. It's been a model program. We're not going to compromise."[7] He does not say that this model program was cut in half in the first place or that plans to decentralize were curtailed only after public pressure.

These headlines tell the story of a sexual assault unit begun during a citywide crisis and almost terminated due to lack of funding less than five years later. The articles address increasing rates of reported rapes, budget cuts, continued community advocacy for victims, multiple perspectives on staffing needs, communities of color being hit harder by crime, and repeated threats of closure. Nowhere could I find mention of victim outreach or increased investigations. There were no articles about any of the rapes occurring in the summer of 1984 having been connected or solved.

These archived articles offer a snapshot of one sexual assault unit in one U.S. city. Other cities also have specially trained sex-crimes officers working in what is often referred to as a special victims unit. Why we are "special" victims, I can't say. Maybe it's a euphemism for precious. Perhaps it's a unique category for those who are special victims of special crimes, the kind where evidence isn't tested, investigations are underfunded, reports are frequently deemed unfounded, and arrests and convictions almost nonexistent. That sounds pretty special to me.

Over all these years, I had remained unaware the Boston Sexual Assault Unit existed. I still didn't get *The Boston Globe.* I didn't like to watch the news, and I hadn't been contacted about my case. It's ironic, when I look back, that my reflex is to think that I might have learned about the unit if only I had read the paper or watched the news. Even years after my attack, my first instinct was to feel that it was up to *me* to find out about *them.* I was never contacted, even though I was a victim of the crime spree that helped spur the unit's creation, and the attack, my roommate's name, and our address were publicized on TV and in the newspapers. Given that, it felt more than fair to ask whether the unit was created merely for public relations or whether it truly set out to make a meaningful difference in the city of Boston in addressing crimes of rape. I was flailing around trying to rebuild my life, busy with the hardest work I would ever do, work that continues, to a certain extent, to this day. Victims shouldn't have to advocate that their cases be pursued; that's law enforcement's job. And the impact of their disregard is deeply felt.

I realized how crucial it is to communicate with victims in the right way—how the precious moments where agency can be restored and legitimacy given are few and crucial to grab hold of. One concrete thing that resulted from my own experience and that informed my work over the years is an understanding that how we train the myriad of professionals who interact with sexual assault victims matters.

A few years past my surgery, I still couldn't shake the post-traumatic stress it triggered. It was exacerbated by the work I did running health services at Tufts University. We held a training every late August before students return to campus, and making sure we responded skillfully to sexual assault was my job. It had been some part of my job since I'd begun, but our university had received a federal grant from the Department of Justice for campus violence prevention and my team was working specifically on improving skills for medical personnel.

"I have a great idea," the medical director said to me one morning during her supervision. Margaret was a tall, thin woman with curly blond hair and wire-rim glasses. I used to fret about how she might feel having someone who is not a doctor as her boss. No matter what I accomplished, the embarrassment of my earlier incapacitation was a constant. The innocent question "How did you go from majoring in English to working in public health?" required a long answer if I were being truthful. I'd resorted to dodging with a surface narrative and hoped no one would pry.

"I think we should fill at least two days of the week having staff from the Beth Israel Hospital and the Boston Area Rape Crisis Center come and talk about the impact of sexual assault," Margaret said. "They can discuss what services are available, what happens when someone goes to a hospital for evidence collection, how to respond during a clinical visit if someone discloses, and the impact rape has on survivors."

I stared above her shoulder at the empty field outside my window. Soon it would be filled with students' shrieks of excitement as they reconnected after a summer apart. I tried smiling at her, nodding my head.

She continued. "I'll plan the whole thing. The staff is capable; they already have the skills, but they would benefit from this specific training."

I willed my face to neutrality. "Go on."

"We shouldn't be referring students to a hospital when we have the capacity to help. Besides, most don't even need or desire that level of care."

I wanted to change the subject but instead said a brief "sounds good."

"It's all I can do to get up in the morning" was a sentence I'd heard from rape survivors and had uttered myself. The act of returning to the world and functioning in it is a high bar for many of us, and it's something I was proud to have managed most of the time. I cared deeply about the students and the number of health issues that beset them at this age, sexual assault being a major one. In this moment, my passion for the work I did was overshadowed by the memories that gripped my body.

In truth, Margaret was years ahead of her colleagues in this area, understanding students' health care needs pertaining to sexual victimization. She conceived of this advanced training long before the federal government addressed the critical need for colleges to improve their response to sexual assault survivors. In 2011 the United States Department of Education issued guidance on how universities should respond to students reporting sexual assault. It was written after a handful of schools were investigated for their abysmal handling of survivors' complaints and referred to as the Dear Colleague letter.[8]

Nineteen single-spaced pages long, the letter gave direction on dozens of specific items, but one of its signature features was framing sexual assault policies and response requirements for higher education as a Title IX issue. Since the victims of rape and sexual assault are overwhelmingly female and Title IX guarantees an equal right to education, schools were required to have appropriate sexual assault policies in place to avoid creating barriers for victims/survivors to be able to continue their education. This meant schools had to look at how their current policies, or lack thereof, impacted sexual assault victims' ability to stay and thrive in school *and change them.*

The letter itself took a confounding position regarding sexual assault as a crime of violence. It stated explicitly that "sexual violence is a form of sexual harassment prohibited by Title IX" while also asserting that in "cases involving potential criminal conduct, school personnel must determine, consistent with State and local law, whether appropriate law enforcement or other authorities should be notified."[9] So, according to the letter, sexual violence was *definitely* sexual harassment and must be addressed as a Title IX issue but maybe only sometimes constituted criminal conduct. I'm not sure any legal statute would describe sexual violence any other way. For the purposes of this guidance, sexual violence *must* be classified and addressed as sexual harassment, when in reality it is not only or even primarily that.

Before this document, some schools lacked policies for adjudicating complaints of sexual assault or misconduct. Many, like ours, used panels to decide general conduct cases, which meant a student would have to sit in hearings while other students— friends and classmates, potentially—would hear the details of their assault. This discouraged many from coming forward. There were often no standards of training required for individuals to sit on these panels or for the deans who wrote the policies and created these processes. Many schools also had nothing in place to help support victims/survivors or to provide academic or other accommodations while their complaints were in process. Before the Dear Colleague letter, it was more often the survivors whose grades suffered, who felt unsafe in their living environment or classrooms, and who declined to participate in an adjudication process they knew would be further traumatizing.

On a national level, there was immediate pushback that the new guidelines had gone too far in favoring those making complaints of sexual misconduct and unfairly affecting students who had been accused.[10] In 2018 the Department of Education proposed new regulations that, in essence, undo much of the Dear Colleague letter's guidelines, and suggested a higher threshold for what constitutes sexual harassment, among other changes.[11]

Sometime after 2011, the American College Health Association published a "toolkit" for medical practices at universities titled *Addressing Sexual and Relationship Violence: A Trauma-Informed Approach.*[12] It addressed many of the topics our staff had been trained on at least five years earlier, thanks to Margaret. Understanding how to respond to the physical and emotional needs of sexual assault survivors is a key skill for medical providers, but in a college setting, like any community, it cannot stand alone. The Dear Colleague letter had made that clear.

We finished our meeting, and Margaret headed out the door. "By the way," I said to her back, "you are so right about the sexual assault training needs here. Responding well to rape victims really matters. It can mean everything when it comes to how the next few years might go for them." I pictured my younger self, hanging up after calling the police detective I'd met only once after the break-in. "Responding poorly matters too and can impact someone for longer than they could ever have imagined."

Margaret closed the door behind her and a memory intruded. This time, I saw the detective pulling the knife in the baggie out of his briefcase. "Recognize this?" he said. "Look familiar?" There had been no warning, no acknowledgment of my fear. My heart was pounding at my desk as hard as it had in that moment, and I put my hand on my chest to slow it down, trying to will myself back into present time. *What was with that guy, anyway?* I thought. I remembered his green short-sleeved, button-down shirt and how it clashed with Emmy's antique chairs. This thread led me to think about Emmy and how happy I was when she and her family lived in Connecticut so we could visit them by car in only two hours' time. Then I thought about calling her to set up a date now that they were moving back to Boston. I then remembered a visit where the basset hound that smells funny had knocked over Becca. Then, I tried to remember all the names of their many pets.

Time is unreliable. Was I still twenty-four or in my forties? Which body did I currently inhabit? I was back in my current life once again, in my office, in the present day, trying my best to do my job.

—

Margaret's training program was three weeks away, and I could no longer get myself to bed. Late that night, I channel surfed well beyond the time Mary had gone to bed.

Rest had become elusive.

The small TV clicker rested quietly in my hand. Twilight turned into nighttime and the house was still. The worn red couch had pillows strewn about, a familiar groove molded over time to fit my small frame, inviting me to relax and remember that I am safe. This was my home and I was surrounded by love. Mary was waiting for me upstairs and the children were asleep.

Nightmares crept into my brain and sleep's vulnerability prevented me from being able to shoo them away. There were the smells of night, the creaking of trolley cars, the feel of damp skin and fear. Dread followed me around from morning till night.

I am not an avid TV watcher, but when I am alone and flooded with memories, it provides an odd comfort. The people on the screen remind me what it feels like to be transported into different worlds with little preparation and no understanding of what comes next. Surviving to the next moment becomes a singular goal. It's apparent to me that the actors on the screen are not simply playing a role but existing in a life scripted by others and must be undone by their lack of agency. Before I get a chance to care too much about what happens, I abandon them.

It's television, I told myself; it's almost always a happy ending.

With that, I turned off the TV and headed to bed. The padded stairs felt scratchy on my bare feet. Mary had left a light on for me on my bedside table that cast a lemony shadow into the hallway. The children were asleep, each in their own small room. I rested my hand on their chests as I said goodnight silently to their slumbering bodies, until the movement of air on my palm convinced me they were alive. Soft cotton pajamas laden with yellow and blue trucks, hair that smells of kid shampoo, bedrooms overflowing with stuffed animals and books. The many sounds of love whispered to me.

—

Margaret finalized the agenda for the training. The clinicians from BARCC would present first, followed by the Beth Israel staff, who would explain the care students would receive when they went to the emergency room, which included collecting evidence. Students, however, rarely needed or wanted evidence collection. Studies estimate that between 80 and 90 percent of college students do not report their assaults to law enforcement.[13] Our jobs were not to convince them to get care at an emergency room or report what happened but to meet them where they were and give them the health care they needed. More commonly, students spend days or weeks wondering if they could call what happened to them sexual assault or rape, if they should tell anyone, and, should they tell someone, if they will be blamed for what happened, whether because they were drinking, because the perpetrator was a nice guy until he wasn't, because they feared being judged over previous sexual activity, because they were good friends with the perpetrator, because, because, because.

But even when sexual assault can't yet be named, a student knows that something was wrong about what happened. Take the case of a student who goes to campus health services for medical care, perhaps for a concern seemingly unrelated to what happened: a headache, not sleeping, a bothersome wart on their toe. They show up in our building looking for some care, some help. We had to get it right. As one trauma researcher states, "When 'experts' doubt survivors, hold them responsible for the assault, or refuse to provide assistance, survivors may question both the effectiveness of such services and the usefulness of reaching out for help to anyone at all."[14]

Sometime during the visit, often when walking out the door, the student might turn and ask if it would be all right to ask one more question, if the clinician has time before the next patient, if it isn't too much of a bother, because something else is troubling them. Maybe the student feels as if they can trust the provider, who had smiled warmly and been careful when grabbing their wrist to look at an itchy, annoying rash that had been present for weeks. "May I take a peek?" the doctor had asked. "Let's see if I can help with that; it looks like it might be uncomfortable." And the student wasn't certain they could blink back the tears welling in their eyes in time to avoid notice.

Kindness, asking permission to touch, awareness of the pain they might cause—every bit noticed when it was there, every bit noticed when absent.

It was almost more than the student could bear, but it gave them enough information to risk turning around and asking for more, telling more.

If they took a deep breath, if they were very brave and took their time.

The practitioner signaled with one finger in the air. "Just give me a second and then I'm all yours." She picked up the phone. "Can you move my next patient to walk-in, if possible? I'm going to be awhile."

"I didn't drink much, but I don't remember anything. I woke up with a guy I think I had been dancing with. Maybe I was drugged, but I don't know what happened. I thought he was nice, but when I decided I wasn't into it, it happened anyway. Then, when I told my friends—who are his friends too—they said since we were both partying, how could I be sure? One of them said it wouldn't be right to create a bunch of drama, and now they're all acting weird with me."[15]

These kinds of questions need proper, skillful answers, challenging for even the most experienced medical provider. A health practitioner's job is to ask questions during a visit, but the nature of the query can feel like victim blaming to someone who is reeling and filled with self-doubt.

"Has this ever happened before?" may be a reasonable question if someone reports a blackout from drinking, but for someone describing an assault, it can be heard as focusing on their behavior rather than on what happened.

"How well did you know this person?" is a question often heard as, "Don't you have better judgment?"

Asking what kind of party it was might be interpreted as, "Why did you put yourself in harm's way?" And being curious about why a student waited to make an appointment could be taken to mean, "You waited, and now you might be pregnant or have an STI. Aren't you better at self-care than that?"

Any insensitive question or improper response by a clinician can shut down the conversation. Well-meant but artless inquiries might repeat in someone's head for years. I heard the voices from my past saying to me:

Do you know how they got in?

Did you lock your windows?

Didn't you know there've been other break-ins in this area of town?

A student who does not want or need rape evidence collected at a hospital may still need an examination for sexually transmitted infections, medicine to prevent pregnancy, or simply a compassionate person to talk to about their options. By doing this training, we were signaling that even the most skilled clinician would benefit from understanding how trauma can impact a patient's experience of medical care—in the moment and for a lifetime. The case examples above were used to help clinicians learning more about trauma-informed care understand the stakes and how to respond.

Time is an imperfect healer, massaging the edges of an experience, but it is inadequate as a stand-alone remedy. It's a fact I couldn't ignore, as much as I tried. As a rape survivor, I lived then and forever in a world with a different sense of safety and reason than most. The fear one pushes down during a violent assault in order to survive takes up permanent residence in the synapses and nerves of the body—like the old man who lives in a rent-controlled apartment in New York City and intends to be there until they carry him out in a box. It is stubborn and determined; it will not be dislodged.

There have been so many moments over so many years when

I've felt thrust back into quicksand by a noise, a news story, or an ambulance siren. I'm not sure which would have been worse as a passenger on the *Titanic*, drowning quickly in the frozen waters of the Atlantic or sitting safely in a lifeboat and hearing the screams. The fact that trauma memories were triggered by the work I did every single day felt catastrophic.

It seemed impossible for me to sit in a sterile conference room and listen to people from the very agencies I used almost two decades before during the worst days of my life explaining the impact of rape to my staff. Almost no one at the university knew what happened to me, and why would they have? We maintained a professional relationship. My body tingled and twitched just thinking about the work of the day ahead.

The morning of the training, I sat at the conference table, waiting for our guests to arrive, despite Mary having urged me to come down with a sudden bout of the stomach flu. When Margaret walked through the door with three women, I stood up and introduced myself.

"I'm so happy you've come to work with us. I'm not a clinician and I want people to be able to speak freely about their experiences with survivors, so I won't be staying the whole session."

"No problem." The BARCC trainer smiled at me. "Most of the morning is just a basic overview."

Following Margaret's introduction, the trainer powered up her slides. "Let's begin by reviewing how trauma impacts the nervous system, moving to why informed interactions with professionals matter so much in forestalling development of chronic PTSD." I started a fake coughing fit and left the room.

On my way up the stairs, I ran into Mary, the business office supervisor. "You lasted longer than I predicted," she remarked. "Are you going back, or can we meet?"

"I'm going to skip it," I said. "I hope no one's offended."

"Who cares what they think? You don't need the training if you've walked the walk. Bringing those people here for the clinical staff is what matters; you don't have anything to prove."

I felt my eyebrows rising, almost touching my hairline. Had I let something slip? If I had, I wouldn't have minded Mary knowing, anyway. I'd come to respect and trust her. Besides, she was Somerville born and bred and loved to remind me that her city had a code of silence and that breaking it meant you'd be "a rat."

"How do you always seem to know things without people having to tell you?" I asked, curious.

"I'm the oldest of seven—you learn to figure things out without being told. I kept a lot of my siblings out of trouble that way."

"Okay, then." I needed time to process my conflicting emotions. "I'm going upstairs to see if I can get any work done. If not, I'll head home."

"Maybe get a case of the flu or food poisoning," she said.

"Hey, my Mary said the exact same thing last week. Did she call you?" I was smiling.

"No, but we Marys tend to be a wise bunch." She stated this as fact. "Sorry to break it to you, but you've been a wreck for weeks. I just pay attention more than most."

"Yes, and it's something I've grown very fond of about you." I headed to my office, exhausted.

One down and only hundreds more to go, I thought as I climbed the stairs. Maybe telling more people would help ease my distress. Silence has a way of keeping things bigger than they are, in truth.

What was I so scared of? I thought about it—telling others—with the details scrubbed, just saying that I'd been the victim of a break-in a long time ago and was attacked. Imagining telling incited the feeling of the blindfold on my face and the cord around my wrists and ankles. And then I heard old voices, not of the rapists but of the law enforcement professionals I expected help from.

Just like a woman, can't keep her mouth shut.

Didn't I say I'd call you if we knew anything?

And I felt the silence of my telephone as I waited years for just the tiniest update, even one that said they had no news, that the men responsible for the crime spree evaded them but they tried—a call, a note, anything that would signal to me that what happened was considered a serious matter to the people who were in charge of investigating the crime.

At the time, I thought it was shame I felt, but now I realize that there was rage bubbling below the surface—anger at this crime's impact, anger at all the ways I'd seen and heard it minimized, anger at the thunderous silence from the Boston police. And since there was no other place yet for this rage to go, it stayed inside of me—in every single cell, in my twitching back muscles, and in the tear ducts I struggled to keep dry.

The violence-prevention grant funding allowed us to continue employing two campus outreach workers who were likely to lose their jobs when it ended. They had worked hard to gain the trust of students over time, facilitating campus-wide conversations on masculinity, hookup culture, and the need to obtain consent in sexual situations. They supported students' work sponsoring annual Take Back the Night rallies, bringing in survivor speakers, and working directly with students on prevention messaging and bystander intervention.

Because the staff members worked so closely with students, conversations on how the university could do better on a number of fronts became a frequent topic—a student might have reported to them being upset with an administrator's response, finding the policy used to adjudicate sexual assault complaints inadequate because it left victims feeling unsupported, or feeling like there were areas in the university where no one "got it."

A coworker had recently called me while I worked on wrapping up paperwork we needed to submit to the funders. "I never understood how mandating staff to attend conferences in Honolulu, San Francisco, and other awesome places on the federal government's dime was supposed to change the experience of students who'd been sexually assaulted on campus," she said.

"No grant is perfect; all they're ever meant to do is jump-start needed work and hopefully create momentum," I wanted to argue, but she had a point. Not all university departments had sent staff to these conferences, and many still didn't see sexual assault prevention or response as central to the work they did—even if it was. Training some of us only seemed to highlight the need for a comprehensive shift for the entire institution. It did little good if some staff understood the impact of sexual assault and others did not. Students come into contact with hundreds of staff and faculty during a semester. Nothing short of a university-wide expectation that this issue be addressed comprehensively would do, and none of us were exempt from criticism or responsibility. While I believed change was a process, I also knew from my own experience how assault victims suffer when institutions fail them.

The unmistakable parallel between how the students felt about our failures as administrators and how I felt about society's inadequate response to rape victims was an almost unbearable irony; I felt split in half and ashamed. Mary and I had begun to talk seriously about whether I should look for new work. Every story about a student, every well-meant but insensitive comment from a work colleague, every article in the student paper describing the experience of a survivor—I experienced them all as a hammer to my skull. I sweated, my heart raced, and I had to close my office door to quiet down my conflicting emotions. The situation didn't feel manageable, but neither did leaving a job I loved. University structures have often been described as having "every tub on its own bottom." Individual silos may have the sense of progress without understanding fully how or whether other areas were addressing the same concerns. Creating comprehensive, collaborative, and sustained change in such an environment required standards and leadership that brought together staff and faculty. Over the next few years, an environment for changing the response to sexual assault on campus was created through a larger national conversation, guidance at the federal level, and, most critically, students at our university and around the country who demanded change.

—

"I need something to shift," I said to Mary one night after the kids had gone to bed. "There's so much content about sexual assault at work now and I can't take it. But it's also my job to do just that— handle it, work to make change." I shook my head side to side so hard I got dizzy.

Mary grabbed my cheeks and whispered, "We'll figure this out together."

Later, she added, "Maybe one of the reasons it's hard is because you don't feel like you're bringing your full self to the work." I imagined the end of that sentence being *and at home too,* but she hadn't voiced what I knew was true.

"I honestly have no idea anymore." I picked up a book and stared at some words, not comprehending, just trying to end the conversation.

With work having become so challenging, it took every bit of leftover energy I had to recalibrate at home. That long-put-away life catastrophe sat next to me most of the time now, the faraway years coiled inextricably with the present, though I tried hard to push it away. Kids aren't fooled by whatever façade their parents put forward. I wore my fear like a shield, and my kids poked and scraped at it whenever they could, trying to find me. Vulnerability defines parenting. When struggling with trauma memories, it's hard to feel present. Even when kids are too young for a parent to explain what happened and its impact, they can sense something is amiss. It can be challenging for the whole family. The last thing I wanted was for something that tormented me to have a deleterious effect on the beings I loved more than I ever thought possible. I urgently needed to find a way for this experience to live outside me and not to take up the entirety of my life and body.

Something had to change—me or my job. I chose the former, knowing running away wouldn't help, the fear and shame chasing me until I dealt with it. Any job in higher education would likely, and tragically, deal with the same issue, a pervasive one on campuses across the country. I kept my suffering to myself. I had yet to start a single sentence with, "As a rape survivor . . ." I knew that had I been able to utter those words, it might have helped when I was trying to counter a statement made by a colleague that showed a basic misunderstanding of issues related to sexual assault. And I couldn't be fully effective in my professional role if I was behaving in a way that affirmed that sexual violation was unspeakable.

Students would soon demand we did better. They would demand we own our history as an institution and move forward to create an environment where survivors do not feel disregarded, unfairly treated, or unseen. The more I watched their courage and rage push them forward, the more my silence felt like a betrayal to the larger meaning of societal disregard of these crimes of violence.

I began looking for a way forward—looking for my voice and my power. Being a victim isn't a badge of honor one can wear to deny responsibility when serving in a role that requires it. I was an adult, had a college degree, supported myself and my family, was white and cis gender, and was no longer as vulnerable as the students were. I had to be able to live with this dual identity—survivor and administrator—and the pain it elicited. I grabbed hold of my own experience as one part of a much larger societal ill, and in this I started to find internal strength as well as resolve.

I was one of many who needed answers and one of thousands who needed the way in which crimes of rape are addressed by law enforcement and by society in general to change.

—

When my name was called to give a speech at a party organized to celebrate the work our grant funding had provided to our institution, I crumpled up the paper I'd scribbled notes on and walked to the microphone. I held on to the podium as my knees shook.

"Sexual assault is never the victim's fault and shouldn't be unspeakable. And if I believe that as a core value in the work I do, I have to believe it for myself." I moved away from the microphone so that my deep sigh wouldn't get captured.

"I am a rape survivor."

I told my story about the break-in during a citywide crime spree and how overwhelming the experience had been for many years—and continued to be. I described how I'd felt like a different person and how destabilizing the experience was in every part of my life.

"I'll be honest—sexual assault isn't something you survive and then fully move on from. It never becomes only a thing that once happened to you. Parts of it may sit with me for the rest of my life, and I say that not because I want to dishearten the student or staff survivors in the room, but to acknowledge the personal challenges in the aftermath of assault and also the responsibilities of those charged with addressing sexual assault survivors' concerns and needs. That would be most of us in this room working with students."

I left the stage feeling more my genuine self than I had in a while. In the aftermath of my speech, a few of my work colleagues, people I had known and considered friends for many years, disclosed their own histories. I realized that one's own pain and silence can lend itself to a self-absorbed distortion—*no one else knows how I feel*—when the statistics on sexual assault tell us that in every room, close to 20 percent of people are likely to have experienced sexual assault or abuse.[16]

I would never be silent about my experience again, and my newfound voice allowed me to find ways to thrive, make meaning, and demand accountability.

Twelve

A decaying warehouse sat somewhere in Detroit. Birds flew in
and out of open windows, the floor littered with stray feathers and
rat droppings. Long ago, its thermostat had broken, and what lay
stored inside became subject to temperatures that sweltered past
one hundred degrees in summer and dropped below freezing in
the cold Michigan winter. Inside the building in 2009 boxes sat
stacked from floor to ceiling, filled with forensic evidence: more
than eleven thousand untested rape kits. For the eleven thousand
human beings each one of those uninvestigated cases represented,
no call ever came. Worse still, when the city finally began to go
through the evidence kits, they found matches to serial rapes that
might have been prevented had they been tested sooner. In fact,
817 serial rapists were identified and 50 of them each had 10–15
"hits" among the evidence tested.[1] In human terms, hundreds of
individuals in Detroit would have to be told the news that the
person who hurt them committed the same violent assault over
and over and over and over again and that their DNA had sat in

a crumbling structure holding a secret that could have changed their and other victims' lives had the serial perpetrators been identified sooner.

What happened in Detroit was no anomaly; human rights groups identified cities that ignored rape evidence for decades: Dallas, Los Angeles, Cleveland, Memphis, Las Vegas, Houston, Milwaukee, and dozens more. Estimates of how many evidence kits in the country had never been tested were as high as 400,000.[2] The kits were abandoned, the stories tied to them left behind. Those responsible would argue that the numbers of cases were overwhelming, that these "backlogs" weren't due to disregard of the crime of rape, and that inadequate funding existed for testing them all.[3] In truth, though, the piles upon piles of kits found in U.S. cities were not awaiting funding for testing; many were swept aside before any investigations had happened.[4] As one law professor wrote, a backlog "implies that the untested rape kits were in a queue awaiting testing by overburdened labs. That does not reflect the reality across the United States. In fact, untested rape kits were often simply discarded in warehouses, trash depositories, or storage closets with no intention to ever test the contents of the kits."[5]

The juxtaposition of the inaction with the circumstances of how those kits came to be, gathered from the private folds and spaces of victims whose bodies had been transformed into crime scenes, defies understanding. The hundreds of thousands of untested rape kits existed because hundreds of thousands of individual victims agreed to submit to an exam consisting of head and pubic hair combing; vaginal, anal, and oral swabbing; retrieval of saliva, blood, and fingernail clippings—evidence taken carefully under the bright light of an emergency room by strangers following a violation that defines vulnerability. The victims endured this examination for a reason; they wanted justice. Instead, their bodies and the evidence taken from them were treated like useless trash. When multiple cities began attending to their untested evidence kits, many rapists were identified, but often the statute of limitations had expired and prosecution was no longer possible.

District Attorney Kym Worthy had to start a fund-raising campaign a few years after the massive numbers of rape kits were found, when the monies given to Detroit ran out and there were still rape kits needing attention.[6] Crowdsourcing funding for investigations into murder, burglaries, arson, or home invasion is nonexistent. Rape appears to be the only crime requiring this outrageous funding mechanism.

In 2004 a major piece of federal legislation was passed. The Debbie Smith Act, part of the Justice for All Act, provided money to states to reduce their large numbers of untested rape kits.[7] It was named after survivor Debbie Smith, whose story illustrated the life-altering impact of using DNA in investigating crimes of rape. The woman who lent her name to the legislation had been abducted from her home while her husband, Robert, a police officer, slept upstairs after his night shift. The attacker threatened to come back and kill her family if she reported the crime. When she made her way back to her home after the attack, she and her husband first went to the hospital and then to the police department.

Over the next few years, Debbie became severely depressed, fearing harm would befall her family because she'd reported the attack. Only when the DNA from her rape kit was tested six years later did she learn that her rapist had been in jail for the last five years for another crime.[8] Had the match been discovered sooner, she could have been spared years of torment. This very personal and painful lesson set Debbie on a mission to ensure that every single rape kit would be tested so that no victim would be denied the peace she had been given when her rape kit was processed and a match found.

Since passed, the Debbie Smith Act has distributed over one billion dollars to test rape evidence, but loopholes in the wording of the initial legislation gave law enforcement discretion to use the funds more broadly than originally intended.[9] As Sofia Resnick writes in "Rape Kits: A Decade and a Billion Dollars Later, Why Can't We Fix the Backlog?" the act as first drafted "did not specify that *only* rape kits could be tested. . . . Rather, grants could be used to test backlogged DNA samples from a variety of offenders and crime scenes, including crimes unrelated to sexual assault, such as homicide and property crimes."

According to a 2019 *Washington Post* article, "Nearly 200,000 DNA matches have been made . . . because of the Debbie Smith DNA Backlog Grant Program."[10] This is a remarkable number and should not be taken lightly or minimized. Debbie and Robert Smith have spent years advocating for public awareness of untested kits and for resources for testing them, which deserves respect. Yet, even with this landmark act and the additional monies sent to crime labs and police departments around the country, the problem of untested rape kits *and* uninvestigated sex crimes continued—some cities still have vast amounts of untested evidence going back decades. Lack of funding was not the only reason this evidence was ignored—a larger systemic problem was at play. There are so many ways in which investigating officers have leeway to decline to investigate rape cases. Referring to hundreds of thousands of untested rape kits as a "backlog" of evidence is a misnomer if there was never intent to test them in the first place.

In 2012 the Austin Police Department reported four hundred untested kits, with police officials saying, "none of that evidence needs to be analyzed because an internal review shows they are part of cases where criminal charges likely cannot be pursued and where the DNA profile identified would not be eligible to enter into . . . CODIS."[11] This is similar to what was said in Boston about the samples found in the state crime lab, and in other cities as well. It is indisputable that when backlogged kits were tested around the country, matches were found and perpetrators identified. This tells us the standards used to decide whether to investigate rape cases had no merit and were deeply flawed.

In the fifteen years since it was passed, Congress reauthorized the Debbie Smith Act more than once so that monies for DNA testing could continue to be allocated. Advocacy groups and rape survivors pushed for the act to be amended and the loopholes closed to demand accountability from the agencies distributing the funds and those receiving them. It would become the life work of Debbie Smith, a determined survivor who still believes that every victim deserves justice and that law enforcement should do everything in their power to help solve crimes.

After coming out to more people as a rape survivor and researching whether my own rape kit could be in the state crime-lab backlog, I become increasingly focused on activism outside my work at Tufts. The effort to publicize the existence of this rape evidence nationwide and to advocate for testing it needed survivor stories so that the full tragedy of ignoring these cases could be understood. And there were plenty of us already feeling twice victimized—by the crimes of violence that changed our lives and then by the news that no effort had been made to investigate. For me, the deeper I got involved in advocacy work, the more questions I had. My public health training led me to ask why this situation had existed for so long—the many complicated root societal causes. That frame shone a light on the deep injustice and systematic failures in our criminal justice system and on the factors that allowed these crimes to be treated in this manner on a vast and unforgivable scale.

If it were one city or one bad cop. If it were one DA who wanted a high win rate so declined to prosecute rape cases. If it were one judge who voiced empathy for the perpetrator and culpability on the victim's part. If it were one isolated police department where kits were lost, shelved, or thrown away. If it were one crime lab where felony evidence sat untested. If it were one politician who made a throwaway comment minimizing rape. If it were one dean at one college who thought that they didn't need training to decide a sexual misconduct complaint because their untrained but clearly stellar judgment on these matters would surely suffice.

But it wasn't just one. It was repeated dismissal and minimization over decades and throughout multiple systems, without any larger societal understanding of how this neglect regarding crimes of rape and sexual assault might be related. Far too little had changed in three decades. Regardless of the years that had passed, my case was still inextricably linked to present-day societal beliefs, behaviors, and policies. Even where some progress was undeniable, the foundation of rape culture and misogyny continued to have a wide and unremitting impact on rape investigations nationwide.

In 2008 Human Rights Watch (HRW), a social justice nonprofit, began investigating how much rape evidence went untested and what the implications of this neglect were. A year later they published a comprehensive sixty-eight-page report on the situation in Los Angeles County, where over twelve thousand untested kits had been counted.[12] The report stated, "National studies have shown that cases in which a rape kit was collected, tested, and contained DNA evidence of the offender's contact with a victim were significantly more likely to move forward in the criminal justice system than cases in which there was no rape kit collected." It further warned that the clock was running out and that thousands of these cases would be unprosecutable if not attended to in a timely manner.

Before this reporting, many survivors who'd never heard a word about their cases believed that they weren't solved because someone had tried and failed, that law enforcement had used every tool at their disposal and had come up short. The work of HRW told a very different story, and their reporting on Los Angeles County led to more articles being written, which led to increased awareness about the state of rape investigations in this country.

Other articles were being written about untested rape evidence around the same time HRW was doing its research in Los Angeles and subsequent reporting. "The Rapist in the Freezer," published in the *Huffington Post*, states, "It's probably safe to say there are serial rapists roaming free in America and it's our own justice system's fault."[13] *Marie Claire* published the story of a woman who waited over a decade for her case to be solved, its tagline offering, "If you think being raped is your worst nightmare, read what happens next. Women across the country are waiting years, even decades, for their rape kits to be tested."[14] An online report from HRW in 2010 on untested evidence in Illinois begins with this survivor quote: "I learned a lesson when I found out that the police had closed my case without even interviewing [the rapist], or testing the rape kit. I learned that you cannot trust that the justice system will bring hope to you or bring your rapist to jail. You cannot hope that what went wrong will be righted."[15] *The Texas Tribune* reported that "in police departments across Texas, tens of thousands of rape kits have been sitting on the shelves of property storage rooms for years—thanks to strained budgets, overworked crime labs and a law enforcement philosophy that such kits are primarily useful as evidence if a stranger committed the assault."[16] Nicholas Kristof, one of the most respected journalists writing for *The New York Times*, covered the topic as well, in a piece titled "Want a Real Reason to Be Outraged?" that brought the issues mentioned above to the attention of his wide readership.[17]

A few years after the original crush of articles, Sarah Tofte, the writer of some of the first articles on the state of "backlogged kits" around the country, began reaching out to rape crisis centers looking for survivors who'd been in touch with them about their own rape evidence possibly being mishandled. A friend of mine, Peggy, worked at BARCC as the director of outreach. When Sarah called BARCC, Peggy called me, and soon Sarah and I were talking. She told me I deserved to know what happened in my case and supported the efforts I'd made thus far. "If you need some help, I'd be happy to assist. These calls are hard to make ourselves when it's our lives we're talking about," she said.

She then invited me to be part of a roundtable in Washington, D.C. "There's a lot more attention being paid now to these untested rape kits and what the delay means to survivors," she said. "Your search—and the fact that your kit is currently unaccounted for—is an important part of what's probably happening in other cities too. We're putting together an event and inviting survivors to meet with government officials to discuss this further. I know your voice and story would be welcomed. You can get back to me when you've had time to think about it."

I closed my eyes, wondering what it might feel like to take this step—fly to another city and talk to a group of strangers about a topic that consumed me. I wondered if I would have the words to express the pain and diminishment I'd felt reading about the mishandling of rape evidence in multiple cities, for multiple years. I didn't feel as if I had a choice anymore to step aside and attend to my own wounds.

"Sarah—I don't need any time to think about it. Count me in."

Working as an advocate whose story might help change the way rape cases are investigated felt important, even with the growing doubts that surfaced the more involved I became. I didn't want to simply stand up and tell my story and then move aside. I had yet to be convinced that law enforcement, nonprofit agencies, and government would fix everything because they listened to details from survivors about how bad rape can be. That hardly seemed the point.

I still ached and raged when I thought about the silence from the Boston Police Department in response to my case and about all I'd heard in subsequent years about crime lab delays and the treatment of rape investigations locally and nationally. I thought, by being part of a larger effort, my voice and perspective would help lead to meaningful reforms. Then, perhaps, I'd muster the courage I needed to go back and get some answers about my individual case. This contradiction sums up so much of the irony related to the impact of sex crimes on victims. Here I was, willing to have some role in a national effort while feeling scared beyond words to walk into a police station and ask them to journey back with me to a time and a memory I still found impossible to confront directly. Part of what added to my reluctance was a conviction that it was not my job to make them do theirs. But if I didn't act, who would?

I joined the BARCC Speakers Bureau and soon would meet Debbie Smith and a handful of other women called upon to help cities as they began to go through decades of untested rape kits attached to "cold cases." These cases often only became cold because there was no investigation at the time the crimes had been reported. How to deal with victim notification was one of the key reasons we had been called together as a survivor group.

—

My first major invitation to speak about the impact of untested rape kits would be a roundtable discussion at the Department of Justice in Washington, D.C. I had said yes to Sarah, but I needed to first attend to something else I'd been dreading. When you are a parent who has experienced trauma, eventually you have to tell your kids—and this had to be the moment I would do just that. It was time.

When our daughter, Becca, was three, she began having nightmares.

"I need to sleep here," she said, running into our room for the third time in one week. "The bears are going to come in my room and take me." She whimpered while we both rubbed her back until she fell asleep.

"It's my fault," I said to Mary. "She's absorbed my fears through her pores. Come on, she thinks something is going to climb through a window and hurt her. That doesn't take a genius to interpret."

"Lots of kids have fears," Mary said, but her reassurance fell flat on my guilty heart. I had read a book recently about how children of Holocaust survivors experienced high rates of anxiety or depression regardless of whether their parents acknowledged what happened to them. I saw a potential parallel in our family but still didn't know how to address the topic of rape at Becca's tender age.

Now, almost a decade later, Becca was in middle school. I'd bought my ticket to D.C. and friends had been inundating me with questions without filtering who was in the room. *Are you nervous? Do you know what it's going to be like?* We wanted Becca to hear my story from us, not by accident or incidentally.

"Before we tell Becca, don't you think we should tell Ben? He *is* two years older." Mary and I were out walking the dogs. It was February in New England and the wind was blowing. Over the past few weeks, I had started to worry my constant questions were becoming annoying: Do you think going to D.C. is a mistake? What am I getting myself into? What if it makes me feel worse? Mary had taken to answering me with, "What do you think?" And

I realized my anxiety had made me lose confidence. I caught myself this time and changed my question into a statement. "I think we should tell Ben if we're telling Becca."

"He already knows," she said. I was instantly mad at her. She must have known that information would be important to me, but hadn't shared it.

"Say more," I said.

"It wasn't very long ago, and I didn't mean not to tell you. I just haven't had the chance; it was a brief interaction that didn't feel all that monumental at the time, but I should have realized it would to you."

"So you're sorry," I said, making it clear by my tone I thought she should be.

"I'm not really all that sorry, to be honest, but I can tell you'd like me to be, so, yes, I am sorry." It wasn't her best apology, but I accepted it, desperate to hear more. "He went into our room looking for something and saw a stack of papers—that article you've been working on—he was curious and read it. Later, he came to me and said, 'I read Michy's essay. It was really sad.'"

The essay I was working on was in response to yet another article I'd come across about law enforcement's response to rape. The essay, and whatever point I hoped to make by writing it, included some details of my case—blindfold, knife, phone cord, two men. Ben had never said a word to me.

That night, I went into his room at bedtime. "Ben, I heard you read my essay. Can we talk?"

"I'm sorry that happened to you." He looked down at his book.

"And I'm so very sorry you found out the way you did. I didn't mean for that to happen. I'll answer whatever questions you have."

"It's okay, Mom. There's nothing you have to apologize for. You didn't do anything wrong. I don't want to talk more about it right now; I have to finish this book tonight." And he went back to reading.

"I think you should tell her," I said to Mary the next day. "It will be easier for her to have her reaction, and we can all discuss it after." Becca was changing and needed a ride to basketball practice.

"Okay; I'll be brief. Remember the rule from when they were little? Say just enough and wait to see if they're ready for more."

"Call me when she gets out of the car. Or just hurry home."

The distance from our house to the school was about two miles. I paced, ate some chocolate chips from the freezer; opened a book I didn't read. Twenty minutes later, I heard the garage door open.

"I kept it simple." Mary sat next to me on our living room couch. "I said to her, 'We want you to know something you're old enough now to understand. When Mom was a few years out of college, she was raped during a break-in. It was very hard but she got a lot of help to feel better. This trip to D.C. is to help the government learn how to do a better job dealing with survivors. I'm proud of her.'"

"What did she say?" My left shoulder began to twitch.

"You know how sensitive Becca is, and she adores you," Mary said. "She was quiet at first and then yelled, 'What, Michy was raped? That's terrible.'"

"Was that all?"

"A few minutes later she did ask if that was why you turned into a lesbian." Mary made quotation marks with her fingers.

I chuckled. "That's interesting. Did you ask her if she ever wondered why you turned into a lesbian?"

"No, I think she thinks it's more obvious with me. You should pick her up." The car keys glinted up at me, blinding my sight.

Becca hopped in the car. "Michy, I am really sorry that happened to you," she said as she slammed the door. "Did they ever catch him?" My heart pierced, and I did not correct the pronoun to "them."

"No, Becca, they didn't. It didn't matter to me at the time because I was focused just on trying to feel better, but now I kind of wish they did." We seemed to hit every red light.

"Maybe it was the Boston Strangler. It sounds like him and you lived in Boston," she said, unzipping her jacket. "I bet it was."

"No, honey, the Boston Strangler was convicted in the 1960s, and I think he died in prison soon after."

"I think it was; you can't be sure it wasn't." She turned on the radio. "Is that why you're gay?"

"No, love, I was gay before this happened. They aren't related," I said, feeling inexplicably sad. "It doesn't work like that."

"It could," she said, and the conversation ended—maybe because we were home and maybe because we had both said as much as we could right then.

Weeks later, Becca asked me, "Mom, if you were raped, how come you can't swim? It makes no sense."

Mary's head tilted, and I heard her take a quick breath to ask for clarification. But I understood.

"Becca, are you saying if I could go through something scary like that, how could I ever be afraid of anything, especially something like a big dumb bunch of water?" In that instant, I pictured her tiny frame squeezing between us in bed, spooning me and holding on for dear life, lest the bears come and take her away. I saw her big brown eyes staring at me all the times she asked me to go on a roller coaster or join her in the water to play, wishing I could do more than I seemed able.

"Yes, that's exactly what I mean. You don't need to be scared. Please take lessons with me." I tried to think of every possible way to say no. The thought made me lightheaded—going under, unable to get air, helpless, waiting for it to just be over.

"I'll teach you," she said, taking my hand.

"Okay." I sighed, startled by her touch. "But you have to go easy on me. Being raped doesn't actually prepare you for the rest of your life."

She smiled and closed her math book with a loud whack. "We'll see about that! You won't be afraid when I'm done with you."

A nearby health club had a pool that stayed open year-round. We went the next day and the day after and the day after that.

"Bob up and down like I'm doing, and each time go a little further." Becca and I stood face-to-face in the shallow end of the pool on the first day. She took my hand and led me out to where the water was just below my chest and her neck.

"That's far enough, Becca," I said, trying to feign calm. "Let's not get ahead of ourselves. I'm pretty pleased I made it as far as getting in the water. Maybe that's enough for our first lesson."

Her bluish lips became a straight line. "Don't be so negative. Now, let's try to get your head underwater." The lesson had started in earnest. "If you can do that, it'll make swimming easier." We bobbed up and down, and I got as far as the tip of my chin touching the water. Since Becca's head was completely under at each submersion, she didn't notice my face was still dry.

"See? It wasn't that bad. Try holding your nose, and you might go a little deeper."

After our interminable bobbing, Becca lifted me up in her arms and carried me like a baby. I relished the delicious feeling of being in her arms until I saw we were heading to deeper waters.

"Stop, Becca." I thrashed, trying to escape her grasp and land on my own two feet before the water went above my head. "You have to give me some time to do this." She let go, and my heart stopped racing once my feet touched the pool bottom. As far as I was concerned, the lesson was over.

Being raped did not successfully inoculate me from ever feeling fear again, as Becca imagined it might. Most times, it felt more like the opposite was true. I would have done anything to give my daughter that love letter of a successful swim—to show her that fears can be conquered if you just try your hardest, but that would have been the wrong moral to this complicated fable. Fears are not always conquered; some can't be. Maybe it's enough to stand side by side with them and look them straight in the face instead of letting them crush us with power they have no right to wield.

—

The Department of Justice Sexual Assault Roundtable was scheduled midweek, and I had taken two days off from work to attend. In less than twenty-four hours, I would be sitting in a circle in a windowless conference room with twelve strangers—other rape survivors—along with close to twenty government officials and law enforcement authorities, who would sit in chairs directly behind us. "We're here to listen," the moderator would say when we took our places. Later, when the day concluded, they would say they were grateful and that we were brave.

We were brought together to address the complexities of notifying victims that forgotten forensic evidence was being tested in cities across the country and entered into the national DNA database. I didn't yet understand why a tool that provided the highest standard for matching a perpetrator to a crime was available but remained underutilized in rape cases, even with legislation written and funding allocated for that specific purpose. More reform was needed than compelling crime labs to test the old kits and enter them into the FBI database; analysis of what caused this state of affairs was needed, or else it seemed likely that victims raped in the present day would be speaking out about their ignored cases twenty or thirty years from now and someone would be thanking them through tears for their courage.

The National Center for Victims of Crime—a cosponsor of the event—had sent an email that included an attachment with a personal narrative from each of the attendees in which we described our assaults as well as any encounters we had with the criminal justice system. The moment the email arrived in my in-box, I printed the attachment and closed my office door. The stories described shocking levels of violence and terror, and yet, in a way that made me feel ashamed, I was giddy. Until this moment, I had never met anyone who experienced anything like the violence I had. This fact left me deeply lonely. I believed no one else could understand what that felt like and what it took from me since I barely understood it myself. But now there were others, a little group. Groucho Marx's line "I wouldn't want to be part of any club that would have me as a member" went through my head. It felt like my bare foot had found a missing puzzle piece on the carpet.

I couldn't wait to meet them.

Mary drove me to the airport, insisting on parking the car and walking me to my flight.

"It's going to be okay," she said at the terminal, adjusting my collar, which was both cockeyed and turned in, a not-uncommon phenomenon. The look I aimed for was casual as opposed to disheveled, but there were days I had to fight not to look like a mess.

Mary gave me a hug that lasted.

"I'm okay; this is so good for me," I said, hoping she wouldn't see the fear in my eyes.

Mary looked at her watch as we stood near the security line, with plenty of time before my flight. "Do we have time for a cup of coffee?" she asked.

"I think I'm better off just going to the gate." My blue carry-on had a homemade rainbow luggage tag Becca had made years ago in her after-school program. One side read MOMMY MICHY and the other MOMMY MARY. I had made sure my side showed when I'd dragged the bag to the car that morning. "Thanks, Becca," I'd said, planting a kiss on her cheek before she ran to the bus stop. "My luggage definitely won't get lost now."

"When are you going to get rid of that embarrassing tag? You might as well shout 'Hey, I'm a lesbian' to the whole airport." Becca threw her arms around me and held me tight. "Knock 'em dead," she whispered in my ear.

Mary and I stood off to the side to let others get into the security line. "I have about five hours after landing before I'm supposed to meet everyone for dinner. Hopefully, the name of the restaurant is in my packet." I inched toward the line, rambling. "I'll walk around D.C. till it's time to meet, find some souvenirs."

I blew her one last kiss. "Maybe I'll get a haircut and try to look a little less like an aging hippie." She waved as I turned and walked away.

I'd be home in two days with chocolate for Ben and Becca and a suitcase full of stories for Mary. And although I didn't know it yet, I would also return with a kernel of resolve—knowing it was time to find out what happened in my case, no longer satisfied with the tiny speck of information I had.

—

Washington, D.C., in February was about twenty degrees warmer than Boston, and the day was bright and sunny. My cab passed the Washington Monument and the Capitol, and nostalgia overwhelmed me. As an undergraduate, I traveled there on a bus filled with Brandeis students. We slept in a church basement and then stomped our way over to the National Mall for the first national march on Washington for lesbian and gay rights. I felt powerful and proud surrounded by chanting throngs.

What do we want? Gay rights!

When do we want them? Now!

Maybe being back in D.C. would provide me with a physical memory of how I felt then—fearless, with an unflinching belief in myself and the power of engaging in efforts to right society's wrongs. Perhaps I could find that young girl across space and time and keep company with her while I waited with jangled nerves to meet the other participants in the focus group.

The taxi deposited me at a downtown hotel, and I checked in, dropped off my suitcase, and walked out the door. I had hours to go before introducing myself to women I knew only from their stories, which I'd reread twice more on the plane. When I got to my story in the packet, I pretended I was someone else, to see how it might sound to a stranger. What small detail had they winnowed me down to?

The one from Boston with two assailants.

The one held at knifepoint and hog-tied.

The lesbian.

Or, maybe they weren't thinking of me at all.

I arrived at the restaurant a few minutes after the slated time and saw a swarm of women gathered at the front alcove waiting to be seated. I introduced myself, hoping that would be enough, since I had no idea what to say after that.

Almost sixteen of us squished around a table meant for ten, unwilling to split into two smaller groups. I told my brain not to connect the city or name with the stories I had in my briefcase— the one in the stairwell, the one at the bus stop, the one sleeping in the living room. Most of us talked about our lives only in the present and stayed far away from the past. For this evening, anyway, we decided not to be defined by our rape stories. That changed when we went around saying our names and the cities we lived in. Four of the women were from Dallas, and someone asked, "Is that a coincidence or do you know one another?"

"Oh, we know each other now. A detective in Dallas started going through their old rape kits, and he got in touch with each of us with news about a match. We became friends after that."

A woman named Lavinia said, "I'm the oldest one here, I think." She laughed. "I'm not really old, but my case is from 1985, so my case is the oldest one that was solved."

Carol chimed in. "No, Lavinia, mine was from 1984. Remember? We talked about this." The Dallas group started sharing stories, dates, and memories of getting the news.

I didn't hear much of what was said after that. Both of them were attacked near the time I was and knew who their assailants were. The DNA testing had yielded results in both their cases. If the police could find my rape kit, maybe I could learn the identity of who had attacked me as well. I excused myself to call home. I needed to hear Mary's voice.

"Hi, Mary, I'm in the bathroom of the restaurant," I whispered. "So far so good."

"We're good here too, except I left the chicken in too long and it came out really dry. The kids managed to eat it with some ketchup but wanted to know when you'd be home so I don't poison them. What's it like there?"

"Kind of impossible to describe. I'll call you later from the hotel to talk more," I said. "Can I say goodnight to Ben and Becca?"

"Okay, wait; I'll point the phone at them. Go ahead in one second." I heard her yell, "Kids—it's Mom. She wants to say goodnight."

The dogs started barking, and Ben and Becca yelled over them and each other. "Hi, Michy. Come home soon. We love you. Have fun. Mary burned the dinner. Good luck tomorrow. I did good on my math test. Love you. Night, night, Mom. Did you see the president?"

I wanted them to go on forever. The life I had built and the love our family shared filled me with light, and I felt ready for whatever might come next.

I rejoined the dinner; our meals had arrived. We were strangers with one deep thing in common, and I wanted to find out if there was more—books, hobbies, kids—anything not rape related that affirmed the lives we'd built. We talked, ate dinner, and ordered dessert. I was the first one to leave. "It was so wonderful to meet you, but I have to go to bed. I haven't slept well leading up to this, and I'm exhausted." Debbie Smith's husband, Rob, the only man there, offered to walk me back to the hotel.

"I insist," he said. "I'm not letting any woman walk in D.C. alone at night."

I looked at him and tried to imagine being the person seeing their loved one immediately after being attacked. "We never leave each other's side," he'd said when they introduced themselves. His face mirrored Lise's when she first found me in the emergency room and I felt so fond of him in that moment that I almost accepted the offer for his sake but declined. "I wouldn't feel right taking you away from dinner. I'll take a taxi; I promise."

I passed a few occupied cabs and kept going. The hotel was a ten-minute walk away in a well-lit, well-traveled area of the city; there was no reason to be scared. While I understood Rob's need to be protective, I didn't want an escort. Earlier in the evening, when we were waiting to be seated, I had put my seltzer down on the bar. He grabbed it and held it to his chest protectively and said, "Don't you know never to leave a drink unattended?" I thought it unlikely someone would slip something in my drink and lead me away, but there was something about him I liked, so instead of arguing I simply said, "Good point." Later that evening, he revisited the moment and apologized. "Forgive me for being a bit overprotective. I may be retired, but I'm still a cop."

"I do understand," I said, and he smiled.

"Thank you; it means a lot."

Following a night of Benadryl-induced sleep, I took a taxi to the DOJ building. Heavy glass doors and a metal detector greeted me. *Truly, I mean you no harm,* I thought as the security guard went through my briefcase. I texted Mary before the meeting in the first bathroom I could find. "This place makes you feel like you're about to be arrested for something," I wrote as I hid in the stall. Her responses came in rapid succession:

"Just breathe."

"We miss you already."

"What did you say I should make for dinner again?"

After we were seated, someone introduced themselves as the moderator. "We are here to get your thoughts on survivor notification. Your experiences are critical for us to hear. Can I ask you to go around and give your first name and tell your story?"

Perhaps she meant we were supposed to talk about what it was like to learn our evidence was never tested or how we were informed of the results when they were, but her lead-in was vague, and each woman started describing the horrific violence that had been in our summary pages. It took hours. During a break I walked outside with Debbie. We had been sitting next to each other all morning. Our seats were at the end of the semicircle, and we hadn't been called on yet.

"I don't get it," I said. Tall buildings surrounding us created a wind tunnel and I had to shout to be heard. "How is telling the details of our attacks again going to help them with what they're trying to figure out? The impact of our attacks is one thing; telling victims their case has been solved twenty-five years after the fact quite another."

She smiled. "I thought it was just me. I don't generally talk about what happened to me unless I have a chance to gear up for it in advance. It's too hard."

"Tell you what. I'm going to use my work voice and do what I do in meetings when there's no agenda set. I'll say some version of, 'Since you've read my story in the summary, I'd like to get a clearer understanding of how we can be of help today.'"

"Sounds perfect; I will as well if they call on me first," she said, and I felt closer to her than I would have expected, given we'd met less than twenty-four hours ago.

When it was my turn, I made my brief statement as planned, and no one balked or insisted I provide more detail. By then, it was time for lunch. "After everyone eats," the moderator said, pointing to a tray of sandwiches, "we'll begin with some specific questions we've prioritized for today. We want to hear how you were informed that your rape kit had been run through CODIS and a match found."

Most of the women around the table belonged to a small co-hort who knew the identity of their perpetrators now that the evidence had been tested after years had gone by. Our hosts were interested to know how they had been told and how they had re-acted, anticipating more evidence being tested and more matches found.

What if the survivor had never told anyone about the rape in the first place?

What if a DNA "hit" showed someone had gone on to rape several more people? Might the city be sued? What would be their public explanation?

How could they even begin to contact these women and break the news? What if no one in their current life even knew? What wounds might they be opening?

It was a muddle, and they needed us. Because many of these

women had been among the earliest "survivors" of untested rape evidence and prematurely closed cases, they could speak to the concerns being laid out. Their riveting stories ended in their kits being tested, a match being found, and their finally knowing the name and seeing the face of the man who had raped them. I, on the other hand, was still searching and could only speak to that uncertainty. There were many times during the day that I wondered why I'd been invited at all.

The tale of testing "backlogged" kits and "solving" cold cases would soon create an uncomfortable celebrity from tragedy and neglect. The scripts were similar. An innocent woman lives her life until a random violent attack occurs where she is brutalized, tortured, and almost killed. After years of feeling the impact of trauma and being ignored by those charged with protecting the public, her dusty kit is finally tested and a match found. Maybe there's a court case; maybe the perpetrator is tied to other violent crimes; maybe she gets to speak at a victim-impact hearing. In the end, "justice" is finally served and healing occurs. Later, many of these women testified before Congress. They stood side by side with Vice President Biden to announce progress and funding. They spoke globally about their stories. One woman's story, which culminated in her rapist's trial, was featured on an HBO true crime series, and another woman's story was told on Lifetime.

But aside from these DNA matches uncovered from long-ago forgotten cases, another story desperately needed voicing. If there were hundreds of thousands of uninvestigated rape kits that cities acknowledged having collected and still only a small number of women whose cases had been solved, thousands more like me must have had their evidence lost, degraded, destroyed, or thrown away.

I still didn't know enough about my case to know if the elusive concepts of justice or closure were even possible for me. I knew only that my rape kit was missing, and I still hoped that if I searched, it would be found. Then, I thought, I'd be even more like my new friends, and some of my anger and invisibility would abate. Maybe I would feel less broken because someone had bothered to take what happened to me seriously and do something about it—decades too late, but still. I could lift that blindfold and not wonder anymore what the two men who had changed the course of my life looked like, what their names were, and what their stories were. That nagging feeling that my thinking was flawed wouldn't subside. My belief that these women had closure or peace of mind and that I would as well didn't seem to capture the full essence of this tragic situation.

As I sat listening to the women around me, I couldn't help thinking that nothing could erase the trauma of being the victim of a violent crime. Nothing could erase the fact that these rapes could have been solved years before. Nothing could undo the fact that society had seemingly abandoned rape victims by tacitly according these crimes a different status than other felonies. The "solving" of cases after decades may have been highlighted as something to be celebrated, but in truth it was evidence of tragic and inexcusable neglect on a massive scale. We, the survivors, held on to one another as we continued to understand the underlying meaning of our efforts to create change. Our own stories felt unreal to us. Feeling understood by others helped. I needed my newfound group; we needed one another.

In a 2018 *Washington Post* article addressing what to do with decades' worth of untested rape evidence, Jessica Contrera writes, "Until just last year, there were no national requirements or guidelines on what to do with them. Most states had no laws dictating which kits should be tested, meaning every police department could have its own rules about what evidence to test, keep, or throw away. Some even let individual detectives make those calls.

What happened to a woman's rape kit could depend not only on what state she was in, but which side of a county line she was on, or even who was on duty when she asked for help."[18]

Not long after the trip to D.C., a group of us were flown to Los Angeles to provide our perspective on victim notification for a project to develop national written standards for law enforcement and care providers. We stayed in a luxury hotel, and our consultation day was interspersed with a drumming circle, gourmet food, dancing, and a break to "paint our feelings" so we could tolerate the subject matter. Later still, we were brought to a world-renowned DNA lab in Maryland to learn how to be effective advocates by a coalition of national nonprofits. Change would be imminent now, the problem fixed.

My "club" celebrated every TV appearance, every story published, every lecture delivered, since it brought the issue into the light. I came to love these women and considered it a Faustian bargain that the larger world was potentially exploiting our tragedies, hoping to alter, even a little, how rape crimes would be treated in the future. That didn't mean I didn't see it. But it never occurred to me on my way to D.C. for my very first invitation to speak as a "survivor" that I might ultimately find such endeavors so unsatisfying.

A year later, at a different event, I met a woman named Meaghan who said our efforts to address what was increasingly being called the "backlog" were grossly misinformed and that the entire issue was a symptom of a wider problem. The next words she uttered—a question, really—halted my breath.

"You really have to ask yourself if rape is considered a crime," she said as we sat in a hotel lobby waiting for a cab. "This is just more of the same of how we were treated by the police when we were raped. Our investigations weren't backlogged; there were no investigations." She was facing me, her eyes focused over my left shoulder at the expansive foyer. "Now these agencies want our stories and our time, but how will that change anything?"

The roundtable I attended took place in February 2012, but the concern about "backlogged" rape evidence continues to this day. The indignation continues as well. Why it happened, why it's happening still, and whether there are effective solutions continue to be debated. Some states have enacted legislation focused on tracking rape kits so victims can follow where they are in the process.[19] Other states have passed laws that "all kits need to be tested,"[20] but there can be nuance about which kits are actually considered CODIS-eligible. For example, if an officer dismisses a claim as unfounded or a DA declines to move a case forward, it's unlikely that evidence would move ahead. Other states are writing more funding into their budgets for rape kit testing or mandating that officers receive training on responding more appropriately to victims' reports of sexual assault.

If we don't change the attitudes of those responding to rape victims, if we allow categories like "unfounded" and "exceptionally cleared" to inflate solve rates, if we continue to have district attorneys declining to prosecute and judges making public statements about why the victim's behavior is problematic, legislation alone will not make a difference. Further, I still do not understand why so much legislation is needed as a kind of "watchdog" to fix a problem that shouldn't exist in the first place. Rape cases should not need extraspecial support to make sure law enforcement do their job and rape crimes are investigated.

Maybe Meaghan was right. I had spent the last decade of my work life asking colleagues not to say "he said/she said" because it implies it's as likely as not that a woman would lie about something as deadly serious as rape. I played and replayed video clips of ignorant comments by politicians, forwarding them to friends and posting them on social media. It shamed me how many hours

I sat in front of the computer looking for additional proof that no one cared about these specific crimes or understood their impact. Maybe some part of me hoped that by searching to confirm the disregard, I'd discover something different—someone working to counter the assertions that rape reports are overblown, products of a woman scorned, an outright lie, or merely a misunderstanding during consensual sex. What I found, instead, endorsed the notion that the "backlog" exists in large measure because most rapes are considered baseline illegitimate and police turn away from them to solve crimes that no one doubts happened and whose harm is not being exaggerated.

Like me, most of the women I met in D.C. were met by skepticism from the detectives interviewing us in the immediate aftermath of our attacks. Their questions had indicated they didn't believe that what was reported happened.

"I was dragged from a bus stop into the trunk of a car. I escaped hours later. My mother brought me to the police, and we were both sobbing. I was only sixteen," one of the women had shared, tearing up. "The police officer said right in front of my mom, 'It's okay. I know you don't want your mom to know you have a boyfriend, but it's important you tell us the truth.'"

Several women then told similar stories, and the space filled with both sadness and outrage.

Those whose cases resulted in DNA matches described what it felt like to get the news.

"I'm glad to know. I really am, but it makes me so mad it took so long," one said. "If they could do it now and get a match, why not ten years ago, or fifteen? We could have had a trial. I could have made a victim-impact statement and let out some of what I've been living with for far too long."

While all these women agreed that finally knowing who had raped them had been life-changing, their experiences seemed quite layered and complex—while having received the news mattered to them enormously, the fact that it was delayed could not be ignored.

I voiced my frustration. "Are we supposed to think this is justice of some kind, given that these cases could have been solved years ago and just weren't? Officials in these cities not only need to inform survivors; they need to apologize."

Someone behind me replied, "We'll be doing more work on the complexities of victim notification soon. This is just a beginning. Can we go around the room and talk about how your lives have changed since you got your news?"

And I had nothing to add, again.

My experience at the roundtable sat with me for months. Up to this point, I had only tiptoed into researching my cold case. But now something had shifted. What had been made clear to me was that I had a right to ask what had happened in my case, and I now knew several women who had seen their lives change when they had done the same. I also understood the history of efforts to address the nationwide problem of untested rape kits that began almost a decade earlier, marked by the passage of the Debbie Smith Act, and I knew that a vast number of rape cases still remained uninvestigated, even with these efforts.

I wanted—needed—to have whatever information could be found. Obtaining it would be an exercise in self-regard and a small effort at political action. Daring to ask for accountability felt like an enormous step away from the silence I'd maintained and the shame I felt. The Massachusetts state crime lab had just announced yet another new scandal in late September 2012 when a chemist was fired for falsifying results in perhaps as many as thirty-four thousand drug convictions over the nine years she worked at the lab.[21] I felt like "scandal at the crime lab" could be a standing headline at this point. Picturing my new friends around the dinner table and then at the Department of Justice, smiling at one another warmly through our tears, my resolve hardened. I finally felt as if I could accept wherever walking down this road would lead me, no longer believing it would break me.

It was time.

Thirteen

2013

In 2013 I entered the Boston Sexual Assault Unit for the first time. The head of the department and I had been in touch by email for several weeks. I introduced myself to him initially with just the facts, providing a link to the archived story in *The Boston Globe* about my case and the other break-ins in Boston that summer, "A Series of Rapes Alarms Allston-Brighton."[1] His name was Sam Thomas. He had a good reputation and was known to care about victims. I referenced this in our emails in a weak attempt to win his favor, but my heart wasn't in it. The summer before, I'd seen him receive an award at the BARCC fund-raising walk. After the ceremony where Saundra had given him a plaque in recognition of his work, he joined the rest of us, devoting his afternoon to walk a 5K along the Charles River. At the end of my note, I snuck in how I had been searching for any information on my case for a while now, after learning about the problems at the state crime lab, and

I reminded him that Jennifer from BARCC had made inquiries on my behalf a while back.

The *Boston Globe* article I sent, along with my name and former address, gave him everything he needed to locate my file. Whatever he found made him apologize to me, both by email and then on the phone. He seemed unconcerned about acknowledging that there had been some kind of screwup. I could tell that my phone voice with him was appreciative, even obsequious—not my typical work tone, which projected confidence and authority. It didn't seem to worry him that I could use these emails to embarrass the department or seek redress, or both. Maybe the number of years that had passed made my inquiry seem more like an archeological expedition than a grave matter. I kept all his emails in a folder and waited. After a few more months, I finally decided I was ready to meet in person.

"I'm completely at your disposal," he said, "but think it's best if we talk face-to-face. My schedule is flexible as long as I don't have any police trainings booked. Part of my job involves teaching officers about responding to survivors." This last sentence irritated me, perceiving it as an expression of self-regard—*I'm good at my job; I teach other officers how to behave with people like you.* I could feel myself taut, unwilling to give him much of a break, but worried that if he perceived it, he'd be less forthcoming.

The detective consistently used the term "survivor." It seemed to be the term in common use to describe people who had lived through all sorts of maladies. If uttered more than a few times in a conversation or in reference to me, I bristled. People survive sometimes. It didn't seem appropriate to be lauded as an Olympian for the effort. I was the victim of a violent crime. I didn't die. Let's get on with it.

"Let me find out when my wife is free, Detective, and I'll be in touch."

"Great, but you must call me Sam. I'd love to meet her, and you'll probably like having someone with you anyway. Most people do." I didn't give him any special points for his easy response to the mention of my same-sex coupling, but he'd passed my test. Detective Thomas confirmed they had not located my rape kit, but that he would share with me what they did have. "We'll talk more about it when you come in," he said.

The indication that he had some information enticed me into following through every time I thought about canceling. He had something to tell me and would gladly do so if I were willing to sit down with him. "I prefer to talk in person," he'd said when I called to see if a face-to-face was really necessary. Any further questions would have to wait.

In this same conversation, he had told me that, in addition to my case file, they had found a bloody sheet and an electrical cord still in evidence. "Yep, that sounds about right," I said, my voice robotic. That stain had seeped through the sheet and onto my futon; it was the size and shape of a medium pizza. Lise told me she and our other roommates heaved it into the dumpster the day after the break-in—their last day ever in that apartment—as they took what they wanted out of the rubble and scattered.

Until I began my advocacy work, even after being the victim of one, I did not understand why solving a crime mattered to people in the slightest. If you solved a murder, the person was still as dead as ever. It changed nothing. What could be gained seemed utterly insignificant to what was lost. I was drawn to crime shows on TV but sweated during scenes where victims' relatives sat in the spectators' booth savoring the moment the murderer was strapped into the electric chair, as if it were the happiest day of their lives. As if it could erase the saddest day. There was nothing about this I understood. It made my throat constrict, and all I could focus on was how scared that poor sucker in the chair looked. That wasn't the kind of justice I sought, but I was looking for something, in spite of my skepticism and confusion.

All the things I celebrated in my life daily—love, parenthood, friendship—had not fully taken away the devastation of that sightless and violent night. I was open to a last-ditch effort to find a modicum of peace by revisiting it with the only people who could help me understand what happened. Since the rapists—whom I longed to confront about what they did and what they took from me—had seemingly vanished, I chose the police. Maybe there was something I could learn from them, and then, with some grace, I could allow my memories to rest.

—

Mary and I rehearsed the questions I would ask: "What happened to my rape kit? Why are you so sure it didn't wind up in the state crime lab with those other untested samples?" She suggested I leave out the phrase "scandal-ridden" when referring to the crime lab to prevent shutting down the conversation. I wrote my questions on a sheet of paper with the instructions *crescendo* and *fortissimo* in case my voice needed a reminder not to disappear.

Mary played the role of the detective. "Why is this important to you now?" she asked, gesticulating with one hand. "Don't you realize the statute of limitations has passed? The CODIS system wasn't even fully functional for years after your rape."

I made her break character for a moment. "You're just saying what you think he might say, right? You don't really feel that way, do you? You don't think this is a fool's errand and you're humoring me?"

"Honey, of course not," she said, placing her open palm over my heart. "I support you one million percent. But maybe we should pay attention to how vulnerable this makes you feel. Let's take a tiny time-out." Our meeting at the Boston Sexual Assault Unit was scheduled for the next day. Mary tried to convince me to take the day off work, but I refused.

"I made the appointment for five in the evening on purpose. Work is really busy right now." She didn't argue while I opened my computer and started answering some work emails, knowing I wouldn't get much done tomorrow.

One of the things trauma took from me was the sweetness of the earth. And I longed for the world around me to come alive again. I ached to smell the bread baking in the oven. The soft, sticky wetness under my hands as I kneaded the dough the moment before it went into the loaf pan. To have noticed the fly buzzing around my head, fearing it would wind up in the bread and be mistaken for a raisin.

But if someone asked what I did over the weekend, I would most likely say, "I made bread."

Since going to D.C., I'd remained in contact with my rape friends—as I referred to them, much to Mary's chagrin—and I was getting more of myself back. My mind wandered less, no longer missing half of what was said in a conversation. On one day, my nose had actually noticed the smell of an orange in my hand, its prickly fragrance, and the way it turned the tips of my fingers white after peeling it. Being alive rather than merely not dead offered thousands of tiny moments that required attention and held the possibility of joy. There simply wasn't time to wait and ponder what to do while another twenty-five years flew by. Maybe I'd learn more about my crime, and—a long shot—the rape kit would be found and the case solved. Or maybe none of this would happen. But I would move ahead, learn what I could, and then we'd see.

Hope is so often a prelude to heartbreak, and yet we persevere.

That space where hope resides holds possibility, promise, success, a taste of victory.

Maybe this dream I wish for will happen after all. I'll get the job. She'll fall in love with me, too. The acceptance letter from the college of my choice is on its way.

While we are in the space of waiting, magic is possible, which may be why we can wait so very long. I planned to move through this process with the Boston Police Department and draw conclusions later, even though a positive outcome was far from guaranteed.

—

I got no sleep the night before. Mary made me take a scalding hot bath and drink some calming tea, but it was no use. My stomach flipped as I imagined the day ahead and the meeting I had both dreamed of and avoided. She found parking on Commonwealth Avenue right away, something she referred to as "intention"—if you pictured a space waiting for you, it would be; and, this time, it worked. Her optimism was so reliable, always there in one form or another and showing up to wave at me when I needed it most. Mary had stashed four quarters in the car's cup holder, enough for exactly one hour.

"Do you think that will give us enough time?" She deposited the last coin into the gray slit of a tilted meter that looked like it had been rear-ended by a parallel parker.

"God, I certainly hope so," I replied, wishing I could pull a couple of quarters out of the meter and reverse time.

"It's all the change I have. A ticket wouldn't be the worst thing in the world now, would it?" Mary took my hand and we walked, looking for the street number the detective had provided.

"I don't get it," I said. "Wouldn't the police want people to know where to find them?" Every edifice looked the same to me: a few stories tall, in varying shades of dirty red-and-tan brick. Most housed retail shops on the first floor with apartments above. "I'm so curious about who lives in them." Mary craned her neck, looking skyward, while I concentrated on the task at hand.

Commonwealth Avenue stretches through Boston for miles. The section we walked through, just a few blocks west of Boston University, bordered my old neighborhood. I looked for any familiar signs of my life from twenty-five years ago. Maybe I'd see the corner market or my favorite coffee shop. I half-expected my friend Laura to run toward me from her old apartment building to ask if I wanted to get a Chinese lunch special, the good kind that comes with soup *and* an appetizer.

"Mary, I think we're going to be late if we don't find it soon. Maybe we should break down and ask someone. I must have left Detective Thomas's number at work; it's not in my contacts." I slowed down as I looked at my phone. "Should I try looking it up on Google?"

Mary squeezed my hand and kept walking. "Let's give it a few more minutes. We got this." She stopped and raised my chin toward her. "Look up, sweetie. You're going to trip and fall if you keep staring at that phone. Let's not add a tumble to our day."

We eventually found our destination—the street number of the building appearing just as I reached into my pocket for my phone again. Our meeting would be with both Detective Thomas and the chief forensic scientist. Detective Thomas was affable in person, greeting us with a deep bellow of "Well, hello there!"—as if we were long-lost relatives arriving for a holiday meal. He shook my hand hard and squeezed tight. I half-expected a hug and planted my feet firmly to resist. John, the scientist, looked at the floor, his head bent down at a forty-five-degree angle. He reminded me of a toddler fighting bedtime who had fallen asleep standing up. It was finally time to have our "sit-down" about my case, which was older now than I was at the time the crime had occurred.

A swirl of information spun in my brain as we were buzzed through a locked door into a long hallway. The detective was a tall man, close to six feet, with graying hair and a high forehead. Despite myself, I thought his face looked open and kind. "I am so glad to meet you both. God bless. What you've been through is just horrible." He opened another locked door with his card access and gestured for us to walk through first. We arrived at a small conference room in which every available surface was piled high with stacks of paper, with the exception of a round table. I spied a pizza box in the trash and wondered if we were taking over the office lunchroom. He gestured to the table. "Have a seat."

Mary and I had discussed various strategies both the night before and on the way in. She said I could pinch her or hit her leg under the table if I needed help.

"Feel free to speak your mind, too. You do not have to defer to me," I said. After all, she had been through much of the emotional struggles of the last few years and was as invested in this meeting as I was. "Based on my past phone conversations with Detective Thomas, my hunch is he may fill up the silent, empty spaces, so maybe we should both be very quiet and let him talk away and see what comes of it."

Mary nodded. "Okay, sounds like a plan."

—

My case file sat in front of the detective, his hands laid flat across it like a poker player protecting his cards. It looked thin. I could see my last name on the aging manila folder, and the 1984 archived *Boston Globe* article sticking out of it. He must have printed it out from the link I'd sent. He and John sat across from us. I stared at Mary, she stared at them, and they stared at me. We said no thank you to coffee. We made small talk.

Did you have any trouble finding the place?

How old are your kids?

"I can't believe you found a parking spot so nearby. I should have remembered to tell you we have visitor spots in front," Sam said, slapping his forehead.

He filled me in on the history of the sexual assault unit. "I did a little research with some of the veterans here because the timing of your assault rang a bell. The unit we're sitting in now began a week after your break-in—not this location, but the sexual assault unit itself, started in late June or early July 1984."

"Wow," I said, and looked at Mary, the enormity of that information hard to take in. She gave me a familiar look. *Let him continue,* I thought.

"The purpose of creating the sexual assault unit was to ensure coordination between neighboring jurisdictions. Before that, detectives from separate police departments were assigned cases from their towns, and it was rare they would consult one another, even when the crimes happened close by. These cases—yours and the others that summer—seemed likely to be linked. If they were investigated by one central division, potential patterns might be uncovered." He took a deep breath to say more, but I had a question that couldn't wait.

"Were any of the cases solved? If they were, maybe we could learn something now about whether any of those perpetrators could be tied to my break-in."

Sam said he was looking into it and would let us know.

There we were—Mary, Sam, John, and me—sitting at the headquarters of the unit formed specifically so that crimes like mine would have a greater chance of being solved. Cases with so many similarities were meant to be handled with coordination and care. The city had intended to do something to make the city safer and take care of rape victims.

I had the unshakable feeling that they had created it just for me, even though I hadn't known anything about it until this very moment, thirty years too late, it seemed. And yet here we sat. The Boston Sexual Assault Unit had been formed to address a problem and improve responses to rape victims. *We* had demanded action. *We* had begged for help in response to break-in after break-in. The act of creating the unit certainly calmed down everyone in the city, but had it done its job? I still didn't know.

My brain started doing a little dance as I sat in this building as a victim, wanting answers and wanting help, hoping the people in charge would provide them to me. Wasn't it because someone hadn't responded fully to me almost three decades ago that I was sitting here with them now looking for answers? It seemed that the Boston Sexual Assault Unit might have come to exist specifically to respond to the wave of publicity around crimes of rape in the city. Its name reminded me of the Sexual Assault Task Force we had set up at my university to respond more fully to students' concerns about our policies and treatment of survivors. I started thinking more about these parallels as I stared at Detective Thomas, wondering how this meeting might end.

The fact that the term "Sexual Assault Task Force" had a similar moniker to the unit started in Boston a week after my assault seemed important. Something victims already experience as deeply problematic is named as an "urgent concern" that only something as serious as a task force or special unit can address. In the Sexual Assault Task Force at my university, students voiced their anger about how policies and decisions had impacted them and so many others from years past. Their careful research and strategic efforts demanding change, along with their leadership on needed next steps, helped us develop reforms. As an administrator watching them in action, I experienced with a personal sense of responsibility my failure to push reform forward. And sitting across from Detective Thomas, I felt an even deeper empathy for their frustration and anger: Why had any part of this been their responsibility to fix?

They had come to their institutions for help, accommodations, or justice, and if there was not an adequate process in place that protected them or the adjudication procedure was untenable, or if the policies were complicated and drawn out and did not serve them, then what? The place they had loved became the place they left, feeling abandoned, unseen, and betrayed.

They were devastated and angry, and they had a right to be.

And here I was, having the conversation it took me years to get to with Sam Thomas in the Boston Sexual Assault Unit, tiptoeing into the past. I wondered, as I did working with students, why did it take victims' voices to usher in reform?

My leg bounced nervously under the table as I looked into the sad eyes of a chagrined detective.

"I'm not sure where we should start," Detective Thomas began, now looking only at me. "John, why don't you explain how Boston deals with our DNA evidence? Michelle is worried her rape kit was with all those untested samples at the state lab."

I hated it when someone described me as worried. It implied the thing I focused on wasn't important and that my anxious self demanded attention only so that my worry could be soothed. I wasn't worried; I was angry and confused, wishing mostly the thing that put me in this seat had never happened.

John looked up and talked without interruption about DNA technology during the 1980s. "It was called the Johnson test. It provided some information, but the very process destroyed the DNA for further testing. So even when the technology improved, they couldn't retest the evidence. And it wasn't all that helpful if there wasn't a suspect to match the results with, since there wasn't a national database yet."

Sam made a crack about the Johnson test's unfortunate name, and Mary spoke up. "No jokes, please" was all she said, but her tone made it clear we should move on.

"Boston has no backlog," John said. "We weren't happy to hear about the state crime-lab problems, but that's not the case here.

"The national DNA database didn't get traction until the late nineties. I tested everything I had available to me then, even if the statute of limitations on the cases had expired, but yours wasn't. There's no indication it was ever logged in. It's missing."

"Where could it be?" I asked. "You told me you had the cord and sheet from my case. Maybe the kit was sent to the state lab in error." I grabbed Mary's hand under the table and made sure our knees were touching so I wouldn't float away. I took a short detour to talk about the women I had met over the last few years, whose evidence was tested and whose perpetrators were identified. "I've seen what a difference just knowing makes, and . . ." My voice trailed off.

"Let me tell you what we think *might* have happened, although it doesn't reflect all that well on us," Detective Thomas said. "I can only hope you understand this is not how we do things now." I thought about stopping him right there to argue this point. I had just spent the last eighteen months attending focus groups and victim forums learning about how cities were dealing with years of untested rape evidence precisely because "things" had not changed. I didn't doubt there were some departments in some cities that did a somewhat better job than others, but I hardly thought it worth a brag, especially given the many scandals that had beset the Massachusetts state crime lab. Maybe Detective Thomas and John did a good job; maybe there were other officers or departments or crime labs out there that were slightly less abysmal than others. I wasn't prepared to be impressed by people who did jobs they were supposed to do. He didn't have the right to assert things were so much better now. I'd heard too many present-day stories about victims to believe such a claim.

Detective Thomas opened my file and read it, his lips pursed. "As we have established, you were raped in late June and the sexual assault unit formed a few days later. Detectives working on the recent break-ins were supposed to turn their cases over to the unit. Yours never was." He took a sip of coffee, shaking his head.

"I can't say for sure, but I have a guess . . ." He closed the file and put it on the table, almost within my reach. "Your detective, he's retired, but there are still fellows here who knew him. He was old-school. Some of these guys got pissed when the higher-ups tried to take their cases and hand them over to this brand-new unit." He paused and let me draw my own conclusions. "Your rape kit was never logged. The last line of the file says something like, 'evidence in locker.' We've looked everywhere. I'm pretty sure we never had it. I'm really sorry on behalf of the entire department."

Detective Thomas's face and neck were red. "I haven't been able to sleep well since you first wrote to me. This is harsh news, and I understand if you're upset. You have the right to be."

I reviewed all the feelings Sam just told me I might be having and his opinions about them. He thought it likely I was upset; it was okay with him and understandable if I was. I really didn't feel much of anything right then—maybe numb or frustrated. I'd need some time to figure it out.

Apparently, it was not inconceivable—although I found it astonishing—that a law enforcement officer might reasonably speculate that an "old-school cop" had withheld evidence or hadn't investigated a violent felony because his ego was bruised. My ability to learn more about a life-altering trauma depended on what this person had done with my case, and, it seemed, he had done nothing.

Didn't I say I'd call you if we knew anything?

There was never going to be any news.

Just like a woman, can't keep her mouth shut.

I had no words. I had no questions. I'd been struck mute.

Fourteen

"Here," Detective Thomas said. He handed me the folder, allowing me to touch it and feel its fragile bones. He held it out to me as a sacrament, the blood and body mine.

As he placed it in my reluctant hands, I readied myself for third-degree burns. How brief it was, how ancient and worn. It smelled of a basement, dank and mildewed. I touched the folder bearing my name.

"We don't usually do this. These files belong to the department, not to the victims, just to be clear. But you deserve to see it." His voice was soft. I think if I'd picked up the file and walked toward the door, he would have done nothing to stop me.

"I can't let you take it or copy it, but you can look at it briefly. I don't see the point of just reading it to you." He sighed, and his cheeks turned the color of a scraped knee. "Please don't take any photos."

I handed the file to Mary the moment Sam handed it to me. She pulled her reading glasses down off her head and read it.

"There's not much here," she said. "Is this normal with such a major crime?" My heart burst with gratitude for her ability to speak her mind. It never ceases to stun me how very different we are.

"I asked if it's normal in a case like this, such a terrible crime?" she repeated. "It's pretty appalling. It doesn't look like there was even an investigation."

Sam puckered his lips and looked down. "No, I wouldn't say it's normal. I can only say I'm sorry. I don't know what else to do at this point. The detective is retired, as I've said, and I'm not even sure it would be all that helpful to talk to him about it given the volume of cases we handle every year. I honestly don't know if he'd remember one case."

"I don't have the luxury of forgetting," I whispered to Mary, and she leaned her leg against mine under the table while she stared at the open folder.

That phrase—*evidence in locker*—three words with no perceivable punctuation attached, was the last entry in blue ballpoint ink on a single page in a manila folder yellowed with age, charcoaled with grime. At least I think that was the last line. Maybe there was another word or two, a sentence of purported conclusion. Maybe there was an observation contained within, a reflection or insight. My eyes couldn't bear to look at the file directly when Mary passed it back to me, so I skimmed it as if I'd been asked to read *Moby-Dick* in its entirety overnight. The task at hand is impossible; a best effort will have to do.

"Towards thee I roll." Ahab shouted this famous line to me, about me, with me in this pursuit of nothing. I was a white whale, beached and speared.

—

I had left my body and stopped taking anything in, something I still did when emotions overwhelmed me, a classic byproduct of trauma. A line I read from Virginia Woolf's *The Waves* gave me words for what happened to me when I was there somewhere but had also disappeared. "I am above the earth now. I am no longer upright, to be knocked against and damaged."[1] First, I saw Detective Thomas's mouth moving, no longer able to hear the words. Slowly, sounds reemerged, Detective Thomas still talking. "The only thing I can think of is to test the bloody sheet. John isn't all that optimistic there'd be anything useful, but he's willing to try. Why don't you and your wife think about it?"

I didn't move. I didn't speak. If we stayed any longer, we'd soon be talking again about blood and semen and how quickly body fluids degrade. I wanted to go. I needed to get out. Maybe if I blinked my eyes I'd disappear some more and wake up at home.

Mary looked at me and knew. "That's enough for today. I don't think we can take in much more." She lifted me by my elbow and guided me out, her hand holding on tightly.

—

I didn't speak much for days unless I was around the kids and then could marshal a parenting voice:

"Dinner's ready."

"Can I get into the bathroom before you take your shower?"

"How was school?"

But otherwise words failed.

Really, sometimes, only silence will do.

—

"What did it actually say?" I asked Mary as soon we got in the car. In a way, she'd been present for an event I'd been forced to skip.

"Let's talk about whether there's a next step after we've had a chance to absorb this. I'm feeling pretty emotional and upset, so I can't even imagine how you feel." I had no idea how I felt, so I tried to imagine it, too. My brain searched my body for a clue.

After we had gotten home and sent the kids off to bed, Mary had told me that the file had a record of the single conversation the original detective and his partner had with me at Emmy and Steve's apartment, briefly rendered in less than half a page.

What was not in there began filling the empty spaces of my brain. There was no mention of any contact with the Boston Sexual Assault Unit. There was no mention of logging fingerprint evidence from my room, looking to see whether it matched fingerprints from the other half dozen eerily similar and potentially related crimes that summer. There was no mention of checking in with me a few weeks after, a few months after, a few years after, or a decade after, when DNA technology improved and John the scientist was busy testing older kits, as he had relayed to us. There was no notation of a brief call done simply out of concern or kindness—just to say hello, to give an update—even if the update was that there was no news whatsoever.

My experience was not just a single failure by a single detective long ago. Closing a rape complaint without an investigation continues to the present day. Searching the internet for "uninvestigated rape cases" yields dozens of recent articles where cases have been dismissed with no investigation. A 2019 *New York Times* article, "These Rape Victims Had to Sue to Get the Police to Investigate," highlights a growing trend of women suing police departments for this very reason.[2] The article reports on examples from seven

U.S. cities: a plaintiff from Austin, for whom "police collected no evidence from the crime scene after a rapist broke into her apartment"; a college student "whose screams for help were recorded but whose case was dropped when her attacker, a stranger, claimed the sex had been consensual"; and another woman "forcibly taken to a motel and raped by three men, one of whom was not arrested even when his DNA was found in her sexual assault kit." In a case pending in Illinois, a police commander said under deposition that "he believed that half of the reported sexual assault cases in his precinct were false." In one of the cities mentioned, the district attorney found it necessary to create "an Interagency Sexual Assault Team to examine why sexual assault cases do not proceed through the criminal justice system."

A scathing report from New York City's Department of Investigation in 2018 found massive structural failures in the city's sex crimes investigations—the lede in the press release accompanying the report says it all: "DOI Investigation Finds NYPD Has Routinely Understaffed and Neglected the Special Victims Division, Negatively Impacting Sexual Assault Investigations."[3] This unit, for what it's worth, has been depicted in the long-running show *Law and Order: SVU*, almost every episode of which seems to fervently investigate and solve a case—within an hour, mind you. In reality, though, the report finds that "documents as well as current and former SVD staff, sex crime prosecutors, service providers, and victims' advocates all confirmed to DOI that chronic understaffing and inexperience have 'diluted' and 'shortened' investigations, jeopardized prosecutions, re-traumatized victims, and negatively impacted the reporting of sex crimes, thereby adversely affecting public safety." Analysis of the report notes that the "DOI found there are only 67 investigators for more than 5,000 adult sex crime cases a year. That's compared to about 100 homicide detectives to handle less than 300 murders a year."[4]

It is impossible to fully grasp how this wholesale, decades-long, ignorant disregard of rape cases has impacted victims.

As for me, I felt as small as my file.

—

This entire unprocessed jumble whirled while I scanned my work emails, wondered if the kids had homework, and noticed we were low on milk and almost out of coffee. I simply did not know what to do on the most fundamental level. My feet were ice, stuck in a snowcap. As I had suspected, knowing this little bit was perhaps worse than knowing nothing at all.

While trying to remember that the original detective's failure said nothing about me and volumes about him and the larger system he functioned within, I continually thought about what I would do if I had that job. I would want rape victims to know that law enforcement was committed to investigating cases with all due respect and the seriousness a felony-crime complaint deserved. I wouldn't use my time finding reasons to dismiss most rape complaints or reflexively find victims unreliable. Finally, I would counter rape victims' feelings of invisibility and insignificance, hoping more victims would come forward to report sex crimes if they knew that law enforcement wouldn't further traumatize them.

The emptiness on that one single page spoke volumes. By absence and brevity, it told me everything I needed to know.

Mary and I still had a decision to make. Detective Thomas had said that John's team could try testing the sheet but weren't hopeful. The blood on it was obviously mine, extracting one of the perpetrators' DNA from it unlikely. It seemed unwise to experience another disappointment so soon after the one we'd just had. I needed to catch my breath, to find where my body had disappeared to. Still, I wondered if I owed it to myself and my little club to do everything I could, to leave nothing undone.

"Before I take that step, I need to think more about what it is I'm doing and why I think it still matters to me," I said to Mary a few days after our trip downtown. She was making us a second pot of coffee on a Saturday morning. Ben and Becca were both down the street shooting baskets with friends.

"I had this fantasy I would feel better if I knew who the rapists were and what happened to them, like all those women I met in D.C. Maybe that's a false assumption."

"Go on," Mary said.

"Maybe this pursuit of mine is stupid and says more about my need to look inside myself than it does about some magical path to peace of mind. Maybe I need to focus my efforts on thinking *less* about all this."

"I don't think just telling yourself to think less about it will work," Mary said.

I ignored her. "A lot of them told me how great it was to see someone functioning as well as I was—working in my field, raising a family, stuff like that. They thought I was the one doing so well, and yet I've been envying them and the closure I imagine they now have." I couldn't catch my breath; a dribble of coffee spilled onto my sweatpants.

Mary nodded. "How about we give it some time? That meeting was a really big deal. Let's absorb it a little and deal with our feelings for now."

"Sure, okay."

"Whatever we decide, you have to stay in touch with those women, the other survivors. It really helps people feel less alone just having a peer group," she said. I thought about them—Helena, Natasha, Debbie, Yvonne, Lavinia, Amy, Julie, Joanie, Susan, Carol, Meaghan, and the rest. I could write to them anytime I

needed to feel understood in a particular way. We thought about
each other; we acknowledged anniversary months. We encouraged
one another's work. Sometimes, a text was as simple as "I'm thinking of you," or "You've been a little out of touch, I hope all is well."
Having them in my life made me feel less damaged—my reactions
similar to theirs, a normal response to abnormal events. I found
them to be bold and kind and caring people who had suffered an
event that fundamentally changed them. Even when we lost touch
for months at a time, they were a lifeline.

Mary continued. "You always have us, and we love you to
pieces, but having people who truly understand what you went
through and why it still hurts is helpful. And you all are doing
the best you can. Whatever happens next, you need them and
they need you, too. Why don't you let them know what happened?"

"I already did. I sent an email letting them know about the
meeting at the unit. They wanted to know, so I told them," I said.
"And I've already heard back from most of them."

"And?"

I started to cry, not the kind where you slowly well up but the
kind of guttural roar that follows devastating news so shocking
that your feelings need time to catch up with your brain. Without
a word, Mary picked up Wrigley—the younger of our two dogs,
who always seemed to know when someone in our family needed
comfort—and placed her in my lap. She nestled in, and I hugged
her round middle. "I'm just so tired" were the only words I could
say for a good long while.

Then, finally: "They said they were sorry and sent me all kinds
of love. A few said I should call if I want to talk."

"Do you?"

I cried some more. "I have no idea, but I have no doubt they'll
be on the other end of the phone if I need them."

—

I spent a long while considering Sam's offer to test the sheet. Every time the phrase "bloody sheet" entered my brain, I felt a zing and a lurch. The fact of its existence stung. An object from that night had survived and held the experience of the attack in a particular way. I had spilled my blood on it; two strangers had lain next to me on top of it; it held me when I thought I was about to take my last breath. That sheet held every secret and memory of that night; its sight had not been robbed.

If I decided to have it tested, I'd have to say the words aloud a few more times. *Bloody sheet, bloody sheet, bloody sheet, bloody sheet.* There was a thing in the world associated with me called bloody sheet. I wanted common, everyday thoughts to replace the ugliness: whether there was a good sale at the garden store, whether Mary and I would follow through on our goal of a daily two-mile walk. I considered getting out my kids' chalkboard and writing the words a few hundred times, like a student punished for talking in class. Maybe the repeated exposure would ease my fast-beating heart and allow me to follow up with the detective.

"Call me when you're ready," Detective Thomas had said. "It's not going anywhere."

While trying to decide what to do, I found myself sitting in one of the country's premier DNA labs, invited by nonprofits needing survivors' voices to help advance their efforts on rape-kit testing. Geillo Labs is located in a Maryland suburb, about an hour's drive from Washington, D.C., tucked into an office park off the highway. We were there to learn more about the power of DNA in solving sex crimes. I agreed to go because I wanted to see my friends and thought some additional advocacy efforts could help take away the sting I felt after learning about my case. I still wanted to help publicize the problems of untested rape evidence, but I'd started having so many questions. Who paid for our trip, hotel room, and dinner last night, and what was their investment in the work we did? The more we advocated for legislation requiring more rape kits to be tested, the busier already overwhelmed state crime labs would be, maybe outsourcing the work to private labs. It didn't necessarily mean they had malevolent intentions, but I found myself increasingly wondering what everyone's motives were. There were those who did crime victim advocacy for a living and those who profited from the change in rape kit–testing policies. There were politicians patting themselves on the back for reauthorizing legislation that released funds to enable law enforcement to respond more effectively to sex crime complaints. And then there were the rape survivors, the folks who had words like "kidnapping," "torture," "knives," "sodomy," "statute of limitations," "rape kits," "parole hearings," and "bloody sheets" taking up space in our psyches. I had begun noticing that our roles were often limited to telling our "stories" instead of being more seriously involved in the work of change.

Once again, the people who organized the event thanked us and told us how much they needed us in this important work.

"You are all so amazing," one of them said at the start of the day.

"It's an honor to have you here," said another.

We were sitting in a semicircle in front of a large screen, and soon we would be going on a tour of the facility. Later, a TV reporter would coach us on packaging our stories for maximum effectiveness. By now, I felt sure that this endeavor attended to a symptom rather than the underlying cause of the problem, but I was unwilling to walk away. Something kept me there, and I thought I'd figure out what that might be by continuing to participate.

"Before we start," an organizer said, "can we introduce ourselves and say a bit about why you're here?"

My stomach sank. I should have spoken to someone beforehand about this inevitability. Once people shared—even if I already knew their stories—my head felt like it had been pushed underwater. I looked around the room at each of the participants, trying to convey with my eyes that they were so much more to me than their trauma.

What tiny human detail could I remember about each of them? The woman on my left was from Ohio, three hours from where I grew up. I had met the woman on my right at a Los Angeles focus group, and she'd apologized to me when I saw her smoking a cigarette during a break. Another woman loved dogs and filled her social media pages with them. We were not defined by what had happened to us, though it sat with all of us still, and I refused to only see these lovely people through that lens.

We began going around the table. By now, every one of us had become accustomed to brevity, winnowing down extreme terror and violence into a few sentences. Brevity, it turned out, was no less devastating.

We were scheduled to take a tour of the facility after lunch. As we waited in the hallway for our guide, I noticed framed news clippings on the walls, each touting a DNA "success." They described infamous murders and rapes that had remained unsolved for decades—and then an eyelash or fingernail found in evidence was tested, and the perpetrator identified. DNA could, apparently, perform miracles. The framed stories proved it.

"Do you test items from police departments in other states?" I asked our guide.

"Yes, if they request it."

And in that moment I decided to call Detective Thomas when I returned to Boston and see if he could send the sheet to Geillo. I didn't want the Boston crime lab involved, and Geillo, I'd just learned, was one of the best in the country.

Sam coordinated sending the sheet off with a woman named Ilse, someone from one of the nonprofits addressing rape-kit reform whom I had come to trust. She thought it would take at least two months before we'd hear anything. "It goes into a queue at the lab; eight weeks is an approximation."

"What's two more months after two-plus decades?" I replied.

"Call me sooner if you just want to talk. It can be brutal balancing hope with the very real possibility of disappointment."

"I get that it's a long shot."

"Understood," she said. "But I've seen miracles with DNA testing. There's no harm in hoping."

I wasn't so sure about that.

I sent a text to Ilse after three months. "Just checking in," I wrote, trying to sound casual.

She replied, "I was about to write. Sam and I just got off the phone. Can you talk in an hour?"

"I'm free then, but can you at least give me a hint?" My phone rang.

"It's not good news; I'm so sorry," Ilse said. "They recovered only one person's DNA on the sheet, and since we know the blood is yours, there's nothing more to test." There was no next step; there would never be a way to identify the men who had hurt me.

"Your story is no less important than anyone else's." Ilse sounded emphatic. "There are hundreds of thousands of victims out there who wonder why they never heard more about their cases and whose cases will never be solved. You're a voice for them, a powerful one. Whether you know it or not, your insistence on accountability already shows how much you've healed. I promise you, that's true." I wanted to hug her across the phone line, grateful for the crumb of hope her words offered.

"And one last thing, my friend. Your persistence is not erased or your value determined because your rape kit was lost and there was no DNA on that stupid, stupid sheet."

If I were honest, I still wanted an ending. I wasn't sure how not to want one. But she was right. Taking some action felt better than despairing if those were the only two choices left. A few days later, I searched for the email address of Yvonne Abraham, my favorite columnist at *The Boston Globe*. She and I had spoken a couple of years back, when she was writing a story about the "backlog" at the state crime lab.

"I have some information to share with you," my note started. "I've reached a dead end in my case and want to get it out there for others who feel forgotten, too."

Yvonne responded within the hour. "Are you free later this afternoon?"

And before I had much time to think about it, I said, "Sure."

We met in my office after work and talked awhile to get comfortable with each other. "Tell me your story," she finally said, placing a small recorder on the table. And I did.

A few days later, the article appeared on the front page of the Sunday *Boston Globe* Metro section, accompanied by a picture of me over the lede with the title, "After Night of Terror, and Years of Anguish, She Finds Meaning."[5] Yvonne had pared the issue down to its essence: "There are thousands of women like her, victims of crimes that were minimized, or forgotten. They submitted themselves to examinations in the hours after their rapes because they wanted to help police find their attackers. Their investigations went nowhere, sometimes because their rape kits were allowed to languish for lack of will or funding. It's still happening."

I heard from dozens of people who thanked me for sharing my story and, often, then shared their own. Someone felt less alone; someone felt their anger or pain could now be spoken. What I'd previously experienced only as a disaster—a bomb that had gone off that then impacted the rest of my life with no discernible meaning or respite—shifted. The meaning for me went beyond victims feeling "seen." Through the many years I'd spent seeking answers about my case—desperate to understand this calamity—I found the resolve to address more broadly the pervasive neglect of sex crimes. The injustice of ignoring rape evidence, not investigating complaints, shaming victims who come forward, and minimizing the impact of sexual violence continued and needed redress. The type of societal change needed wouldn't be fixed by highlighting one individual victim's experience of disregard, but the fact that it is happening still and tolerated still—that's where I would find meaning.

My frame shifted slowly, moving not because of an epiphany but a low simmer as I considered two distinct questions: Why had I believed "solving" my attack would lead to individual healing, and what is the value of personal justice if not tied to systemic change?

Before I could think further about where I wanted to put my energy next, given that all hope of personal closure had been dashed, I'd be tempted to find closure one final time.

—

It was a normal night at home and Mary had just gone to bed. My phone buzzed from a text sent by a work colleague.

"I want to tell you something but don't want to upset you," it said. This text couldn't wait till morning.

"Tell me," I responded, thinking she was giving her notice at work.

"Have you seen the story in the *Globe* about the arrest at the homeless shelter this week?"

"No."

"There was a man arrested for breaking into an apartment in Boston and raping two women. What he did to the victims then seems eerily like what happened to you. I'm sorry, but I thought you'd want to know."

"Send me the link and thank you!"

It appeared moments later. "More than three decades ago, R. B. broke into an apartment in Roxbury, gagged and blindfolded a woman in her bedroom, and raped her twice, court records show. The brutal attack sent him to prison for more than 20 years."[6]

The article then described the most recent attack for which he was arrested.

Two women in the apartment were blindfolded—check.

They were bound, hands and feet together—check.

They were gagged—check.

They were raped repeatedly—check.

My heart pounded. This man was arrested a few months after my attack and later convicted. The timing worked; the details of the attack were almost the same. How many people in the mid-1980s in Boston were breaking into apartments and blindfolding, binding, and gagging their victims?

I texted Detective Thomas and forwarded him the link.

He responded within seconds.

"I was there when he was arrested. I haven't been able to stop thinking about you. I'm in the middle of something now, so let's talk in a day or two. I might have more information by then."

I woke up Mary. "Listen to this," I said.

Two hours later, wrapped in each other's arms, we fell asleep. Telling her made it seem more real, and I had completely forgotten all about my new resolve to create a larger meaning out of my experience, caught up in this new possibility.

—

I called Sam a few days later. "What if I decide it's him right now, just because I want to?" I pressed the phone to my ear. He was outside somewhere.

"The case from 1985 sounds a lot like yours, and so does the one we got him on last week." He sighed. "What kind of bastard would do the same thing again after spending all that time in prison?"

"Would it help if I went over the details of my case with you again, like things the men said to me?" Detective Thomas didn't respond. "They introduced themselves. I'm sure their names were fake—Mike and Dave. But what if this guy used one of these same names this time?"

"I need time to do the work here."

"Maybe I've watched too many crime shows, but I have this idea that you can get him to confess by offering him a better cell or something."

"Let's talk in a few days," he repeated.

I thought about my first meeting with Detective Thomas a year ago and all the questions that day left behind. "Okay, but in the meantime, I'm just going to try on what it feels like imagining it's him."

I thought he hung up. But then he said, "It's not just you who's feeling there's some hope here. We need to take a good look at this guy, and we will."

Sam and I went back and forth about getting together. I kept having the feeling I was forgetting to do something. I'd look over the chores I'd written down for Mary and me, hoping they'd prompt my memory.

Do budget, send sister birthday card, return library books.

"Have you set up a time with Sam yet?" Mary asked. "I need to make sure I get it in my schedule."

I ran over to the kitchen island and added *Call Sam and I mean it* to the bottom of the list. "I think I'm scared he's going to have some little piece of information that makes us rule out this guy and I've been so happy imagining it's him I'm not sure I want to go at all."

"I understand," she said. "We don't need to do this. We can just leave it alone . . . or not. I'll do whatever you want."

Later that day, I wrote to Sam and made a date.

—

I took the day off; our appointment was at 1 P.M. Mary returned home from work late, and we had just enough time to make it into Boston if there was no traffic.

"Can I eat first?" she asked, holding a piece of Tupperware with last night's dinner.

"I'll drive and you can eat in the car." I grabbed the keys and headed out.

I raced through yellow lights, passing Fenway Park and Boston University in a blur. "I'm surprised more students don't get hit by cars around here," I said, almost hitting a few who darted out into traffic trying to catch the T.

"Maybe I should drive," Mary said.

"No, it's right ahead." Sam was waiting for us and handed Mary a pass for our dashboard.

"Welcome, ladies," he said, gathering me to him in a bear hug. He was wearing a button-down shirt and tie with his gun strapped onto his waist, and I did my best not to touch it when we embraced. He released me and reached for Mary, who had her hand out for a handshake, no hug.

"Hello, Sam," she said.

We followed him through the now-familiar locked doors and

hallways, and he motioned us into his office. "Wait a minute. Let me get your liaison," he said. He shepherded a silent woman into his office, who was wearing tan jeans and a T-shirt. Sam offered no explanation of her role as she sat down.

Here's what I thought would happen.

"Okay, let's go through this step by step," Sam would utter. He would say he compared the recent case to the one in 1985, for which R. B. had been convicted. The way the victims were disabled was so parallel—blindfold, weapon, scarf, hands and feet bound together—he was certain this had to be the guy.

He would have the report from the most recent arrest and read me the things this man had said to other victims, and there'd be an uncanny similarity.

"I won't kill you; I just need the money. You know, it's the economy."

"My name's Mike" or "My name's Dave."

It's not like there are hundreds of people at a time in one city breaking into apartments and raping women with a particular signature pattern that reemerges soon after being released from prison. There would be some additional detective work needed, but soon he'd utter words I never thought I'd hear: "We got him!" Bloody sheet, lost rape kit, disgruntled detective be damned.

Or maybe Detective Thomas had already interviewed him and used the strategy I'd seen in a thousand crime show interrogations. "Listen, pal, you're going away for a long time. I'm interested in what you know about the break-ins in Boston a few months before you were arrested in 1985. If you can tell me what you know, I'll tell the judge you cooperated. What do you say?"

I think some part of me knew that my quest for a storybook ending was bound to disappoint. I had driven wildly through traffic, almost hitting a few college students along the way, because I hoped—for the very last time—that the TV-crime-show fantasy

I concocted was about to become real. There would be justice, a conclusion, a period to mark the end of my story instead of an irascible question mark.

Instead, he said the following.

"I don't feel quite as confident that this is the guy as I did when we first talked. There are a few things I'm not sure fit."

And, "We don't technically have what people call a cold case division; I wish we did. As it is, we're flat out on current investigations."

The energy in the room fizzled. In the end, Mary and I asked for a couple of things. They had taken fingerprints from my house; I wanted them to try to locate them and see if they matched R. B.'s. I also wanted to know if Sam would interview R. B. "Maybe he'd admit it." I did my imitation of a crime show detective yet again. "You know, you go in and promise him some privileges. You ask if he's willing to help you out."

Sam didn't think the latter request plausible. "That's not what happens; it's never in their best interest. Prison hardens people; he wouldn't care about helping you."

I signaled to Mary we were leaving. "It's not my fault the case is cold—or old, for that matter. That detective never turned my case over to the sexual assault unit and left evidence in his locker. I'm asking you to do a couple of final things and then we're done."

"I just didn't want you to have false hope," he said.

"Sam, I think by now it's safe to assume I don't have much hope at all."

Mary and I got in the car. This time, she drove.

———

Weeks later, Sam and I spoke again, but it was clear that things were going nowhere.

"I want to make sure I didn't miss anything," he said, asking me to repeat my list.

"Compare the fingerprints."

"See if anything the guy said to the victims matches what my attackers said to me."

"Compare what he did in 1985 to what my attackers did—the details, the specifics."

"Find out if you can meet with him."

I hung up the phone and sat for a good long while. I considered whether the department had done enough on my behalf or could ever make up for the detective's behavior so many years ago. But I had moved on. This wasn't how I wanted to spend my time anymore. I would call and leave a message for Sam later, hoping he wouldn't be there to answer the phone—some version of "thank you but never mind."

I didn't want to hear him say my decision made sense. I didn't want his approval or for him to weigh in at all.

The search for something external to give me peace was over, and ironically giving up the hunt helped me begin to find my way toward it. That big-haired girl from Brandeis was sick of lying dormant. That very day, she rumbled from a place deep inside me and grabbed my hand. "Let's get to work," she said, her voice gentle yet resolute.

—

Embrace your life fully, the one almost robbed from you. These were the words beckoning to me for weeks after saying goodbye to Detective Thomas. The *how* still eluded me, but I felt its insistence as an itch, increasingly uncomfortable and impossible to ignore. Even after deciding to discontinue the investigation with the Boston Police Department, I still needed to find a path forward—a way to integrate this experience with an intellectual understanding of the systemic dismissal of rape and failure to take it seriously. In that state between awareness and action, while trying to gain my strength back after two failed efforts to close my case, I grabbed snippets of meaning from the past and sharpened my resolve.

Mary had gone out for a long walk with our new puppy to try and wear him out. I stayed home to nap. As I began to let sleep blanket me, a memory emerged of a time when our tiny family took a vacation. My children's need to have me present shook me out of the distance I often created when overwhelmed by trauma.

"Mom, you promised you'd go in the water with us." Becca sits on my lap in her soaking-wet bathing suit. Her pink-and-green beach towel lay on the floor next to her feet, heavy with lake water and sand. My shorts absorb the lukewarm water dripping from her suit, and I try to keep my shirt dry by holding my arms up across my chest as she presses her back into me. At the time, she is eight years old and sixty pounds of solid muscle. I am no match for her strength or determination.

"Please, Michy, you're already wet now, and you said you'd play in the water with us on this trip." Becca jumps up, hoping I'll be uncomfortable in my wet clothes and have to change.

"Go put your suit on while I have a snack," she says, her eyes twinkling. "Don't worry; we'll keep a good eye on you. The water isn't over your head until way past the dock. Ben and I will be with you the whole time, and we know what we're doing."

I stand up, trying not to drip water on the Astroturf carpet that covers the bottom level of the lake house we're renting for a week in New Hampshire. It's day 3 of our late-August vacation, and Becca hopes for more than my day 1 dip in the water up to my ankles, and my day 2 ride on a blow-up raft wearing a life jacket

and yelling multiple times, "Don't rock the boat so much!" This
does not qualify in her mind as keeping my promise to get in the
water.

"Okay, I admit I said I'd go in the water; I didn't say I'd try
swimming. Would a canoe ride do?"

Becca puts her hands on her hips. "Why didn't you learn how
to swim when you were little like we did?"

"That's a really good question." I stall. "Did I ever tell you my
dad was a lifeguard?"

Now Ben is interested. He looks up from *Robinson Crusoe,*
a book from his summer reading list. "Your dad was a lifeguard?
He must not have been a very good one if he couldn't teach his
own kid to swim."

"Remember I told you he died when I was seven and I hadn't
learned yet? My mom didn't know how to swim, so she couldn't
teach me and that was that."

"We've been swimming since we were two years old. Why
didn't you learn before he died? Did you try and just sink like a
stone?" I look at his lanky preadolescent body. He reminds me of
a Great Dane puppy, his arms and legs growing so fast he doesn't
know what to do with them.

"We lived in Chicago. The only time we were near water was
when we went to the community pool, and we didn't do that very
often."

"Go put on your suit already and we'll wait for you outside."

"Okay, but don't go in the water unless Mary or I are down
there with you." I bluster. "That's the rule. You have to have a
grown-up with you."

"What are you going to do? You couldn't save us anyway. We'd
have to save you saving us," Ben says. "I think the rule should be
that *you* can't go in the water unless one of *us* is there."

I walk upstairs, feeling like I'm heading to my own execution. It's my dearest wish for my children to see me as someone who makes an effort not to let her fears get the best of her, but this feels like more than I can do. I pull the one-piece suit on and sit on the side of the bed, trying to collect myself. Do they know what a hard time I'm having? Do they ask Mary when I'm not around what's wrong with me, or is it possible they can't tell how jangled my nerves are? It seems to me they go to her more often these days—for both fun and comfort. I'm so ashamed about the anxiety that washes over me and feel helpless when it does.

"I can do this," I whisper.

"Come on, Mom, hurry up!" I hear them both shouting from the small sandy beach. "We know you're up there."

I look out the window and see them playing in the sand, staying out of the water as instructed, and my heart flutters.

"I'm on my way!" I shout back, zipping up my life jacket.

The afternoon in the water goes better than I expected. Becca uncovers a blow-up tire near the dock, and I plop myself down inside it. We agree they can push me in it as long as we stay in the shallow end—which goes on for a mile as long as we stay near the shoreline. Becca suggests a game so we can take turns in the tire: I spy with my little eye. The tire sitter names a color of a secret item, whoever guesses the right object gets a turn being spun, and then they spy something with their little eye. I prefer being the one spinning the tire rather than the one in it, so I make my clues super easy, saying I spy something blue while staring straight up at the sky. Still, we manage an afternoon of delight with some glorious memories made, and I survive the effort. I even suggest a repeat the next day, rushing down ahead of both kids with my life jacket in hand.

This memory danced in my mind as sleep found me. *Hold on*

to those memories; hold them tight, I repeated, reassured to be reminded that love and joy sat somewhere deep inside my body, waiting to be elevated into the light. Somehow, I understood this was the foundation for my way forward.

I grabbed hold.

Part III

A Manifesto

*When we speak we are afraid
our words will not be heard
nor welcomed.*

*But when we are silent
we are still afraid*

So it is better to speak.

—AUDRE LORDE

It's hard not to crave an ending—to my story, to the many unfinished stories of rape victims everywhere who are too often dismissed, blamed, and outright ignored.

After the last meeting with Detective Thomas, Mary and I ate ice cream cones on a stoop in Chestnut Hill, unable to speak. I had mint chip; she had pistachio. My conversation with him consisted of a stream of words I didn't want controlling my life anymore: semen, cold cases, sorry, really sorry, burnt-out detective, hard job, PTSD, rape, prison, weapons, rape, rapists, evidence, sorry, really sorry, brave girl, bloody sheet, rape kit, I'll get back to you, complicated, sorry, really sorry, not sure, not easy, not a slam dunk, rapists, knife, phone cord, prosecution, poor girl.

I was done with all that.

Somewhere along the way, in my effort to find closure, I'd lost track of one of my core tenets: sustained change takes time and persistence and is never only about one person. I began telling my story by asking a question. Can we really say that rape is a crime given the way this felony is addressed by law enforcement, politicians, and the larger world? For many intractable social and political issues, progress gets measured by whether things are slightly less bad than they once were. Unfortunately, sex crimes are still placed in that category. Slight improvements to issues that never should have been tolerated are celebrated, and the deeper and pervasive issues remain barely touched.

Spousal rape is illegal! Parental rights for rapists have been mostly terminated! Some men in positions of power whose sexually abusive behavior was an open secret for years are finally being exposed! Each of these pronouncements carries beneath it devastating and lasting harm to victims caused by behavior tolerated over years. Their effects persist. They cannot be erased. The fact that these conditions existed at all and for so long is a tragedy and an outrage.

How many more books will need to be written by victims of sex crimes describing devastating violence, the minimization that followed, and the impact both experiences have had on their lives? How many more public hearings will we see in our lifetimes where credible, poised, and highly respected persons like Professor Anita Hill and Dr. Christine Blasey Ford are pummeled in public and then subjected to death threats for daring to speak out about their experiences of sexual violation at the hands of powerful men? How many more judges will make "unfortunate" comments about rape victims' culpability as a way to justify ignoring sentencing guidelines? How many more times will dozens of women have to accuse the same famous man of assault before anyone takes even one of them seriously? How many more cities will announce they "discovered" a "backlog" of untested rape kits?

We have to do better than this. We can't be satisfied with celebrating small shifts that have done little to change either society's view of sex crimes or how they are addressed in multiple arenas.

While the "me too" movement has garnered a great deal of attention and a few newsmen, actors, celebrity chefs, comedians, and CEOs have lost their jobs as a result, we see backlash already—a common theme when pushing against norms that protect those in power. A recent article in *Forbes* reported that in some business environments women are less likely to be hired for jobs where they are required to interact with men in one-on-one situations and that "attractive women" are especially impacted by this hiring bias.[1]

The forty-fifth president of the United States, someone himself accused of sexual assault by over a dozen women, said, "It's a very scary time for young men in America when you can be found guilty of something that you may not be guilty of."[2] Given that estimates of false reporting are 2–8 percent, that the vast majority of rapes go unreported, and that those that are reported rarely go to trial or result in conviction, the idea that there is an epidemic of men being falsely accused of and found responsible for sexual assault is simply inaccurate. This statement asks us to give equal weight to the exceedingly rare experience of being falsely accused and the experience of life-altering trauma exacerbated by minimization at almost every level of society. We should pay close attention to which consequences and whose experiences get noticed, spoken of, and attended to.

Even when a man is found guilty of rape or sexual assault, it is often his experience that becomes the focus rather than the victim's. In 2012 a young girl in Steubenville, Ohio, was raped at a party, and video footage taken. The two boys who perpetrated the attack were convicted in juvenile court. A CNN reporter covering the sentencing said on-air, "I've never experienced anything like it; it's incredibly emotional . . . these two young men, with promising futures, star football players, 'A' students, literally watched as their lives fell apart."[3] In order to avoid "ruining" a young man's life, rape is often framed as a "mistake," "youthful transgression," or miscommunication rather than as an intentional, violent act. What is too often articulated in the public sphere is the tragedy befalling the perpetrator, while victims and the consequences they suffer are rendered invisible.

If rape is perceived as a shared tragedy rather than a crime of violence, then victims are seen as having a role in a mutual experience. A judge in Montana gave a high school teacher who had raped a freshman student a multiyear sentence and then required only thirty-one days be served, declaring that the victim looked older than her years and was "probably as much in control of the situation as was the defendant."[4] How is it even possible that someone adjudicating a rape case can believe and feel comfortable articulating that a teenager is culpable for her own rape by an adult—and a teacher, no less?

A bus driver was given a multiyear probation but no jail time after being convicted of the third-degree rape of a fourteen-year-old because, as the judge noted, the driver "had no prior arrests and only one victim."[5] How many more victims would there need to be before he would be held accountable? Across the ocean in Ireland, a twenty-seven-year-old man was acquitted by a jury because the seventeen-year-old victim wore thong underwear when attacked in an alleyway.[6] Apparently, the jury was swayed that what one puts on in the privacy of her home excuses a man of an attack begun before he had any idea of what underwear she was wearing, as if this has any relevance whatsoever.

A judge from New Jersey declined to prosecute a sixteen-year-old male as an adult for raping a young woman, taping it, and referring to his actions as rape in text messages to friends because he "comes from a good family" and will most likely go to a "good college."[7] Whether one believes it is appropriate to try a juvenile as an adult—I do not—the judge's reasoning showed that privilege all too often impacts decisions in court. The judge also commented on the young man's text messages as "just a 16-year-old boy saying stupid crap to his friends." Because of this case and several others, the Supreme Court of New Jersey announced that they would require statewide training for judges hearing sexual assault cases.[8]

—

So, no, Detective Thomas, I don't believe that things are different now and rape survivors are getting the treatment they deserve. In fact, they seem to have gotten worse, because now we have the technology at our fingertips, and we still do not investigate sexual assault or treat victims as we should. Sex crimes are still uniquely minimized, the focus staying on whether the victim is lying, is seductive, is mistaken, is making a big deal out of nothing. There remains no other felony crime where a victim must first pass a test of veracity and legitimacy before her complaint will proceed—and, too often in our current world, she will fail that test.

—

Many of us are experiencing outrage fatigue as one story of sexual assault after another bombard us, attended by shameless denial of the gravity of the crimes and no meaningful solution. Another "me too" case, another story about how old rape kits reveal serial perpetrators matched on cold cases, another report about police who don't investigate crimes of rape, another city where the percent of reported rapes deemed unfounded exceeds national norms, another victim being told she might be charged with filing a false report, another victim suing because her case could have been solved but no one investigated, another politician saying they care about rape victims and making empty promises about laws they will fight for to create needed reforms.

Until we collectively raise our voices, little of significance will change. We must move beyond the celebration of one or two data points that show some things are improving incrementally while that progress is thwarted by backlash and legislation designed to undo advancements. Justice should be based not on who is in power but on fair laws that grant equal protection. We should all heed the lessons of those writing about rape culture in the 1970s, then again in the 1990s, and once again in the present day. Naming the systemic misogyny that has allowed rape to be treated like it doesn't matter, isn't real, and doesn't deserve equal treatment under the law is not enough. We must speak up and call out the neglect.

Early in my graduate education, a professor told a story that illustrates how the chaos resulting from a crisis often prevents us from understanding the root cause of the problem and developing strategies that bring about effective change: A man is walking through a meadow and hears someone crying for help. He runs to where he hears the noise and sees that someone has fallen into a raging river. He rescues the person, and by the time they both reach the shore, exhausted and terrified, he hears another call for help. Someone else has fallen in. All day long, he rescues one person after the next. In fact, he is so busy rescuing these individuals that he never has time to see that the bridge nearby is broken. If we have any chance of changing the way sex crimes are addressed and the "rape culture" that allows such disregard to continue unabated, we must fix the bridge.

The broken bridge is societal tolerance of violence against women; it is complacency for data that shows rape is investigated and prosecuted at shockingly low rates and results in almost no convictions, even when cases do go to trial; it is the absence of awareness that rape evidence sat for decades untouched in cities around the country until a massive effort to uncover this neglect led to some reforms; it is politicians who minimize rape, comedians and their audiences who laugh at rape, entire industries where sexual harassment and assault were hidden secrets and perpetrators' careers thrived. It is all this and so much more.

—

And then there are the survivors.

To them, I say: Your case may not have been investigated. You may have told no one. Your life may have been destabilized by this violent crime, potentially impacting your ability to hold down a job, have a healthy relationship, and take care of yourself on a basic level. And everywhere around you there are repeated reminders that what you went through, your experience of violence and its aftermath, matters to no one.

While none of us can escape our experiences, we do have a little more control over the meaning we assign to them and the choices we make as a result. And this is my attempt to do just that—make meaning and address what can no longer be tolerated.

The crimes perpetrated against you were real and they were, in fact, crimes.

The impact they had on you says nothing about you and your emotional "shortcomings."

There are voices out there who are working as hard as they can to counteract those who minimize rape and rape survivors' experiences.

My case was never investigated and never solved. I am like so many of you. What happened to me was not extraordinary. In fact, it is unbearably common, an ordinary tale of violence and terror

that left a deep impact on me, and yet seemed of little import
to those assigned to investigate. I will spend the rest of my life
working to change this reality and I invite you along—if you can,
in whatever way you can, when and if you feel ready.

To repeat my spouse's wisdom on a day I felt despairing, "You
aren't crazy; what happened to you is crazy." We needn't blame
ourselves for a normal reaction to terror when a memory comes
flooding back. We are not our rape stories; they are one part of a
rich life that may still offer the possibility for joy.

More and more of us refuse to have our experiences minimized and silenced.

And we are raising our voices and demanding change.

Note

This book spans almost thirty-five years' time. In many instances, I have confirmed my memory of events and conversations with friends, loved ones, and colleagues.

While I did my best to recall events in this book as they occurred and believe them to be accurate, my memories and perspective are my own. I have changed some names and details and thank all those who see themselves and our shared experiences rendered on the page.

I have survived and thrived because of many of you—too numerous to name.

Acknowledgments

This book took shape over a number of years, and there are so many people to thank. If I have missed anyone, it is not for lack of my deep my appreciation and gratitude.

Thank you so very much to Bryn Clark and Flatiron Books for giving me the opportunity of a lifetime and believing in my work and championing it throughout the entire process. I couldn't have asked for a better thought partner than Bryn, and I am eternally grateful. To Nicki Richesin, who has been a dream agent and worked side by side with me in this process. I offer my deepest gratitude as well to Wendy Sherman Associates, Inc. Literary Management and to Cherise Fisher. Thank you as well to Amelia Possanza, my publicist, for her tremendous work; Elizabeth Catalano, my production editor, and Angela Gibson, my copyeditor, for helping to make this work its best self; and the entire team at Flatiron Books.

Additional thanks to MacDowell Artists Colony and Ragdale for the space and time and delicious food that made possible early drafts of this work and to the many, many wonderful and talented artists I met there.

To the Barbara Deming Foundation for believing in my work and supporting it and for all the work they have supported over decades as the oldest feminist granting agency in the United States.

To Boston's amazing GrubStreet for offering a program like the Memoir Incubator for emerging writers and to instructor and mentor Alex Marzano-Lesnevich, whose talent is endless and who never stopped believing in my book and the various projects of all their students.

To my mentors: Alison Smith, who read and gave comments on an early draft of my manuscript and continued on as a friend and a writer of many recommendations; Honor Moore, who reminded me clichés don't make for good writing and who shared afternoon tea and chocolates at Ragdale, sharing wonderful stories, great wisdom, and friendship; and to Priscilla Cutler Bourgoine, who met with me regularly during the Memoir Incubator year for conversation and support.

To Emmy Novick for being my first writing teacher, lifelong friend, and honorary big sister. To Steve Goldstein for being my dear friend and, along with Emmy, providing me a home when I needed it most.

To the entire Memoir Incubator class, including Gita Brown, Alicia Googins, Ananda Lowe, Jay Moskowitz, Gail Nastasia, Catherine O'Neil, Kristen Paulson-Nguyen, Lara Pelligrinelli, and Mike Sinert. Never stop believing in your talent, as I am in awe of all of you. Various classes of Memoir Incubator students over the last several years have produced incredible published essays, have many forthcoming books, and have begun a nonfiction live-reading series in Boston. Thank you all for your support and encouragement in seeing this book take shape.

To colleagues who confirmed the research component of my

memoir: David Hemenway, Lisa LaChance, Peggy Barrett, Janet Yassen, and Karlo Ng.

To the many dear friends who read drafts or listened to sections and encouraged me throughout: Lise Brody, Julie Reuben, Lisa Lovett, Julie Ross, Regina Corrao, Vanessa Britto, Stacey Sperling, Laura Gillenwater, Marcia Hubelbank, Catherine Guthrie, Amy Mann, Janet Sullivan, Theresa and Tim Garvin, Beth and Maryanne Ludwig, Susan Mahoney, Grace Talusan, Alysia Abbott, Madeleine Rossi, Susan and Cathy Gorman, and Norma Gorman. Thank you also to the many friends of my children who have been so enthusiastic as this book has evolved.

To Alonso Nichols for taking my photo and for being such a kind friend.

To Hannah Kent for providing outstanding assistance with my references.

Thank you to the friends and colleagues I met doing advocacy work—Meaghan Ybos, Julie Diehl Weil, Carol Bart, Helena Lazaro, Robert and Debbie Smith, Amy Roberts, Joanie Scheske, Carol Dillard, Natasha Alexenko, Susan Kendrick Schuenemann, Yvonne Pointer, and so many others.

To Becca O'Connor and Ilse Knecht for all their efforts on my behalf.

Thank you to Yvonne Abraham, Nick Kristof, Kevin Rothstein, Karen Anderson, and other journalists who promoted this story.

My deepest gratitude to Anita Hill for honoring the work I do and making me feel like it matters, and for her unwavering example of speaking truth to power.

To my many colleagues at Tufts University for encouraging my writing and my voice as a survivor in the work I do.

To my sister, Judy, Aunt Bar, and the memory of my mother and Aunt Marlene, all of whom I love with all my heart and who love so deeply and whose loyalty to family is unmatched. Thank you to Leah Kent, Kim Miles, Allan Garnick, Jeff Hiller, Denise Hiller-Wehrenberg, and Ellene Hiller-Lammers for their support and love.

And finally to my beautiful family—Mary, Becca, and Ben—for everything I hold dear, and to the many dogs we've loved together as a family. I love you more than I can ever express.

My deepest appreciation to the literary magazines and anthologies that have published earlier versions of some of the pieces reworked in this book: *Left Hooks* literary journal, *Burningword Press*, *Gertrude Press*, *The Anatomy of Silence* (Red Press), and *WORDPEACE*. Your generosity and appreciation of my efforts to create this book mean the world to me.

Notes

INTRODUCTION

1 "What Is Rape Culture?" WAVAW Rape Crisis Centre, Mar. 19, 2019, https://www.wavaw.ca/what-is-rape-culture/.

2 Emilie Buchwald, Pamela R. Fletcher, and Martha Roth, *Transforming a Rape Culture* (Minneapolis: Milkweed Editions, 2005), preamble, xi.

3 See, for example, Roxane Gay, ed., *Not That Bad: Dispatches from Rape Culture* (New York: Atlantic Books, 2018); James Hitchings-Hales, "Emma Watson Takes on Rape Culture in Bold Speech to the UN," *Global Citizen*, Sept. 22, 2016, https://www.globalcitizen.org/en/content/emma-watson-rape-culture-heforshe-un/.

4 For more, see Susan Brownmiller, *Against Our Will: Men, Women and Rape* (New York: Random House, 1975); Allie Conti, "A Brief and Depressing History of Rape Laws," *Vice*, Jun. 8, 2016, https://www.vice.com/en_us/article/9bkje5/for-context-heres-how-various-societies-punished-rapists.

5 "Victims of Sexual Violence: Statistics," RAINN, https://www.rainn.org/statistics/victims-sexual-violence. Data taken from the National

Institute of Justice and Centers for Disease Control and Prevention, *Prevalence, Incidence and Consequences of Violence Against Women Survey* (1998). Sexual violence is notoriously difficult to measure, and there is no single source of data that provides a complete picture of the crime. As RAINN states on their website, they "have tried to select the most reliable source of statistics for each topic presented and steer the reader to the original source. The primary data source they use is the National Crime Victimization Survey (NCVS), which is an annual study conducted by the Justice Department."

6   "NISVS: An Overview of 2010 Findings on Victimization by Sexual Orientation," National Intimate Partner and Sexual Violence Survey, CDC, https://www.cdc.gov/violenceprevention/pdf/cdc_nisvs_victimization _final-a.pdf.

7   Asha DuMonthier, Chandra Childers, and Jessica Milli, "The Status of Black Women in the United States," Institute for Women's Policy Research, chapter 6, "Violence and Safety," June 26, 2017.

8   Elizabeth Kennedy, "Victim Race and Rape," Feminist Sexual Ethics Project, Brandeis University, Sept. 26, 2003, https://www.brandeis .edu/projects/fse/slavery/united-states/kennedy.html.

9   Chelsea Hale and Meghan Matt, "The Intersection of Race and Rape Viewed Through the Prism of a Modern-Day Emmett Till," American Bar Association, Jul. 16, 2019, https://www.americanbar .org/groups/litigation/committees/diversity-inclusion/articles/2019 /summer2019-intersection-of-race-and-rape/.

10 Samuel R. Gross, Maurice Possley, and Klara Stephens, *Race and Wrongful Conviction in the United States,* National Registry on Exonerations (Newkirk Center for Science and Society, University of California, Irvine, Mar. 7, 2017), 12–13.

11 Rick Jones and Cornelius Cornelssen, "Coerced Consent: Plea Bargaining, the Trial Penalty, and American Racism," *Federal Sentencing Reporter* 31, no. 4–5 (Apr./Jun. 2019): 265–271.

12 "Highest to Lowest—Prison Population Total," World Prison Brief, http://www.prisonstudies.org/highest-to-lowest/prison-population -total?field_region_taxonomy_tid=All.

13 "The Criminal Justice System: Statistics," RAINN, https://www.rainn
.org/statistics/criminal-justice-system.

14 Department of Justice, Office of Justice Programs, Bureau of Jus-
tice Statistics, National Crime Victimization Survey, 2010–16 (2017);
Federal Bureau of Investigation, National Incident-Based Reporting
System, 2012–16 (2017); Federal Bureau of Investigation, National
Incident-Based Reporting System, 2012–16 (2017); Department of
Justice, Office of Justice Programs, Bureau of Justice Statistics, Felony
Defendants in Large Urban Counties, 2009 (2013). As RAINN's web-
site notes, "This statistic combines information from several federal
government reports. Because it combines data from studies with dif-
ferent methodologies, it is an approximation, not a scientific estimate."

15 Rachel Morgan and Barbara Oudekerk, "Criminal Victimization,
2018," BJS Statistics, U.S. Department of Justice, Sept. 8, 2019,
https://www.bjs.gov/content/pub/pdf/cv18.pdf.

16 Susan Milligan, "Sexual Assault Reports Spike in #MeToo Era," U.S.
News and World Report, Dec. 27, 2018, https://www.usnews.com/news
/national-news/articles/2018-12-27/sexual-assault-reports-spike-in
-metoo-era.

17 Kimberly Lonsway, Joanne Archambault, and David Lisak, "False
Reports: Moving Beyond the Issue to Successfully Investigate and
Prosecute Non-Stranger Sexual Assault," The Voice by the American
Prosecutors Research Institute 3 (2009), 1–11, https://www.nsvrc.org
/sites/default/files/publications/2018-10/Lisak-False-Reports-Moving
-beyond.pdf; David Lisak et al., "False Allegations of Sexual As-
sault: An Analysis of Ten Years of Reported Cases," Violence Against
Women 16, no. 12 (Dec. 2010): 1318–34, http://doi.org/10.1177
/1077801210387747; Melanie Heenan and Suellen Murray, "Study of
Reported Rapes in Victoria, 2000–2003: Summary Research Report,"
Office of Women's Policy, Department for Victorian Communities
(Melbourne, Australia), https://www.secasa.com.au/assets/Statstics
/study-of-reported-rapes-in-victoria-2000-2003.pdf.

18 Bernice Yeung et al., "When It Comes to Rape, Just Because a Case Is
Cleared Doesn't Mean It's Solved," ProPublica, Nov. 15, 2018, https://
www.propublica.org/article/when-it-comes-to-rape-just-because-a
-case-is-cleared-does-not-mean-solved.

19 Cassia Spohn and Katharine Trellis, "Justice Denied?: The Exceptional Clearance of Rapes in Los Angeles County," *Albany Law Review,* Aug. 18, 2011, http://www.albanylawreview.org/Articles/Vol74_3/74.3.1379%20SPOHN.pdf.

20 Lucy Perkins, "Pittsburgh Police Dismiss Nearly One-Third of Rape Cases as 'Unfounded,'" 90.5 WESA, May 15, 2019, https://www.wesa.fm/post/pittsburgh-police-dismiss-nearly-one-third-rape-cases-unfounded#stream/0.

21 Alex Campbell and Katie Baker, "This Police Department Tosses Aside Rape Reports When a Victim Doesn't Resist 'To the Best of Her Ability,'" *Buzzfeed News,* Sept. 8, 2016, https://www.buzzfeednews.com/article/alexcampbell/unfounded.

22 Ken Armstrong and T. Christian Miller, "When Sexual Assault Victims Are Charged with Lying," *New York Times,* Nov. 24, 2017, https://www.nytimes.com/2017/11/24/opinion/sunday/sexual-assault-victims-lying.html.

23 Korin Miller, "Shit Politicians Say . . . About Women's Rights," *Cosmopolitan,* Jun. 24, 2013, https://www.cosmopolitan.com/entertainment/celebs/news/g3309/stupid-things-politicians-say/?slide=20.

24 "Transcript: Donald Trump's Taped Comments About Women," *New York Times,* Oct. 8, 2016, https://www.nytimes.com/2016/10/08/us/donald-trump-tape-transcript.html.

ONE

1 "Parental Rights and Sexual Assault," National Conference of State Legislatures, Jun. 21, 2019, http://www.ncsl.org/research/human-services/parental-rights-and-sexual-assault.aspx.

2 Shauna Prewitt, "Raped, Pregnant and Ordeal Not Over," CNN, Aug. 23, 2012, https://www.cnn.com/2012/08/22/opinion/prewitt-rapist-visitation-rights/index.html.

3 Jessica Ravitz, "The Story Behind the First Rape Kit," CNN, Nov. 21, 2015, https://www.cnn.com/2015/11/20/health/rape-kit-history/index.html.

4 "History and Development of SANE Programs," Office of Justice Programs, Office for Victims of Crime, https://www.ovcttac

.gov/saneguide/introduction/history-and-development-of-sane
-programs/.

5 Brittany Bronson, "Where Are the Rape-Kit Nurses?" *New York Times,* Jun. 20, 2017, https://www.nytimes.com/2017/06/20/opinion /rape-kit-nurses.html.

6 Ellen Goldstein et al., "Medical Students' Perspectives on Trauma-Informed Care Training," *Permanente Journal* 22 (2018): 17–126, http://doi.org/10.7812/TPP/17-126.

7 Molly Siegel et al., "On-the-Go Training: Downloadable Modules to Train Medical Students to Care for Adult Female Sexual Assault Survivors," *MedEd Portal,* Dec. 11, 2017, https://www.mededportal.org /publication/10656/#330656.

8 Monique Tello, "Trauma-Informed Care: What It Is and Why It's Important," *Harvard Health Publishing* blog, Oct. 16, 2018, https:// www.health.harvard.edu/blog/trauma-informed-care-what-it-is-and -why-its-important-2018101613562.

9 "Sexual Assault and the LGBTQ Community," Human Rights Campaign, https://www.hrc.org/resources/sexual-assault-and-the-lgbt -community.

10 "Identifying and Preventing Gender Bias in Law Enforcement Response to Sexual Assault and Domestic Violence," Department of Justice, 7, https://www.justice.gov/crt/file/799316/download.

11 Andrew Van Dam, "Less Than 1% of Rapes Lead to Felony Conviction: At Least 89% of Victims Experience Emotional and Physical Consequences," *Washington Post,* Oct. 6, 2018, https://www .washingtonpost.com/business/2018/10/06/less-than-percent-rapes -lead-felony-convictions-least-percent-victims-face-emotional -physical-consequences/?utm_term=.6ced084fc5a6.

12 Shiloh A. Catanese, "Traumatized by Association: The Risk of Working Sex Crimes," *Federal Probation* 74, no. 2, https://www.uscourts .gov/sites/default/files/74_2_9_0.pdf; "Law Enforcement Officers," National Alliance on Mental Illness, https://www.nami.org/find -support/law-enforcement-officers.

13 John Voilanti, "PTSD Among Police Officers: Impact on Critical De-
    cision Making," *Dispatch* 11, no. 5 (May 2018), https://cops.usdoj.gov
    /html/dispatch/05-2018/PTSD.html.

TWO

1 Joel Epstein and Stacia Langenbahn, "The Criminal Justice and
   Community Response to Rape," National Institute of Justice, U.S.
   Department of Justice, May 1994, https://www.ncjrs.gov/pdffiles1
   /Digitization/148064NCJRS.pdf.

2 Vernon J. Geberth, "30 Years of DNA Technology," *Forensic Magazine,* Mar. 13, 2017, https://www.forensicmag.com/article/2017/03/30
   -years-dna-technology.

3 "Statistics," Center for Family Justice, https://centerforfamilyjustice
   .org/community-education/statistics/.

4 Petula Dvorak, "Millions of Women Understand Christine Blasey
   Ford's Decades of Silence," *Washington Post*, Sept. 20, 2018, https://
   www.washingtonpost.com/local/but-why-did-kavanaughs-accuser
   -wait-37-years-to-say-something/2018/09/20/04118d42-bcdd-11e8
   -be70-52bd11fe18af_story.html.

5 Michele Black et al., "The National Intimate Partner and Sexual Violence
   Survey: 2010 Summary Report," National Center for Injury Prevention
   and Control, Centers for Disease Control and Prevention, Nov. 2011,
   https://www.cdc.gov/ViolencePrevention/pdf/NISVS_Report2010-a.pdf.

6 Martin Beckford, "80% of Women Don't Report Rape or Sexual Assault, Survey Claims," *Telegraph,* Mar. 12, 2012, https://www.telegraph
   .co.uk/news/uknews/crime/9134799/Sexual-assault-survey-80-of
   -women-dont-report-rape-or-sexual-assault-survey-claims.html; Al-
   ana Prochuck, "We Are Here: Women's Experiences of the Barriers
   to Reporting Sexual Assault," West Coast LEAF, Nov. 2018, http://
   www.westcoastleaf.org/wp-content/uploads/2018/10/West-Coast
   -Leaf-dismantling-web-final.pdf.

7 Carolyn Jung, "Sexual Assault Unit Introduced to Help Curb Rape in
   Boston," *Boston Globe*, Jun. 28, 1984.

8 *The Victim's Voice: Sexual Assault Survivor's Stories*, Boston Area
   Rape Crisis Center and the Municipal Police Institute, 2009; video.

THREE

1 "Welcome," Walk a Mile in Her Shoes, http://www.walkamileinhershoes
   .org/.

2 "Take the Pledge," It's on Us, https://www.itsonus.org/.

3 "President Obama's #ItsOnUs Message at the Grammys," YouTube,
   https://www.youtube.com/watch?v=ZAUnjNl7HiA.

4 Nisha Chittal, "Obama Delivers Sexual Assault Message at the Grammys: It Has to Stop," MSNBC, Feb. 8, 2015, http://www.msnbc
   .com/msnbc/obama-grammys-delivers-message-about-sexual
   -assault.

5 Catronia Harvey-Jenner, "Barack Obama Speaks Out Against Rape and
   Domestic Violence in a Video About the Grammys, *Cosmopolitan*,
   Feb. 9, 2015, https://www.cosmopolitan.com/uk/reports/news/a33312
   /barack-obama-grammys-speech-rape-domestic-violence/.

6 Clover Hope, "President Obama Delivers Intense Grammys PSA on
   Domestic Abuse," *Jezebel*, Feb. 8, 2015, https://jezebel.com/president
   -obama-delivers-an-intense-grammys-psa-on-dome-1684590013.

7 Personal communication with Janet Yassen, Oct. 2019.

8 Sarah Snyder, "A Series of Rapes Alarms Allston-Brighton," *Boston
   Globe*, Jun. 26, 1984.

9 Saher Esfandiari, "A Breakdown of Tarof in Iran, and How to Navigate It," Culture Trip, Feb. 2018, https://theculturetrip.com/middle
   -east/iran/articles/breakdown-tarof-iran-navigate/.

FOUR

1 Email from Helena Lazaro to author, Jun, 3, 2019.

2 Email from Lavinia Masters to author, Jul. 21, 2019.

3 Cora Peterson et al., "Lifetime Economic Burden of Rape Among
   U.S. Adults," *American Journal of Preventive Medicine* 52, no. 6
   (Jun. 2017): 691–701, https://doi.org/10.1016/j.amepre.2016.11.014.

4 Rebecca Loya, "Rape as an Economic Crime: The Impact of Sexual Violence on Survivors' Employment and Economic Well-Being,"

Journal of Interpersonal Violence 30, no. 16 (Oct. 2015), https://doi
.org/10.1177/0886260514554291.

5 "Welcome to the National Center for Victims of Crime," National
Center for Victims of Crime, https://victimsofcrime.org/help-for
-crime-victims/get-help-bulletins-for-crime-victims/crime-victim
-compensation.

6 Ashley Fantz, Sergio Hernandez, and Sonam Vashi, "Where Police
Failed Rape Victims," CNN Investigates, Nov. 29, 2018, https://www
.cnn.com/interactive/2018/11/investigates/police-destroyed-rapekits
/springfield.html.

7 Spraya Chemaly, "How Police Still Fail Rape Victims," *Rolling Stone*,
Aug. 16, 2016, https://www.rollingstone.com/culture/culture-features
/how-police-still-fail-rape-victims-97782/.

8 Jennifer Bjorhus, Brandon Stahl, and Maryjo Webster, "Police Overwhelmed and Undertrained," *StarTribune*, Sept. 30, 2018, http://www
.startribune.com/minnesota-police-undertrained-overwhelmed-by
-rape-cases-denied-justice-part-four/488413351/.

9 Application for Crime Victim Compensation, https://www.mass.gov
/files/documents/2019/04/02/application%20for%20web%20040119
.pdf.

10 Judith Herman, *Trauma and Recovery: The Aftermath of Violence—
From Domestic Abuse to Political Terror* (New York: Basic Books,
2015), 7.

11 Ibid. 8.

FIVE

1 Herman, *Trauma and Recovery*, 93.

SIX

1 Michael Planty et al., "Female Victims of Sexual Violence, 1994–2010,"
BJS Statistics, U.S. Department of Justice, Mar. 7, 2013, https://www
.bjs.gov/index.cfm?ty=pbdetail&iid=4594.

2 Interview with Debbie Smith, Jun. 2019.

EIGHT

1 Andrea Estes, "Crime Lab Neglected 16,000 Cases: Evidence Was Never Analyzed, Probe Finds," *Boston Globe,* Jul. 15, 2007, http://archive.boston.com/news/local/articles/2007/07/15/crime_lab_neglected_16000_cases/.

2 Jonathan Saltzman and John Ellement, "Crime Lab Mishandled DNA Results," *Boston Globe,* Jan. 13, 2007, http://archive.boston.com/news/local/articles/2007/01/13/crime_lab_mishandled_dna_results/.

3 John Ellement, "Backlog at Crime Lab Is in Dispute," *Boston Globe,* Jul. 26, 2007, https://www.newspapers.com/newspage/443884859/.

4 "Why Test Rape Kits After the Statute of Limitations Has Expired?" National Center for Victims of Crime, https://victimsofcrime.org/docs/sak-backlog-laws/why-test-expired-kits-victim-centric.pdf?sfvrsn=2.

5 Ruby Gonzales, "Serial Rapist Sentenced to 25 Years for Pico Rivera Attack," *San Gabriel Valley Tribune,* May 25, 2011, https://www.dailybreeze.com/2011/05/25/serial-rapist-sentenced-to-25-years-for-pico-rivera-attack/; Associated Press "Women Express Concern over Police Rape Kit Backlog, *Washington Post,* Mar. 12, 2012, https://www.washingtonpost.com/blogs/crime-scene/post/women-express-concern-over-police-rape-kit-backlogs/2012/03/19/gIQATVRhMS_blog.html.

6 Information about the database can be found at https://www.fbi.gov/services/laboratory/biometric-analysis/codis.

7 Dwight Adams, "Before the Senate Judiciary Committee on Crime and Drugs: Washington, D.C.," FBI Archives, May 14, 2002, https://archives.fbi.gov/archives/news/testimony/the-fbis-codis-program.

8 Brian Ballou, "State Crime Lab Still Behind on DNA Testing—but No Longer Focused on Reducing Backlog," *Boston Globe,* Nov. 27, 2009.

NINE

1 Edwin Chen and Douglas Frantz, "Thomas Denies Sex Harassment, Danforth Says," *Los Angeles Times,* Oct. 7, 1991, https://www.latimes.com/archives/la-xpm-1991-10-07-mn-77-story.html.

2 Derrick Z. Jackson, "Now It's Thomas' Turn to Face the Cameras," *Boston Globe,* Oct. 9, 1991, 19.

3 Walter V. Robinson, "Supporters Rip into Sex Allegations," *Boston Globe,* Oct. 13, 1991, 22.

4 Julia Jacobs, "Anita Hill's Testimony and Other Key Moments from the Clarence Thomas Hearings," *New York Times,* Sept. 20, 2018, https://www.nytimes.com/2018/09/20/us/politics/anita-hill-testimony -clarence-thomas.html.

5 David Brock, *The American Spectator,* Mar. 1992.

6 Anita Hill, *Speaking Truth to Power* (New York: Anchor Books, 1998).

7 Thomas Burr, "Senator Hatch Says Christine Blasey Ford Is 'Mistaken' in Accusing Nominee Brett Kavanaugh of Assault," *Salt Lake Tribune,* Sept. 17, 2018, https://www.sltrib.com/news/politics/2018/09 /17/sen-hatch-says-christine/.

8 Bianca Seidman and Dr. Jonathan Steinman, "Kavanaugh Accuser Christine Blasey Ford Describes Memory Science, Hippocampus in Emotional Senate Testimony," ABC News, Sept. 27, 2018, https:// abcnews.go.com/US/kavanaugh-accuser-christine-blasey-ford -describes-memory-science/story?id=58122 .

9 Andrew Glass, "Senate Confirms Thurgood Marshall, August 30th, 1967," *Politico,* Aug. 30, 2018, https://www.politico.com/story/2018/08 /30/this-day-in-politics-aug-30-1967-797371.

10 "David Hemenway," Harvard T. H. Chan School of Public Health, https://www.hsph.harvard.edu/david-hemenway/.

11 "Violence Against Women: Relevance for Medical Practitioners," *Journal of the American Medical Association,* 267, no. 23 (1992): 3184–89, https://www.safetylit.org/citations/index.php?fuseaction =citations.viewdetails&citationIds[]=citjournalarticle_74010_2; Angela Browne, "Violence Against Women by Male Partners: Prevalence, Outcomes, and Policy Implications," *American Psychologist* 48, no. 10 (Oct. 1993): 1077–87, http://doi.org/10.1037//0003-066x.48.10.1077.

12 Herman, *Trauma and Recovery,* 206.

TEN

1 "Qualified Immunity," Cornell Law School Legal Information Institute, https://www.law.cornell.edu/wex/qualified_immunity.

2 Leonard Shengold, *Soul Murder: The Effects of Childhood Abuse and Deprivation* (New York: Ballantine Books, 1989).

3 Howard Snyder, *Sexual Assault of Young Children as Reported to Law Enforcement: Victim, Incident, and Offender Characteristics*, U.S. Department of Justice, Office of Justice Programs, Bureau of Justice Statistics, July 2000, https://www.bjs.gov/content/pub/pdf/saycrle.pdf.

ELEVEN

1 "New Unit to Target Sexual Assault Cases," *Boston Globe*, May 10, 1984.

2 Sarah Snyder, "A Series of Rapes Alarms Allston-Brighton."

3 Jung, "Sexual Assault Unit Introduced to Help Curb Rape in Boston."

4 "Felonies Overall Are Down 13.5% in Boston; Murders Up Sharply," *Boston Globe*, Sept. 4, 1984.

5 Sarah Snyder, "As Rate Climbs, Boston Seeks Ways to Fight Rape," *Boston Globe*, Apr. 1, 1985.

6 Kevin Cullen, "Some Say Hub Is Phasing Out Sex Crime Unit," *Boston Globe*, Feb. 23, 1989.

7 Peter Howe, "Bowing to Protests, Boston Police to Restore Staff of Sexual Assault Unit," *Boston Globe*, Mar. 22, 1989.

8 Russlynn Ali, Letter to Colleagues, United States, Department of Education, Office for Civil Rights, Apr. 4, 2011, Obama Whitehouse Archives, https://obamawhitehouse.archives.gov/sites/default/files/dear_colleague_sexual_violence.pdf.

9 Ibid. 5.

10 FIRE Staff, "Frequently Asked Questions: OCR's April 4th 'Dear Colleague' Guidance Letter," Aug. 15, 2011, https://www.thefire.org

/frequently-asked-questions-ocrs-april-4-dear-colleague-guidance
-letter/.

11 As of February 2020, the new regulations from the Department of
Education have not been released and were still under review.

12 "Addressing Sexual and Relationship Violence: A Trauma-Informed
Approach," American College Health Association, https://www.acha.org
/Resources/Addressing_Sexual_and_Relationship_Violence_A_Trauma
_Informed_Approach.pdf.

13 Sofi Sinozich and Lynn Langton, "Special Report: Rape and Sexual
Assault Victimization Among College-Age Females, 1995–2013,"
U.S. Department of Justice, Office of Justice Programs, Bureau of
Justice Statistics, Dec. 2014, https://www.bjs.gov/content/pub/pdf
/rsavcaf9513.pdf.

14 Courtney Ahrens, "Being Silenced: The Impact of Negative Social
Reactions on the Disclosure of Rape," *American Journal of Community Psychology* 38 (2006): 264.

15 Note that these are training examples and are not based on actual
clinical cases.

16 M. C. Black et al., *The National Intimate Partner and Sexual Violence Survey: 2010 Summary Report*, National Center for Injury
Prevention and Control, Centers for Disease Control and Prevention, Nov. 2011, http://www.cdc.gov/ViolencePrevention/pdf/NISVS
_Report2010-a.pdf.

TWELVE

1 Nancy Kaffer, "Kym Worthy: 817 Serial Rapists ID'd in Tests,"
Detroit Free Press, Dec. 17, 2017, https://www.freep.com/story
/opinion/columnists/nancy-kaffer/2017/12/17/rape-kit-detroit
/953083001/.

2 Meghna Chakrabarti, "Rape Kits Often Go Untested for Decades,"
On Point, Mar. 5, 2018, https://www.wbur.org/onpoint/2018/03/05
/untested-rape-kit-backlog.

3 Jazmine Ulloa, "Lack of Funding Leads to Backlogged Rape Kits,"
Statesman, Sept. 1, 2012, https://www.statesman.com/article/20120901
/NEWS/309005070.

4 Meaghan Ybos, "No Backlog: Why the Epidemic of Untested Rape Kits Is Not a Symbol of Insufficient Police Budgets but Instead a Failure to Investigate Rape," *Appeal*, Oct. 11, 2017, https://theappeal.org/no -backlog-why-the-epidemic-of-untested-rape-kits-is-not-a-symbol-of -insufficient-police-budgets-but-instead-a-failure-to-investigate-rape/.

5 Corey Rayburn Yung, "Rape Law Gatekeeping," *Boston College Law Review* 205 (Aug. 12, 2016): 208.

6 Anna Clark, "Crowdfunders Say Solving Rape Cases Is Good for Business," *Next City,* Mar. 15, 2017, https://nextcity.org/daily/entry /crowdfunding-rape-kits-detroit-ups-solve-cases-economics.

7 The Justice for All Act, Apr. 2016, U.S. Department of Justice, Office of Justice Programs, Office for Victims of Crime, https://www.ovc.gov /publications/factshts/justforall/content.html.

8 "Profiles in DNA: Debbie Smith, Founder of H-E-A-R-T and Sexual Assault Survivor," National Center for Victims of Crimes, https:// victimsofcrime.org/our-programs/past-programs/dna-resource-center /profiles/debbie-smith.

9 Sofia Resnick, "Rape Kits: A Decade and a Billion Dollars Later, Why Can't We Fix the Backlog?" *ReWire News*, May 19, 2015, https:// rewire.news/article/2015/05/19/rape-kits-decade-billion-dollars-later- cant-fix-backlog/.

10 Tom Jackman, "Advocates Implore Congress to Reauthorize Funds for Backlogged DNA Rape Kits Before Sept. 30 Expiration," *Washington Post,* Sept. 7, 2019.

11 Ulloa, "Lack of Funding Leads to Backlogged Rape Kits."

12 "Testing Justice: The Rape Kit Backlog in Los Angeles City and County," Human Rights Watch, Mar. 31, 2009, https://www.hrw.org /report/2009/03/31/testing-justice/rape-kit-backlog-los-angeles-city -and-county.

13 Diane Dimond, "The Rapist in the Freezer," *Huffington Post*, Dec. 18, 2008, updated May 25, 2011, https://www.huffpost.com/entry/the -rapist-in-the-freezer_b_144087.

14 Ralph Blumenthal, "The Dangerous Rise in Untested Rape Kits,"

Marie Claire, Aug. 10, 2010, https://www.marieclaire.com/sex-love
/advice/a5101/rise-in-untested-rape-kits/.

15 "I Used to Think the Law Would Protect Me: Illinois's Failure to
Test Rape Kits," Human Rights Watch, Jul. 7, 2010, https://www.hrw
.org/report/2010/07/07/i-used-think-law-would-protect-me/illinoiss
-failure-test-rape-kits.

16 Brandi Grissom, "Testing the Evidence," *Texas Tribune*, Jan. 28, 2011,
https://www.texastribune.org/2011/01/28/thousands-of-texas-rape
-kits-never-tested/.

17 Nicholas Kristof, "Want a Real Reason to Be Outraged?" *New York
Times*, Oct. 27, 2012, https://www.nytimes.com/2012/10/28/opinion
/sunday/kristof-Outrageous-Policies-Toward-Rape-Victims.html.

18 Jessica Contrera, "A Wrenching Dilemma," *Washington Post*, Feb.
20, 2018, https://www.washingtonpost.com/news/style/wp/2018/02/20
/feature/decades-worth-of-rape-kits-are-finally-being-tested-no-one
-can-agree-on-what-to-do-next/.

19 Madeleine Carlisle, "A New System to Ensure Sexual Assault Cases
Aren't Forgotten—More States Are Adopting Software That Allows Sexual-Assault Survivors to Track Their Evidence Kits," *The
Atlantic*, Apr. 7, 2019, https://www.theatlantic.com/politics/archive
/2019/04/many-states-are-adopting-rape-kit-tracking-systems
/586531/.

20 Jon Campbell, "New NY Law Requires Timely Rape Kit Testing,"
Democrat and Chronicle, Nov. 30, 2016, https://www.democratand
chronicle.com/story/news/politics/albany/2016/11/30/ny-untested
-rape-kits/94690462/.

21 Brian Ballou and Andrea Estes, "'It's My Fault, I Messed Up Bad,'
Chemist Says: State Police Report Admission of Improper Testing,
Altering Results," *Boston Globe*, Sept. 27, 2012, https://bostonglobe
.newspapers.com/image/444242996.

THIRTEEN

 1 Sarah Snyder, "A Series of Rapes Alarms Allston-Brighton."

FOURTEEN

1 Virginia Woolf, *The Waves* (Wordsworth Edition Limited, 2000) 14.

2 Valeriya Safronova and Rebecca Halleck, "These Rape Victims Had to Sue to Get the Police to Investigate," *New York Times,* May 23, 2019, https://www.nytimes.com/2019/05/23/us/rape-victims-kits-police -departments.html.

3 *An Investigation of NYPD's Special Victims Division—Adult Sex Crimes,* City of New York, Department of Investigation, Mar. 27, 2018, https://www1.nyc.gov/assets/doi/reports/pdf/2018/Mar/SVDReport _32718.pdf.

4 Robert Lewis, "NYPD Misled Public About Response to #MeToo: Report," WNYC News, March 27, 2018, https://www.wnyc.org/story /nypd-misled-public-about-response-metoo-report/.

5 Yvonne Abraham, "After Night of Terror, and Years of Anguish, She Finds Meaning," *Boston Globe,* Mar. 22, 2015, https://www .bostonglobe.com/metro/2015/03/21/after-night-terror-and-years -anguish-she-finds-meaning/PBdZmtjFqxtqlaRNDUmmSP/story .html?event=event12.

6 Laura Crimaldi and John R. Ellement, "No Bail for Sex Offender Charged in S. End Assault," *Boston Globe,* Oct. 12, 2016, https://www .bostonglobe.com/metro/2016/10/12/arrest-made-south-end-home -invasion-sexual-assault-two-people/N16mSiyyCsVRtgnBd0HyuK /story.html.

PART III

1 Kim Elsesser, "The Latest Consequences of #MeToo: Not Hir- ing Women," *Forbes,* Sept. 5, 2019, https://www.forbes.com/sites /kimelsesser/2019/09/05/the-latest-consequence-of-metoo-not-hiring -women/#14fbeb53280b.

2 Jeremy Diamond, "Trump Says It's a 'Very Scary Time for Young Men in America,'" CNN, Oct. 2, 2018, https://www.cnn.com/2018/10/02 /politics/trump-scary-time-for-young-men-metoo/index.html.

3 Adam Clark Estes, "CNN's Not the Only One Peddling Sympathy for the Steubenville Rapists," *Atlantic,* Mar. 17, 2013, https://www.theatlantic

.com/national/archive/2013/03/cnns-not-only-one-peddling-sympathy
-steubenville-rapists/317249/.

4 Joshua Berlinger and Jack Hannah, "Montana Teacher—Initially Given
   31 Days in Rape of Student—Now Gets 10 Years," CNN, Sept. 29,
   2014, https://www.cnn.com/2014/09/26/justice/montana-rape-sentence
   /index.html.

5 Alia E. Dastagir, "A Bus Driver Rapes, a Man Keeps Girl Captive and
   Neither Are Going to Prison," *USA Today*, May 3, 2019, https://www
   .usatoday.com/story/news/nation/2019/05/03/bus-driver-shane-pinche
   -wont-go-prison-rape-hes-not-alone/3653181002/.

6 Casey Quackenbush, "'You Have to Look at the Way She Was Dressed.'
   Ireland Protests After Lawyer Cites a Thong as Consent," *Time*, Nov. 16,
   2018, https://time.com/5456712/ireland-thong-rape-case-protests/.

7 Elisha Fieldstadt, "New Jersey Judge Spared Teen Rape Suspect
   Because He Came from a Good Family," NBC News, Jul. 3, 2019,
   https://www.nbcnews.com/news/us-news/n-j-judge-spared-teen-rape
   -suspect-because-he-came-n1026111.

8 Luis Ferré-Sadurní and Nick Corasaniti, "Rape Case Judge Resigns
   Over 'Good Family' Remark; State Orders Training," *New York Times*,
   Jul. 17, 2019, https://www.nytimes.com/2019/07/17/nyregion/judge
   -james-troiano-resigning.html.